DIVIDE AND QUIT

Divide and Quit

PENDEREL MOON

1962

UNIVERSITY OF CALIFORNIA PRESS

BERKELEY AND LOS ANGELES

Published in the
United States of America
By the University of California Press of
Berkeley and Los Angeles, California

★

Published in Great Britain by
Chatto and Windus Ltd

152716

Contents

Introduction 7

I The Genesis of Pakistan 11

II The Punjab and Pakistan 29

III The Cabinet Mission 42

IV The Mountbatten Plan 65

V The Punjab and Partition 71

VI Bahawalpur State 97

VII Journey across the Punjab 114

VIII Outbreak of Disturbances in Bahawalpur State 124

IX Restoring Order—I 143

X Restoring Order—II 159

XI Disturbances in Bahawalpur City 190

XII Events in Rahim Yar Khan 225

XIII Resettlement 247

XIV Summing Up 261

Note on Casualties 293

Index 295

MAPS

1 The Punjab 89

2 Bahawalpur State 112–113

Introduction

THE dawn of Indian independence was marred by massacres and migrations in the Punjab on a scale unparalleled in world history in time of peace. Within the space of three or four months thousands were killed or died of privation and millions were compelled to abandon for ever their ancestral homes and to start life afresh in new surroundings. These melancholy events attracted attention at the time, but they were so local in their effects that they have quickly faded from the world's memory. Nor have India and Pakistan been sorry that they should fall into oblivion. Yet though sordid and discreditable in themselves—redeemed, if at all, not by striking deeds of heroism (for the weaker party were everywhere driven like sheep to the slaughter), but only by the dumb, patient endurance of the multitude—these large-scale massacres and migrations were sufficiently unusual to deserve more chronicling than is supplied by contemporary newspaper articles or by second-hand propagandist compilations of atrocity stories. Yet this is virtually the only record of them that has so far appeared.

In this book I have attempted, on the basis of my own recollections of these events, to throw a genuine, if limited, ray of light on both their character and causes. The book falls into two fairly distinct halves. The second half contains a detailed, connected, and in places almost day-to-day account of the disturbances that occurred from the end of August 1947 onwards in the State of Bahawalpur—a territory immediately adjacent to the Punjab—and of the manner in which they were handled or mishandled. There are incidental references to the disorders and migrations that were simultaneously in progress throughout the Punjab, but no attempt has been made to give a comprehensive—and necessarily second-hand—account of these. The narrative is confined almost entirely to my own limited but first-hand experience of the troubles in Bahawalpur. Within this narrow scope it is a faithful and authentic record of what

7

actually took place; and though Bahawalpur lay on the outer edge of the area of disturbance, the happenings there do, I believe, illustrate a good many aspects of the whole upheaval.

The earlier part of the book is in a somewhat different vein. It is concerned with the causes of the upheaval and traces political events in India and the Punjab from 1937 until their tragic dénouement ten years later. It is not a purely personal narrative, but it is not objective history. The story is told as it unfolded itself to me at the time, not as it would appear to the disinterested historian; and therefore only those events and those actions and reactions of political leaders receive notice which made a strong contemporary impression on my mind. While some of these are of unquestionable significance—for instance, the Cabinet Mission of 1946 which, being a decisive turning-point, has been treated in some detail—others, particularly the twists and turns of Punjab politics and personalities, loom large mainly because I had some special interest in or connection with them. They may contribute—I hope they will —to an understanding of the final tragedy in the Punjab, but they are petty and parochial in comparison with all-India events, some of which have received in these pages scant mention or none at all.

The earlier part of the book deals with large issues, the latter part with minor local episodes. Though widely different, the two are intimately connected, for all the individual incidents of the Bahawalpur disorders which are described in the second part flowed directly from the broad political decisions of which an account is given in the first. To me this connection was vividly clear at the time; to most of the individual sufferers it was only vaguely comprehensible. They knew in a general way that their misfortunes were the result of the departure of the British and the creation of Pakistan, but the reasons why these two things should cause the sudden disintegration of the social order in which they were living and plunge peaceful Bahawalpur almost overnight into a state of virtual civil war were beyond their powers of analysis. These results were certainly quite at variance with the predictions and proclaimed intentions of political leaders and official spokesmen.

When the clash came, my position in Bahawalpur was like that of a battalion commander in an obscure outlying sector of the field of battle. But during part of the preceding ten years I had held a staff appointment which gave me an insight into the movement and massing of forces leading to the conflict in which I was subsequently involved. Thus, to change the metaphor, I ended by playing a small part in a tragedy the preparations for which I had long watched moving to their appointed but unpurposed end.

In composing this narrative, I had originally laid down for myself the principle of 'nothing extenuate, nor set down aught in malice'. I hope that I have nowhere departed from the second half of it; but it has not been possible to adhere rigidly in all places to the first, and I feel that in addition some extenuatory remarks of a general character are necessary. The narrative depicts mainly an ugly side of human nature and an uninformed reader might derive from it a very adverse impression of Punjabis in particular and of Indians and Pakistanis in general. But just as one does not judge a man from how he behaves when he is drunk or in a fit of rage, so a whole people should not be judged by what they do when temporarily in the grip of mass hysteria; and this was the condition of a large number of people in the Punjab in 1947.

I must add another word of caution. In most of this narrative Muslims are the villains and Hindus and Sikhs the victims. The unwary reader might half-unconsciously slip into thinking that this was the universal picture. But in East Punjab the roles were reversed and Sikhs and Hindus were there guilty of excesses against Muslims which equalled and, in my judgement, exceeded in scale and atrocity the outrages perpetrated by Muslims in West Pakistan. During the course of the disorders in Bahawalpur I continually had to remind myself of this in order to enter into the feelings of the Muslims by whom I was surrounded. The reader likewise, if he is to preserve a fair balance, should bear this in mind.

I am not myself conscious of any bias for or against any of the three communities except perhaps a sneaking sympathy for the Sikhs. All of them, however, will probably be displeased with some portions, at least, of what I have written. The Sikhs in particular are likely to repudiate my interpretation of their part in the tragedy, even though I have endeavoured to explain and partially excuse it. Members of the other two commu-

A*

nities will, I am afraid, resent criticism of persons who have become national heroes. But if one attempts to unravel the causes of the Punjab massacres, it is impossible to disguise these heroes' large, if unconscious, share of responsibility for what took place. If, therefore, I have dragged to light the errors and ill-timed utterances of revered leaders which, though re-marked on at the time, have since been glossed over or conveniently forgotten, this is not done in any spirit of gratuitous disparagement but simply to bring out the true sequence of cause and effect. Furthermore, I recognize that, even if their responsibility for the Punjab massacres was considerable, they were acting in pursuit of ends and ideals which they and their followers may feel to have fully justified these heavy forfeits.

I

The Genesis of Pakistan

THE emergence of India as a free self-governing country
had been foreseen more than a hundred years before
1947. By the turn of the present century it had become
the avowed object of Indian nationalists, and by the end of
World War I it was recognized by British statesmen as the inevitable outcome of the British Raj. Pakistan, on the other hand,
was not thought of till about 1930;[1] three years later Muslim
leaders were describing it to the Joint Select Committee of the
British Parliament as 'only a students' scheme . . . chimerical
and impracticable'; and not until July 1946 could its emergence
as a separate State be deemed inevitable.

In retrospect it is perhaps less surprising that Pakistan came,
as it were, with such a rush at the end as that it was at the
beginning such a slow starter; for as far back as 1888 Sir Syed
Ahmad, the great Muslim leader of the nineteenth century,
had laid down the premises which lead naturally, perhaps even
necessarily, to the idea of Pakistan. India, he had said, is a
country 'inhabited by two different nations' and there would
necessarily be a struggle for power between them, if the English
were to leave India. 'Is it possible', he had asked, 'that under
these circumstances two nations—the Mohammadan and
Hindu—could sit on the same throne and remain equal in
power? Most certainly not. It is necessary that one of them
should conquer the other and thrust it down. To hope that both
could remain equal is to desire the impossible and the incon-
ceivable.'

In the Victorian era the possibility of the English leaving
India did not arise. Sir Syed Ahmad knew that he was asking

---

[1] The first clear expression of the idea is to be found in an address to the
Muslim League in 1930 by Sir Mohammad Iqbal. He had mainly in mind
what is now West Pakistan. At a somewhat earlier date the partition of
India between Hindus and Muslims had been vaguely mooted.

and answering an academic question. His immediate practical
concern was to show that a system of government by elected
representatives—for which the newly-founded Indian National
Congress was beginning to press—could not be safely adopted
in India, for 'the larger community would totally override
the interests of the smaller'. Yet in propounding the two nation
theory and drawing attention so pointedly to the difficulties
of majority rule in a country where the population is not homogeneous, he had not only put his finger on the main crux of the
problem of Indian constitutional development, but also by
implication had suggested a possible answer to it; for if two
nations could not sit on the same throne, why should they not
divide it?

This possible solution, so natural a corollary of Sir Syed
Ahmad's premises, so obvious in the light of what has actually
happened, remained for forty years neglected; not till the eight
years of investigation and discussion that preceded the passing
of the Government of India Act 1935 did it receive notice, and
then only to be dismissed as chimerical.

Of course it was the Muslims alone who could have been
expected to sponsor it. To the Hindu nationalists, who dominated Congress and led the movement for independence, the
idea of dividing India was anathema. To the British, dimly
conscious that the unification of India was one of the greatest
achievements of their rule, it was not in the least attractive.
Though the multi-racial Ottoman and Austrian empires had
dissolved before their eyes, they clung to the notion that their
own polyglot Indian empire should survive as a unity after they
themselves had quitted the throne. The backwardness of the
Muslims in the matter is not so easy to explain. In part it may
be attributed to the fact that some of their most ardent leaders,
including Jinnah himself, were for years in the ranks of Congress and, under the influence of the common urge to shake off
the British yoke, accepted readily the assumption that they
would somehow be able to agree to share the throne with their
Hindu friends. In addition, the inherent difficulties of division
helped to keep the idea in the background. Hindus and Muslims, though they did not intermarry, were closely intermingled
and in many parts of India lived side by side. Division of the
country would, therefore, necessarily leave large minorities in

the new States so formed. Moreover the two regions in which Muslims were in a majority—the north-west and north-east of India—were widely separated, and to form a single State out of such disconnected territories seemed hardly possible. For this very reason the idea of Pakistan, as at first adumbrated, embraced only north-west India.

The Government of India Act of 1935 took no account of the Pakistan 'chimera'. With the full concurrence of Jinnah and the Muslim League, Muslim interests were sought to be protected by other means. The quasi-monopoly of political power which the Hindus' superior numbers would tend to give them was diminished by abandoning the old tradition of unitary government in favour of a federal form of constitution under which the Provinces would enjoy a large measure of autonomy; Sind was detached from Bombay and made a separate Province so that there would be four Muslim-majority Provinces[1] out of a total of eleven; the system of separate electorates for Muslims and 'weightage' was continued; and it was envisaged that the Native States would be included in the Federation and that their representatives would have a neutralizing influence at the Centre. With these arrangements the Muslims appeared to be content. Jinnah, it is true, described the federal part of the Act as 'fundamentally bad and totally unacceptable'. His objection to it, however, was not that it failed to protect Muslim interests adequately, but that it did not provide immediately for full responsible government at the centre, since defence and foreign affairs were reserved to the Governor-General and not entrusted to ministers responsible to the legislature. Jinnah was in fact voicing, though less stridently, the same complaint as the Hindu leaders of Congress. Nevertheless, he and the Muslim League and other Muslim political parties all acquiesced in the Act and were apparently willing to give it a trial.

This was the position on April 1st 1937 when the provincial part of the Act came into operation, establishing in the Provinces full responsible government subject only to certain 'safeguards'. The federal part was necessarily deferred, as it was only to come into force when a specific number of the Native States had acceded to the Federation, and none had as yet done

[1] Bengal, Punjab, Sind and the North-West Frontier Province.

so. Negotiations with their Rulers regarding the terms of their
accession were still in progress and it was hoped that after a
little time their doubts and hesitations would be overcome and
the Federation would be duly inaugurated. There was a possibility that Congress might employ 'wrecking' tactics in order
to wring more concessions from the British, but no hint or suspicion of serious obstruction from the Muslims.

Within the space of a single year the whole situation had
radically altered. A profound change came over Muslim
opinion, and there opened between the League and Congress
a breach destined to grow ever wider and to lead inexorably
to the partition of the country and the massacres of 1947.
The British at first noticed these developments with mild complacency and did not exert themselves to heal the rift. Later
when they woke up to the fearful consequences that might
ensue, they made desperate but unavailing efforts to avert
them.

There is no doubt that the leaders of Congress were responsible, though quite unwittingly, for this critical change in
Muslim sentiment. In retrospect it seems as though a curse was
laid on them at this time which compelled them over the next
ten years invariably to act in such a way as to bring about
exactly the opposite result to that which they intended. They
passionately desired to preserve the unity of India. They consistently acted so as to make its partition certain.

Their first mistake, which may be regarded as the *fons et
origo malorum*, was made in the summer of 1937. In the preceding cold weather elections had been held to the new Provincial Assemblies and both Congress and the Muslim League
had contested them. In all the six Hindu-majority provinces
Congress had been conspicuously successful; it had also done
well in Assam, where it was the strongest single party; but in
three out of the four Muslim-majority provinces, viz. Bengal,
the Punjab and Sind, it had fared comparatively badly. The
experience of the Muslim League had been curiously different.
In the Muslim-majority provinces it still counted for very little
and won remarkably few seats. In these provinces Muslims
were either divided into warring factions or, where united,
belonged to local parties with traditions and alignments of their
own. Thus in the North-West Frontier Province the dominant

Muslim party, the Red Shirts, had long been in alliance with Congress. In the Punjab most Muslims belonged to the Unionist Party, a combination of Muslims, Sikhs and Hindus representing rural and agricultural as against urban and commercial interests. Such success as the League achieved was not in these Muslim-majority provinces but in those in which Muslims were in a minority and could never hope to form a government themselves. Probably its greatest strength was in the United Provinces where Mogul traditions still lingered and Muslims, though only about 16 per cent of the population, had succeeded in retaining a political importance disproportionate to their numbers.

Though Congress and the League had entered into no electoral pact, the League leaders had been careful to draft their election manifesto so as to be in broad accord with the Congress programme. Undoubtedly they fully expected that in some of the Hindu-majority provinces, and particularly in the United Provinces, they would be invited by Congress to form coalition Ministries. But in the summer of 1937 these expectations were rudely disappointed. With overwhelming majorities in the legislatures, Congress had no need for an alliance with the League. The representation of Muslims in the Ministries could be obtained by the appointment of Muslims from within the ranks of Congress.[1] So the League leaders of the United Provinces were plainly told that there would be no coalition and that if any of them were to find places in the Ministry, then the Muslim League Party in the Assembly must 'cease to function as a separate group', and all its members must become members of Congress and submit themselves to Congress party discipline and to the policy laid down by the Congress High Command. In other words Congress were prepared to share the throne only with Muslims who consented to merge themselves in a predominantly Hindu organization. They offered the League not partnership but absorption.

This proved to be a fatal error—the prime cause of the creation of Pakistan—but in the circumstances it was a very

[1] Congress, which always claimed that it represented all communities in India, had within its ranks a sprinkling of Muslims. In the elections Congress Muslims had contested fifty-eight of the 482 Muslim constituencies and won twenty-six.

natural one. There was nothing in parliamentary tradition requiring Congress on the morrow of victory to enter into a
coalition with another party; and a coalition with the League,
which the Congress leaders looked upon as a purely communal
organization, was particularly distasteful to them. They may
also well have thought that if in the U.P. the League could be
lured into dissolving itself it would soon disintegrate throughout the country, leaving no all-India Muslim party in existence,
but only isolated provincial groups. Moreover the idea of
absorption, of gathering all the Muslims into the Congress fold,
was typical of the Hindu habit of mind and the past history of
Hinduism. Nearly three centuries earlier had not the absorptive
capacity of Hinduism impressed the Mogul emperor, Aurangzeb, with the danger that in India Islam might lose its identity
and become a forgotten element in an all-embracing Hinduism?

The Muslim League leaders rejected the Congress ulti-
matum. They were outraged at the suggestion that they should
dissolve their political organization; rather than do this they
were prepared to run the risk of permanent banishment to the
political wilderness. Among the disappointed candidates for
office was Liaqat Ali Khan, a wealthy landowner of western
U.P. who in the coming years was to be Jinnah's principal
lieutenant. Jinnah himself, who before the elections had been
saying that there was no substantial difference between the
League and Congress, at once began to adopt a very different
tone. Previously, though he had often stressed that Muslims
must maintain their separate political organization and that it
was 'no use encouraging individual Muslims to come into the
fold of Congress', he had by no means been an out-and-out
communalist. He had been described in Congress circles as
'the ambassador of Hindu-Muslim unity' and had been more
notable as an anti-British nationalist than as a champion of
Islam. But Congress rather than the British now became his
enemy number one and he embarked on a bitter campaign of
vilification. 'Muslims', he said, 'can expect neither justice nor
fair play under Congress Government' and all hope of communal peace had been wrecked 'on the rocks of Congress
Fascism'.

The reaction was not confined to Muslim League circles and
the Muslims of the Muslim-minority provinces. Muslims all

over India, even in the Muslim-majority provinces, took alarm. If the U.P. sample was to be the pattern of Congress's political conduct, then what would be the position of Muslims when a federal government for all-India came to be formed? There would be no room on the throne of India save for Congress and Congress stooges. Before the year was out the Muslim members of the Unionist Party in the Punjab, under the leadership of the Premier, Sir Sikander Hyat-Khan, had gone over *en bloc* to the League, and the Muslim Premiers of Bengal and Assam had also shown that they supported it. The adherence of the Punjab Muslims was especially significant. In this province the League had failed completely at the elections and almost all the Muslim seats had gone to members of the Unionist Party, Yet now Sir Sikander took all his Muslim followers into the League camp. They remained members of the Unionist Party, but they also became members of the Muslim League. Sir Sikander was very far from being a bigoted Muslim and had little sympathy with the virulent communalism hitherto displayed by Muslim leaguers in the Punjab. But there was now a strong section of his own Muslim followers anxious to join the League as the one party standing forth clearly to champion Muslim rights; and he feared that in the changed atmosphere of Muslim alarm and resentment this section might break away and then draw others after them, leaving him more or less isolated and powerless to mould or guide Muslim opinion in the Punjab. To avoid such a dangerous split he decided to join the League himself with all his Muslim supporters. Subsequent events showed that his fears were by no means groundless.

The League was enormously strengthened by the accession of the Punjab and Bengal Muslims, and Jinnah himself was suddenly raised to an eminence which he had never enjoyed before. Instead of being merely one of several Muslim leaders, without real backing from any of the main centres of Muslim population, he became from now onwards the undisputed leader of Muslims all over India and acknowledged as such even by the Premiers of the Punjab and Bengal.

The Congress leaders do not appear to have appreciated the strong currents which they had set in motion, still less to have perceived where they were likely to lead. So far from repairing their original mistake and seeking to bridge the gulf that had been created between them and the League—grown suddenly much more formidable—they made matters worse by launching, at Nehru's instance, a 'mass-contact' movement among the ordinary Muslims of the countryside. This was a signal to the League to bestir itself and also gave it its cue. Hitherto it had appealed mainly to middle and upper class Muslims and had not sought to enlist the support of the Muslim masses. But for a predominantly Hindu organization like the Congress to try to 'contact' Muslim peasants and artisans on a mass scale was an affront and a challenge which the League could not ignore. So before the 'mass-contact' movement of Congress had made much headway, the League itself turned towards the masses. It reduced the annual membership fee to two annas, began to extend its organization to the countryside and with the aid of unscrupulous propaganda to rouse Muslims of all classes to the danger of Hindu domination. This was an appeal to essentially the same basic nationalist sentiment as the Congress had been playing upon in its long struggle against British rule and it is somewhat strange that the Congress leaders did not foresee that by embarking on a 'mass-contact' movement among the Muslims they would impel the League to invoke this powerful sentiment against themselves. As a means of appealing to the Muslim masses it was far more effective than the Congress programme of social and agrarian reform.

The significance of what was happening did not come home to me till the summer of 1938, when, after several years' service in the districts, I was called up to Simla to act temporarily for six[1] months as Secretary to the Governor of the Punjab. I then became aware of the crucial change in Muslim opinion and began to have a dim presentiment of what it might portend. The Viceroy, Lord Linlithgow, was at that time laboriously attempting to coax the Princes into joining the proposed Federation. Possibly a Viceroy with something of the brilliance and personal magnetism of Lord Mountbatten might have succeeded in this difficult task; but it was quite beyond the scope of the more pedestrian talents of Lord Linlithgow and it never seemed probable that the Princes would yield to his methods of persuasion. It became clear to me, however, that while everyone was still agog to bring in the Princes, their

[1] The six months became three and a half years.

reluctance to enter the Federation had already become of secondary importance and that far more serious and significant was the growing opposition of the Muslims. I realized this when in July Sir Sikander asked me to help him with the 'editing' of a pamphlet, written by him or under his direction, entitled 'Outline of a scheme of Indian Federation'. Sir Sikander was a man of moderate and sober views; I was therefore much struck, on reading through the draft, to find even this level-headed statesman expressing the opinion that the federal proposals of the 1935 Act were no longer acceptable and must be modified so as to remove the misgivings not only of the Princes but also of the minorities—that is, of course, primarily the Muslims. The details of his federal scheme are not of any importance now.[1] His main objectives, as disclosed in the pamphlet, were to limit the authority of the Centre to the barest minimum and to exclude the possibility of 'Congress Raj' by laying down certain provisions regarding the composition of the Federal Executive calculated to ensure a nice balance of interests.

The scheme appeared to me to have little chance of acceptance and to be in some respects impracticable; but Sir Sikander was very keen to lay it before the public. When I asked him the reason for this, he replied with a wry smile that unless positive proposals such as his were put forward for consideration other people would come out with 'something worse'. The 'something worse' to which he referred was the idea of Pakistan— the 'chimerical and impracticable students' scheme' which, I gathered from him, was now gaining a hold in League circles.

Hitherto I had hardly known the meaning of the term 'Pakistan'. I tried now to get to the bottom of it. The essence of the idea was that India should be divided, and a separate predominantly Muslim State created out of the Punjab, the N.W.F.P., Sind, Kashmir and Baluchistan. This would be Pakistan. What should happen to the rest of the Muslims in India had not at this time been clearly thought out, but there was an idea that a second predominantly Muslim State should be created in the north-east out of the provinces of Bengal and Assam. This would provide a division of the country between Hindus and Muslims on a rough population basis. There would

[1] He envisaged a three-tiered constitution such as was later suggested by the Cabinet Mission in 1946.

be large minorities in all the three States, but their presence in *all* of them might ensure their fair treatment. Furthermore it seemed probable that States whose populations had previously been so intimately associated would automatically enter into some kind of close alliance or confederation and never become to one another quite like foreign countries.

I was attracted by the idea. It seemed at first sight to offer a simple solution of the Hindu-Muslim problem and, now that the bogy of Hindu domination at the Centre had been raised, perhaps the only solution. Any system of safeguards and statutory coalitions was all very well on paper but difficult to work in practice. Sooner or later it was bound to break down. I assumed, all too readily, that the Punjab, where three communities (Muslim, Hindu and Sikh) were closely intermingled, spoke a common language, shared a common provincial pride and to some extent a common culture, would remain a unity and pass as a whole into Pakistan without the Hindus and Sikhs raising too much objection.

One day in October 1938 during a conversation with Sir Sikander I began talking to him rather enthusiastically about the merits of the Pakistan idea and suggested that it might after all be the best way of dealing with the communal problem. Sir Sikander, usually so calm and suave, after listening for a few minutes turned upon me, his eyes blazing with indignation, and took me to task in these words:

'How can you talk like this? You've been long enough in western Punjab to know the Muslims there. Surely you can see that Pakistan would be an invitation to them to cut the throat of every Hindu bania.'[1]

I put forward the hostage theory—there would be so many Muslims in Hindustan and so many Hindus in Pakistan that both sides would hesitate to harass their minorities for fear of reprisals. He brushed it aside. The Baluchis and Awans of West Punjab, he said, wouldn't care at all about the lives of Muslims in Hindustan. The hostage idea was a mere fancy. Both sides would kill their own hostages. 'I do hope', he went on, 'I won't hear you talk like this again. *Pakistan would mean a massacre.*'

His words, spoken with unusual intensity of feeling, made a

[1] Hindu trader or shopkeeper, usually also a moneylender.

deep impression on me. My original enthusiasm for Pakistan evaporated, and for the next eight years my hope was that it might somehow be avoided. Sir Sikander, on the other hand, in less than eighteen months subscribed to a resolution calling for its creation.

The Muslim League's slide towards Pakistan was exceedingly rapid. It had first taken alarm in the summer of 1937; a year later it had repudiated the federal scheme of the 1935 Act; by the beginning of 1939 it was considering other constitutional schemes; in September 1939 it declared that Muslim India was 'irrevocably opposed' to any federal objective. Finally in March 1940, at a session in Lahore, it passed what is known as the 'Pakistan Resolution' demanding in plain terms the partition of India and the grouping of regions in which Muslims were numerically in a majority, as in the north-western and north-eastern zones, into 'Independent States'.

The League's rapid and revolutionary change of outlook was very natural; for once faith in the possibility of partnership was shaken, partition was logically the only alternative.

Privately Jinnah told one or two people in Lahore that this Resolution was a 'tactical move'; and the fact that six years later he was ready to accept something less than absolute partition suggests that in 1940 he was not really irrevocably committed to it. In part, therefore, it may have been at this time a tactical move, designed to wring from Congress concessions which would make partnership more tolerable. Certainly the implications of the resolution and even the composition of the proposed 'Independent States' and their interrelations had not at this stage been fully thought out. Some of these matters were clarified later, but Jinnah was never keen to expound the exact nature of Pakistan, and right up till 1947 there was some doubt as to what he would accept as conforming sufficiently to his conceptions.

Sir Sikander was gravely embarrassed by this resolution. His own dislike of Pakistan—or Jinnistan as he irreverently called it—was well known. He had publicly stated that if Pakistan meant 'a Muslim Raj here and a Hindu Raj elsewhere', he would have nothing to do with it. He was the head of a Government and the leader of a political party which included in its ranks or among its habitual supporters Hindus and Sikhs as

well as Muslims. Inevitably on the Pakistan issue there was
serious division. Sikander's Muslim followers, as members of
the Muslim League, became formally committed to the demand
for Pakistan, whatever their private opinions might be;[1] while
his Hindu and Sikh supporters were wholly opposed to it. Sir
Sikander endeavoured privately to explain away the resolution
and to make out that it was not really the intention that the
States into which India was proposed to be divided should be
entirely independent of one another. But his interpretation of
the resolution became more and more difficult to reconcile
with Jinnah's public utterances.

In Bengal, as in the Punjab, the Muslim Premier, Fazl-ul-Haq,
had not yet in his heart accepted Pakistan, though publicly he
stood committed to it. Both he and Sir Sikander were in a false
position, but neither of them at this stage wished to risk a
break with Jinnah. Sir Sikander both now and right up to the
end of his life thought—and with good reason—that if he were
openly to oppose Jinnah, the Punjab Muslims would become
divided and he would lose his hold over them. So outwardly he
bowed to Jinnah, however much inwardly he might chafe.

It was all very well for Sir Sikander, Fazl-ul-Haq and perhaps
even Jinnah himself to have mental reservations about Pakistan,
but once the cry was raised, how would it be silenced? The term
was, no doubt, a vague one; but after the 1940 resolution it
rightly became synonymous in the popular mind with 'Muslim
Raj'—a State where Muslims would be supreme. To the Muslim
masses this held out an ill-defined but alluring prospect of
looting Hindus. With greater clarity of vision, ambitious politicians and civil servants, as also some professional men, perceived
that under a Muslim Raj, with the crippling if not the elimination of Hindu competition, they could rise to positions of power
and affluence unattainable in a single mixed Hindu-Muslim
State. Thus the cry for Pakistan appealed to and excited powerful appetites and individual hopes, and these, once aroused,
would not be readily assuaged.

'The thicket of the people will take furtive fire
From irresponsible catchwords of live ideas

[1] In March 1940 a considerable number, probably a majority, of Sir
Sikander's Muslim followers shared his antipathy to the idea of Pakistan.

Sudden as a gorse-bush from the smouldering end
Of any loiterer's match-splint, which, unless trodden out
Afore it spread, or quelled with wieldy threshing rods,
Will burn ten years of planting with all last year's ricks
And blacken a countryside.'

Responsible statesmen like Sir Sikander might foresee the
dangers inherent in raising the cry for Pakistan, but ostensibly
the League had accepted Pakistan as its goal—a goal which it
would be easy for demagogues to pursue to disaster, difficult
for statesmen to abandon or render innocuous.

The ominous trend of thought in League circles, of which the
1940 resolution was the overt sign, might have been checked if,
soon after the breach in 1937, the Congress leaders had made
positive efforts to conciliate Jinnah and his henchmen. But
for several reasons it was difficult, if not impossible, for them to
do so. Jinnah attacked Congress bitterly, accusing the average
Congressman of 'behaving and acting towards the Mussalmans
in a much worse manner than the British did towards Indians',
and letting loose a flood of malicious propaganda. Reports were
issued regarding the ill-treatment alleged to be meted out to
Muslims in various Congress Government Provinces, in which
mountains were made out of mole-hills and trivial communal
incidents of everyday occurrence painted in lurid colours so as
to inflame popular feeling. Smarting under these largely unjustified attacks the Congress leaders showed a good deal of
restraint, but they would have been more than human if they
had responded immediately with an olive branch.

There was also another obstacle to any rapprochement. Just
as Congress claimed to be the only body representing all communities and alone qualified therefore to speak for the whole
of India, so Jinnah now claimed that the League alone represented the Muslims of India and must be recognized as the only
body qualified to speak on their behalf. To Congress, which had
several prominent Muslims within its ranks—one of them,
Maulana Abul Kalam Azad, became President of Congress in
1940—this claim was unacceptable; and in one shape or another
it remained a stumbling block in the way of any settlement from
this time right up till the final calamitous end of Congress-
League relations.

Nevertheless in the summer of 1939 there were signs that Congress saw the need for a settlement and desired to reach one. Gandhi in June expressed the hope that British statesmen would revise the federal scheme embodied in the 1935 Act and 'try to placate all parties'. Congress spokesmen studiously refrained from criticism of the proposals embodied in Sikander's 'Outline Scheme' which was published in the first half of the year. Gandhi himself obtained six copies of it and during June and July he and Sikander were in communication with one another in the hope of finding some common ground.

But, despite these feelers, up till the outbreak of war there had been no effective reconciliation between Congress and the League; and when war came the gulf widened. Confused by Gandhi's pacifism and blinded by their own violent antipathy to British rule the Congress leaders in September 1939 were unable to view coolly the realities of the situation. To remove or even lighten the British yoke in time of war was impossible; but the days of British rule were obviously numbered and already the crucial problem was not how to get rid of the British but how to preserve the unity of the country when they had gone. Jinnah and the League had already appeared as a potential source of disruption. The threat to unity was quite evident even before the League's 1940 resolution. A united effort in the war might have averted it and paved the way for settlement thereafter. If Congress had been willing to co-operate and accept for the duration of the war the existing Constitution with its inevitable limitations, the moderate Muslim elements, still quite strong in the Punjab and Bengal and not yet wedded to extreme courses or completely under Jinnah's thumb, would have gladly joined hands with them in forming a government at the Centre and thus the foundations might have been laid for a government of a united and independent India when the war was over. Instead, Congress decided to stand aloof, co-operating with nobody and coming to terms neither with the British nor with Jinnah. In October 1939 the Congress Ministries in the Provinces were ordered to resign from office and this proved to be the prelude to retirement into jail. Jinnah was thus left with a clear field and he took full advantage of it.

From every point of view the Congress attitude was unfortunate except perhaps that of the successful prosecution of the war. But this was the aspect which at the time most impressed itself on the British. Congress 'co-operation', it was felt, would take the form of daily and exasperating obstruction to which 'non-co-operation' or even active hostility would be preferable. A section of British opinion was, therefore, not at all keen to have members of Congress in office during the war and secretly welcomed their departure soon after its outbreak. On short-term considerations there was much to be said for this view; and, whether deliberately or not, the Viceroy ensured that events would conform to it. It is conceivable that if on the outbreak of war he had proclaimed in a few stirring words his belief that a war for freedom could only end in the freedom of India[1]—as in fact it did—the Congress would have been swung in favour of co-operation—in which case Jinnah would have had to co-operate too. But Lord Linlithgow did not adopt this course. After several weeks of discussion and cogitation he came out on October 17th with a dreary prosaic statement, renewing previous assurances that Dominion Status was the goal of British policy in India, but giving no indication when that goal was likely to be reached. It was so ill-calculated to appeal to Congress that cynics said it was purposely designed to ease them out of office. Five days later the Working Committee called on the Congress Ministries to resign.

The British disposition now was to leave Congress to stew in their own juice. From the point of view of preventing a widening of the gulf between Congress and the League, this attitude was unwise. But even after the 'Pakistan' resolution had highlighted the danger of drift, no active effort was made by the British to awaken Congress leaders to the imperative need of early reconciliation with the League, if Indian unity was to be preserved. In both camps, however, the more sober elements were profoundly disturbed by the 1940 resolution and, independently of their leaders, endeavoured to come to some understanding. During the summer of 1940 Sir Sikander through various intermediaries got into touch with right-wing Congress

[1] A group of British officers in the Punjab privately urged this course, the most senior of them, Sir Malcolm Darling, approaching the Viceroy on the subject while the rest tackled the Viceroy's private secretary. Their suggestions were ridiculed.

leaders such as Rajagopalachari in the hope of reaching a settlement. Though reluctant to break with Jinnah, Sikander was ready in the last resort to do so and confident that he could carry sufficient moderate leaguers with him, *provided that* he was assured of Congress support. But it was found that such support could not be counted upon, for even right-wing Congress leaders wanted that as part of the plan of settlement the Viceroy's Executive Council should be reconstituted so as to give it an almost exclusively non-official character and a far greater degree of independence than the British were likely to concede in time of war. Lord Linlithgow, when he got wind of these pourparlers, was wholly discouraging and expressed the view that Sikander would burn his fingers; so they petered out early in 1941 without any result except perhaps that Sikander, though still wholly averse to Pakistan, became less inclined even than before to stand up to Jinnah.

A year later, when the Japanese seemed poised for an attack on India, the British themselves did at last make a determined effort to unite all parties in the common defence of the country. Sir Stafford Cripps flew out to India in March 1942 with proposals both for an interim government and for a final constitutional settlement after the cessation of hostilities. His mission failed and with its failure went the last chance of bringing the Congress and League together in a 'National Government' for the prosecution of the war. Congress clung to the demand for virtual independence forthwith, and settlement of all outstanding problems—including the Hindu-Muslim quarrel— afterwards. The British proposals, while they amounted in effect to the promise of Dominion Status immediately after the war, with full liberty to secede from the Commonwealth, contemplated no major constitutional change while the war was still in progress. It was mainly on this ground that Congress rejected them. But Congress also complained that the proposals were 'a severe blow to the conception of Indian Unity'. From the point of view of Hindu-Muslim relations this was much their most significant aspect; for this was the first occasion on which the British publicly admitted the possibility of Partition. The creation of 'Pakistan' was not accepted outright —on this ground Jinnah in his turn rejected the proposals— but the right of individual Provinces and Indian States to stay out of the proposed Indian Union and form separate Unions of their own was acknowledged. This was a triumph for Jinnah. It put him in a very strong position, for if the Muslims of the Muslim-majority provinces stood behind him, he could now, with the right to stay out conceded, bargain for the terms on which those provinces would come in and the dream of Congress Raj over the whole of India would never come true. Even Muslims who did not want Pakistan were impressed by the importance of supporting Jinnah.

Gandhi was mainly responsible for the rejection by Congress of the Cripps proposals. Not content with this he came out soon after with the startling demand that the British should immediately quit India altogether, even if this meant leaving it to chaos and the Japanese. One prominent and courageous Congress leader—Rajagopalachari, the ex-premier of Madras and an old friend of Gandhi—now boldly made a stand. He had for some time been uneasy at the negative, unrealistic attitude of Congress both towards the British and the Muslims. He had favoured reaching a settlement on the basis of the Cripps offer, but had been overborne and Gandhi's views had prevailed. Appalled by the disastrous and irresponsible futility of the Gandhian policy, he now protested both publicly and privately against the 'quit India' demand, asserting that it would be a crime for the British to leave India at this juncture and that their withdrawal without simultaneous replacement by another government 'must involve the dissolution of the State and society itself'. This was plain common sense; but in the policy which he advocated towards Jinnah and the Muslims he showed more than common sense; he showed far-sighted statesmanship. In May 1942 he submitted to the All India Congress Committee a resolution recommending acquiescence in the principle of Pakistan. Statesmanship does not however commend itself to the many except after the event. He was heavily defeated, and soon afterwards, threatened with disciplinary action for his denunciation of Gandhi's 'quit India' policy, he resigned from Congress. Few now would deny that the Congress leaders would have done well to follow his advice. For in 1942 most of the leaguers, perhaps even Jinnah himself, did not in their hearts desire the partition of the country, and to have conceded Pakistan in principle would have smoothed the path for a settlement on other lines. But the voice of reason was disregarded and Congress, following blindly the promptings of Gandhi's own 'inner voice', launched in August 1942 the insensate 'quit India' rebellion. All leading Congressmen were immediately arrested and put in confinement. When nearly three years later, at the close of the war with Germany, they emerged once again, they found Jinnah as intractable as ever and considerably stronger. Almost all Muslims were arrayed behind him in a solid phalanx.

II

The Punjab and Pakistan

BEFORE the general story is carried forward, it is necessary
to explain in more detail the implications for the Punjab
of the demand for Pakistan and the reasons for Sikander's
dislike of it. He had said to me that Pakistan would mean a
massacre. He had referred specifically only to a massacre of
Hindus by Muslims; but there was also the opposite danger of a
massacre of Muslims by Hindus, and this not only in distant
parts of India hardly known to me, where the Muslims were
far outnumbered, but in the Punjab itself—a Muslim-majority
province. In the province as a whole the Muslims constituted
about 57 per cent of the population and in the west of it were
markedly predominant, but east of Lahore both their numbers
and their dominance fell away. Here the non-Muslim population did not consist merely, or mainly, of merchants, shopkeepers and clerks. In the districts immediately east of Lahore
lay the homelands of the Sikhs—the vigorous but violent peasant
stock that only 100 years before had held sway over most of the
province; and in the south-east towards Delhi dwelt the Hindu
Jats—a tough peasantry with martial traditions and racially
akin to the Sikhs. Would all these turbulent folk meekly accept
a Muslim Raj?

Here lay the crux of the Pakistan problem. According to the
ideas of Jinnah and the Muslim League, the Punjab, being a
Muslim-majority province, would be part of Pakistan. But if so,
it would be necessary to square the Sikhs. For how could this
robust and highly self-conscious community be incorporated
in a Muslim State against their will? They would certainly
resist it by force.

The Sikhs had an importance in the Punjab, and even in
India as a whole, quite out of proportion to their numbers.
Altogether there were only about six million of them. Even in the
Punjab, where they were mainly concentrated, they constituted

less than 20 per cent of the population and were not in an
absolute majority in a single district. But they were an enterprising and relatively prosperous community. They held a dis-
proportionately large share of the best land in the Punjab—
in part a legacy from the days when they were its rulers, in
part a result of their remarkable success as colonists of the new
canal-irrigated lands in West Punjab. They had also acquired
under British rule a privileged position in the army—no other
community had such a high percentage of its members serving
as soldiers.

Originally the Sikhs were simply a religious sect. Their subsequent emergence at the end of the seventeenth century as a
distinct and militant community was a result of Muslim rule
and oppression and may be regarded as one of the Hindu protests against the proselytizing zeal of the Mogul emperor
Aurangzeb. The core of the community consists of peasants of the
Jat tribe.[1] A certain number of Hindus of the urban commercial
classes have grown beards and embraced Sikhism and some of
these with their superior education and intellectual qualities
have played an important part in the leadership of the Sikh
community. But the typical Sikh is a sturdy 'Jat' peasant. It
was through his toughness that under the stimulus of Muslim
oppression the Sikhs developed into a distinct community, and
through his fighting qualities that Maharajah Ranjit Singh, himself a Jat Sikh, founded and sustained a Sikh kingdom in the
Punjab on the ruins of the Mogul empire.

Naturally with this background the Sikhs were deeply
alarmed at Jinnah's plan for dividing India and forming an
independent Muslim-dominated State—Pakistan—in which
they and the whole of the Punjab would be included. Their
reaction to it was the exact counterpart of the reaction of the
Muslims to a Hindu-dominated India. Just as the Muslims, with
their memories of the Mogul empire, were not prepared to see
themselves condemned to a position of inferiority under a
permanent Hindu majority, so the Sikhs, remembering that
only 100 years before they had ruled the Punjab, were not prepared to become a tiny minority in a large Muslim State.

[1] The Jats were the predominant agricultural tribe of the Punjab as it
existed before Partition. There are Muslim and Hindu Jats as well as Sikh
Jats. They probably all have a common Scythian origin.

Moreover, just as the Muslims could use the threat of dividing India as a means of extracting concessions from the Hindu majority, so the Sikhs saw that they could use the threat of dividing the Punjab as a means of extracting concessions from the Muslims.

The crucial position held by the Sikhs, if Pakistan were to become a live issue, could not escape the notice of any Punjab civilian. It was particularly forced on my attention; for soon after the outbreak of war I became rather intimately concerned with Sikh affairs, and in 1941 I was appointed Deputy Commissioner[1] of the district of Amritsar. It lay in the heart of the Sikh country and the city of Amritsar itself, built round the Golden Temple, was the main religious and political centre of the Sikhs. Here were the headquarters of the Akalis,[2] the most powerful Sikh political party, representing an extreme form of Sikh nationalism with a strongly anti-British bias. They controlled the Golden Temple—and indeed most other Sikh shrines—and buzzed about the place like angry wasps.

A very senior British official told me that the Deputy Commissioner, Amritsar, ought to regard himself as British ambassador to the Sikhs. The practice of some of my predecessors had conformed to this conception. They had considered it their duty to keep themselves fully informed of the Sikh point of view on all important matters and to represent it to the Government as cogently as possible. With many great issues looming ahead it seemed very desirable that this tradition should be maintained. Inevitably, therefore, I had to try to establish friendly relations with Sikh political leaders and particularly with Master Tara Singh and other prominent Akalis. In this I was greatly assisted both by my predecessor and also by a military officer, Major Short, with whom I had been thrown into close contact since the middle of 1940.

[1] In the Punjab the head of a district was called the Deputy Commissioner.

[2] Akali means immortal. The Akalis (Immortals) were originally a famous regiment of Ranjit Singh. The term was revived during the movement after World War I for the liberation of Sikh shrines (gurdwaras) from the control of hereditary priests. Those who took part in this movement were described as Akalis. Since the priests' possession of the shrines (often very well endowed) was legal, the Government tended to support them and the movement quickly took an anti-Government turn.

Short was a 'dug-out' officer of the XIth Sikh regiment and a great Sikh enthusiast—destined over the next few years to plead their cause in vain. He had come to the Punjab in the summer of 1940 in consequence of a series of disquieting incidents among Sikh elements of the armed forces, which had culminated in April 1940 in the refusal of the Sikh squadron of the Central India Horse to embark at Bombay for the Middle East. A considerable flutter had been caused in Army Headquarters. There was some wild talk of disbanding all Sikh units; and, more seriously, a proposal was put forward to stop all further recruitment of Sikhs. The Punjab Government strongly opposed any such drastic step and a decision was wisely taken to try to restore the situation by more conciliatory methods. At Short's suggestion, he and a number of officers specially selected for their experience of Sikhs were deputed to probe and report on Sikh unrest in certain army units and in the principal Sikh districts. Later, a few officers, similarly picked, were posted in the main areas of Sikh recruitment and required to stimulate sustained and co-operative efforts by the civil and military authorities to allay Sikh disquiet and to induce a healthier attitude among the Sikhs towards the war and recruitment. Short was one of these civil liaison officers, as they were called, with his base at Lahore.

The Sikhs' favoured position in the army, with all that it meant in the way of pay and pensions in a land of chronic under-employment, was something that it was very much in their interest to retain. But if owing to the misconduct of Sikh troops or the disaffection of the Sikh population the recruitment of Sikhs was stopped or greatly reduced, that favoured position would be lost—and lost for ever; for in a free India, which was already in sight, neither of the two major communities, Hindu or Muslim, would have the slightest motive for restoring it. This was a danger which no Sikh could overlook; and it was not lost upon the Akalis. They were, however, in a rather difficult position. Hitherto their attitude had generally been anti-British and they formed along with the Congress the opposition to Sir Sikander's anglophile Unionist Government.[1] Most of their leaders had been to jail and had spent their lives in anti-

[1] A weaker Sikh group, the Khalsa National Party, representative of conservative and relatively pro-British Sikhs, supported the Unionists.

government agitation; indeed it was largely Akali influence that had unsettled the Sikhs and shaken the loyalty of the Sikh soldier. It was not easy, therefore, for them to perform a complete *volte-face* and openly advocate full collaboration with the Unionist Government and the British in the prosecution of the war. But in order to safeguard the position of the Sikh in the army some of them were inclined to modify their attitude of opposition. The danger of becoming isolated, unbefriended by either the Congress, Muslim League or the British, also began to dawn on them. In the jockeying for position in anticipation of the end of the British Raj, who except the British would support a minority community like the Sikhs?

Circumstances were, therefore, not unfavourable to a revival of Anglo-Sikh amity, and for facilitating this rapprochement Short at Lahore, covering also Amritsar and the central Punjab districts and with influential friends in the Sikh State of Patiala, was in a key position. His duties were not strictly political; but obviously, if he was to effect anything in the Sikh recruiting areas, he had to meet, converse with, and try to have an impact on Sikh political leaders. He threw himself into his work with enthusiasm and was soon accepted by leading Sikhs, and not least by the Akalis, as a friend and well-wisher. In addition he became intimate with Sir Sikander and other influential Punjabi Muslims and won the confidence of the Governor, Sir Henry Craik.

Short conceived his immediate and pressing task to be to rally the maximum Sikh support for Britain's war effort by restoring Anglo-Sikh amity and by inducing the largest possible measure of Sikh-Muslim amity in the Punjab. But he also viewed current Punjab affairs in the wider context of India's future, 'Settle the Sikh', he would say, 'and you settle India.' There was an element of truth in this exaggeration; for, as already explained, the Muslim-Sikh problem in the Punjab was a reproduction in microcosm—and in reverse—of the general Hindu-Muslim problem in India as a whole, and a political settlement in the Punjab acceptable to the Sikh minority, besides serving the immediate purposes of war, would contribute to the larger end of an all-India Hindu-Muslim settlement. With a true but ill-fated prescience Short worked for a Muslim-Sikh accord—which in political terms meant an alliance between the Unionists and the Akalis. His first efforts were repulsed, and this was not

B

surprising; for though the Akalis were in process of becoming
rather less hostile to the British and so indirectly—but more
unwillingly—less hostile to Sikander's pro-British Unionist
Government, there was still much suspicion on both sides. To
the Akalis Sikander's ostensible support of the demand for
Pakistan seemed hard to reconcile with any genuine goodwill
for the Sikhs. To Sikander the Akalis appeared insatiable; one
concession, he felt, would only lead to the demand for another
and nothing would win their permanent attachment.

But Short persevered and with good reason; for in face of the
demand for Pakistan some kind of understanding between the
Akalis and the Punjabi Muslims was essential, if first a dissi-
pation of the Punjab's war effort and then a disastrous division
of the province was to be avoided. Both sides knew that division was contrary to the interests of all Punjabis, whether
Muslim, Sikh or Hindu. Both sides dreaded it. But if the demand for Pakistan was pressed it might become inescapable;
for the Akalis were quite determined that the Sikhs should not
become a helpless minority in an independent Muslim State.
Rather than this they would face—indeed insist upon—division
despite all its disadvantages not least to the Sikhs themselves.

At first sight the distribution of population in the Punjab
as it then existed might appear not unfavourable to partition.
The western districts were predominantly Muslim, the eastern
predominantly non-Muslim. It might therefore seem easy and
natural to divide the province into two roughly equal parts by
a line drawn down the centre between the two principal cities
of Lahore and Amritsar. But any such line would be geographic-
ally, ethnically and economically wholly artificial. Save for a
few outlying districts the Punjab was a close-knit unity, and
the population so intermingled, especially in the central
districts, that wherever the line was drawn large numbers of
all three communities would find themselves on the wrong side
of it. Moreover, though differing in religion, the population
in all parts of the province was drawn from the same racial
stocks, spoke a common language and was very conscious of
being Punjabi. Economically too the province was a unity.
Its prosperity rested on an elaborate network of canals, spread
right across it from east to west, which had enabled large tracts
of desert to be converted into flourishing 'colonies'. People

from all over the province had a stake in these colonies and had played a part in their development. A line drawn down the centre of the Punjab might serve well enough as a boundary between two provincial administrations both subordinate to the same central government; but if it were to be made a regular frontier between two separate, sovereign, independent States, it would at best cause enormous economic dislocation and hardship and at worst lead to serious disorders.

Sikander and the majority of the Punjabi Muslims, aware of the real facts of the situation, were utterly opposed to such an artificial division of the province. Even extremist Muslims, who were animated by narrow sectarian impulses rather than by broad feelings of provincial patriotism and regard for the general interest, wished such division to be avoided. Pakistan according to their conception included the whole of the Punjab. Its division on a population basis would mean the acceptance by them of a truncated Pakistan, with large numbers of their co-religionists left just on the wrong side of the frontier and with Hindustan in control of the headwaters of three[1] of the five Punjab rivers. They had, therefore, strong motives for wishing to keep the Punjab intact.

The Akalis for their part also looked at the matter from a narrow sectarian point of view and fully realized how damaging division would be to the Sikhs. On a strictly population basis the likely dividing line would leave two million of them, with all their valuable colony lands not to mention some important Sikh shrines, on the Pakistan side. To a small community of only six million such a division might well be fatal. The Akali leaders sought to comfort themselves with the hope that the line of division might be shifted westwards, even as far as the river Chenab, so that all the rich colony lands of the Lyallpur and Montgomery districts with their numerous Sikh peasantry would fall into East Punjab and be excluded from Pakistan. During my time at Amritsar one of them tried hard to coax me into conceding that this was a possibility and urged that, if it came to a division of the Punjab, the Sikhs' stake in the colony lands and the part they had played in developing them would have to be taken into account. I told him bluntly that such hopes were in my view illusory and that if Pakistan became

[1] The Sutlej, Beas and Ravi.

inevitable either it would include the whole of the Punjab or
the Punjab would be divided on a population basis by a line
down the middle. The Wagah Rest House, I said, would mark
the dividing line—this being a well-known canal inspection
bungalow near the Grand Trunk Road on the border of the
Lahore and Amritsar[1] districts. I did not manage to convince
him. He recurred to the subject more than three years later at
the time of the Cabinet Mission, and in one form or another this
illusory hope persisted to the very end.

But in 1942–3 the Akalis' main hope was that the threat of
Pakistan would not materialize. In the then prevailing mood
of Punjabi Muslims this hope seemed well-founded; but the
prospects of its realization would be greatly improved by a
political alliance between Unionists and Akalis. If the Muslim
and Sikh communities, as represented by these political parties,
stood firmly together, Pakistan would in all probability remain
an aspiration; for without the support of the Punjabi Muslims
it could not come into being. Even if, at worst, the latter were
compelled to translate into reality their nominal adherence to
the idea of Pakistan, a Unionist-Akali alliance was likely to
prevent the division of the province between two sovereign
States and lead to an offer to the Sikhs of special rights and
privileges which would make them feel that their community
had a more glorious future as part of Pakistan, supported by the
combined might of Muslims and Sikhs, than as an insignificant
fragment of Hinbu India.

The prospect, then, of a disruption of the Punjab, which the
demand for Pakistan seemed to portend, made natural and
possible the coming together of Unionists and Akalis; and to
well-wishers of the province an understanding between them
certainly seemed desirable. The death early in 1941 of Sir
Sunder Singh Majithia, the leader of the Khalsa National
Party and a prominent member of Sikander's Government,
provided the opportunity for some political realignment; but
it was not till a year later that through the prolonged efforts of
Major Short and a few others an agreement was reached between Unionists and Akalis known as the Sikander-Baldev
Singh pact. S. Baldev Singh, who though himself not an Akali

---

[1] The frontier post between India and Pakistan on the Grand Trunk road
is, in fact, at Wagah.

was known to be acceptable to the Akali Party, became the Sikh Minister in the Punjab Cabinet and the Akalis tacitly undertook to refrain at least from active opposition. The first fruits of this pact were seen in the Akalis' attitude towards Gandhi's rebellion in August 1942. Only a handful of them took part in it; the majority held aloof and did nothing to embarrass the Punjab Government.

'At present', I commented at the time, 'this pact cannot be regarded as more than a temporary truce. Its significance lies in its potentialities for the future. That a predominantly Muslim Government should have been able to come to terms, even temporarily, with a party of extreme Sikh nationalists is something to the good, and if the truce holds good for a few years it may develop into real understanding between the Unionist Government and the Akalis and bear fruit in the form of a far-reaching Sikh-Muslim compromise regarding the sharing of power in the Punjab. If such a compromise were effected, it would facilitate and perhaps give the clue to a similar solution of the all-India problem.'

A series of misfortunes and mistakes blasted the hopes thus cautiously expressed. The Unionist Party crumbled to pieces, and in consequence the Sikander-Baldev Singh pact instead of being the salvation of the province contributed to its undoing. Jinnah gained complete ascendancy over the Punjabi Muslims, crushing all opposition till there was none left to resist him or even to tell him the real truth about the Punjab. He himself knew no more of the Punjab than Neville Chamberlain did of Czechoslovakia.

This tragic history will be traced in later pages;[1] but the first misfortune occurred at the close of 1942. Suddenly one night without any warning Sikander had a heart attack and died. He was only fifty and his death was entirely unexpected.

Felix opportunitate mortis. I said this at the time and I still feel that it is true. He died at the height of his power and reputation and escaped a future which seemed to threaten both. The truth is that the demand for Pakistan had put him in a quandary from which there was no obvious way out. For nearly two years he had contrived to reconcile the irreconcilable—his own political beliefs, proclaimed by his leadership of the Unionist Party, and

[1] Chapter V.

his acceptance of the Pakistan resolution. But it is doubtful whether even he, with all his skill, could have succeeded much longer in explaining away the contradiction. He would have been compelled to choose between the risk of a break with Jinnah (and consequent defection of a powerful group of Punjabi Muslims) and the loss of all credit with his non-Muslim supporters.

Many of us had been critical of Sikander for his constant submission to Jinnah and unwillingness to stand up to him. He was aware of these criticisms and during a long talk with me, just before I went to Amritsar, defended himself against them with considerable feeling. He said that unless he walked warily and kept on the right side of Jinnah he would be swept away by a wave of fanaticism and, wherever he went, would be greeted by the Muslims with black flags. I was by no means wholly convinced by his arguments. I thought that he underrated the strength of his position in the Punjab and his hold on the Muslims, reinforced as it was in the case of many of the prominent Muslim politicians by ties of personal affection. Subsequent events suggest that his reading of the situation was more correct than mine.

There can be no doubt that if he had lived and nerved himself to defy Jinnah he would have had more chance than his successor of doing so without disaster. The probability is that he would never have taken the risk, but would have continued his temporizing policy and faced the loss of all credit with non-Muslims rather than hazard any defection amongst his Muslim followers. If so, he would at any rate have been a moderating influence on Jinnah during the critical months of 1946–7 and would hardly have allowed him to be driven into acceptance of the partition of the Punjab without making the smallest attempt to reach an understanding with the Sikhs. On either alternative, therefore, his death must be reckoned a great misfortune.

Sir Sikander's successor as leader of the Unionist Party and Premier of the Punjab was Sir Khizar Hyat Tiwana, the scion of a well-known family of West Punjab where he enjoyed much of the status of a feudal baron. He was a man of the highest courage—far more resolute than Sir Sikander—and a strong, attractive personality. But, having only entered politics in 1937, he did not have Sikander's experience and standing, nor was he endowed in the same degree with his diplomatic gifts and charm of manner.

Like Sikander he was at heart strongly opposed to the demand for Pakistan; but he was less willing than Sikander to compromise or to bow to Jinnah's dictation. Compromise was in fact becoming impossible, for Jinnah stood firmly by the demand that all the Muslim-majority provinces should be formed into Pakistan and repeatedly stated that this meant their complete severance from the rest of India with no link save such voluntary agreements as might be concluded between independent sovereign States. He also began to evince a desire to control the actions of the Punjab Government, claiming that as the Muslims, who constituted the majority of the Unionist Party, were also members of the League, the Punjab Government was a 'League' government and should submit to his directives as President of the League. To this Khizar demurred on the ground that his government was not a League government but a coalition government with Hindu and Sikh members.

Jinnah soon realized that in Khizar he had a tougher man to deal with than Sikander. He therefore set himself to undermine his position. There had always been among the Muslim Unionists a clique of communal extremists, out of sympathy with Sikander's moderate policies and wholehearted supporters of the demand for Pakistan. Sikander with his capacity for being all things to all men had contrived to keep them in check. They were however readily available to Jinnah for the intimidation of Khizar or, failing that, for rousing Muslim opinion against him and bringing about his downfall. Khizar was not, however, a man to be intimidated. He courageously resisted Jinnah's attempts to dictate to him till finally in the middle of 1944 there was an open rupture and he was expelled by Jinnah from the League. The Muslim members of the Unionist Party were now forced to choose between loyalty to Khizar and the Unionist Party and loyalty to Jinnah and the League. Thus there opened the rift in the Muslim ranks which Sikander had always dreaded and the Unionist Party, which had dominated Punjab politics for over twenty years and governed the province since 1937, began to disintegrate.

It suffered a grievous loss in January 1945 by the death of
Sir Chhotu Ram, the leader of the Hindu Jats of south-eastern
Punjab. For a generation he had been one of the main pillars
of the Unionist Party. He was a forceful politician of great renown within the province and had considerable influence
among some sections of the Muslims.

Khizar, though weakened by these developments, was not
immediately brought down; most of the Muslims in the provincial assembly continued to support him. But there were
ominous signs of the way the tide was flowing and of what
might happen when a general election was held. Several well-
known Punjabi Muslims of comparatively moderate views
announced their adherence to the League rather than to the
Unionist Party. Where these went others were bound to follow.

Thus by 1945 Jinnah's influence in the Punjab—the key
province so far as Pakistan was concerned—was very much
greater than it had been five years earlier when the 'Pakistan
Resolution' was passed. He had not destroyed the Unionists,
but he had made a breach in their ranks. Elsewhere too he had
strengthened his position. In Bengal Fazl-ul-Haq, the Premier
since 1937, had dared to defy him and had been overthrown in
1943. His successor, Khwaja Nazimuddin, was more amenable
and a whole-hearted leaguer. In Sind and Assam there were
League governments, and even in the North-West Frontier
Province, the one Muslim province attached to the Congress, a
League Ministry was formed during the absence in jail of
Congress's allies, the Red Shirts, and the League established
itself as a political force to be reckoned with.

Jinnah's relentless determination to eliminate all independent
Muslim parties and to marshal all Muslims under his own
leadership was well illustrated in the summer of 1945, when
the Viceroy, Lord Wavell, on the termination of the war with
Germany, made a fresh attempt to break the political deadlock.
The members of the Congress Working Committee who were
still in jail[1] were released and invited to a conference at Simla
to consider proposals for an Interim Government, all the members of which, except the Viceroy and Commander-in-Chief,
would be drawn from the principal Indian political parties.
After the folly of the 'Quit India' rebellion Congress were in a

[1] Some had already been released on grounds of health.

chastened mood and ready to co-operate. But if the Interim
Government was to be fruitful for the future, Jinnah's co-
operation was also necessary, and Jinnah put forward demands
which effectually wrecked the conference. The Muslims, he
claimed, must not only have half the total number of seats in the
government, but all the Muslim seats must be held by nominees of the League. There must be no Muslim stooges of Congress, like Maulana Abul Kalam Azad, nor possible Muslim
'Quislings', like Khizar or any other Punjabi Muslim belonging
to the Unionist Party. On this demand that the League should
nominate all the Muslims Jinnah was adamant. Lord Wavell
had wanted to include a nominee of the Unionists, but Jinnah,
who was bent on eliminating them altogether as a political
force, would not hear of it. If we had acquiesced, he said
afterwards, in the inclusion of non-League Muslims in the
Muslim quota, 'we should have signed our death warrant'. It
was over this issue that the conference broke down.

The Congress had once claimed to speak for the whole of
India. The claim was invalid and they had been compelled to
abate it. Jinnah now claimed to speak for all the Muslims of
India. This claim was also invalid; but unlike Congress he was
not compelled to abate it and soon he succeeded for all practical purposes in making it good.

III

The Cabinet Mission

A NEW Labour Government came into power in Great Britain at the end of July 1945. Despite other preoccupations they were determined to give high priority to the settlement of the Indian problem. The failure of Lord Wavell's Simla Conference left the field clear for some fresh initiative, and the capitulation of Japan on August 14th made it necessary to think not merely of interim arrangements but of a final constitutional settlement. The Labour Government's first action was to order elections for the Central and Provincial Assemblies. Owing to the war these had not been held since early in 1937. It was announced by the Viceroy on August 21st that there would be fresh elections during the ensuing cold weather. Their result, so far as the Hindu population was concerned, was a foregone conclusion—there would be overwhelming support for Congress. But they would be a test of Jinnah's claim to speak for all the Muslims of India.

The British Labour Party had always been sympathetic towards India's struggle for freedom and several of its prominent members had been in fairly close touch with Gandhi, Nehru and other Congress leaders. There was therefore a natural tendency to incline to the Congress' view of things and a reluctance to regard Pakistan as a really serious and live proposition. Though the importance of Jinnah could not be ignored, his firm adherence to the demand for Pakistan was believed to be for bargaining purposes; and in any case, so long as he failed to win the allegiance of the Muslims of the Punjab and N.W.F.P., Pakistan could not come into being and the unity of India could be preserved. These were the hopes and beliefs of the Labour Government as the year 1945 drew to a close.

Early in the new year the realities began to be seen to be a little different. A parliamentary delegation visited India in January. Its members were considerably impressed by the solidity of Muslim opinion in favour of Pakistan and some of them felt doubtful whether Jinnah's demand for it could any longer be regarded as mere bluff. One of those who most stressed the strength of Muslim feeling behind Jinnah was Mr. Woodrow Wyatt, a Labour M.P. and therefore not to be suspected of anti-Congress bias. The correctness of his appreciation was confirmed by the results of the elections. In the Central Assembly the League had already captured all the Muslim seats. In the Provincial Assemblies it now won 446 out of a total of 495 Muslim seats. Its only failure was in the N.W.F.P., but this was of small significance compared with its smashing success in the Punjab. Here in 1937 it had utterly failed, securing only one of the Muslim seats in the Provincial Assembly while the Unionists captured all the rest. But now the tables were turned. The League won seventy-nine seats and Khizar and the Muslim Unionists were reduced to a mere handful of ten.[1] It was for all practical purposes the end of the Unionist Party. The cry of Pakistan, with its vague but alluring connotation for the Muslim masses, had proved irresistible. Jinnah's claim to speak for the Muslims had been triumphantly vindicated.

Obviously the prospects of avoiding partition had considerably worsened; but the British Government were not lightly to be deflected from their aim of preserving, while granting independence, the unity of India which British rule had achieved. They made now a last supreme effort to realize this aim, atoning thereby to some extent for former British complacency over the communal cleavage. It was not their fault that it did not succeed.

The leading figure in this British effort was Sir Stafford Cripps. In March 1946, almost exactly four years after his previous abortive mission, he flew out once again to India, accompanied this time by two other Cabinet Ministers—Mr. A. V. Alexander and Lord Pethick Lawrence. Among the members of his staff was Major Short, who had by this time returned to England. His inclusion in the party was a small but graceful gesture to the Sikhs, suggesting (quite erroneously as it proved) that their interests would be safeguarded.

[1] After several defections to the League subsequent to the declaration of the election results.

The task of this trio of Cabinet Ministers was twofold, to
assist the Viceroy in bringing about agreement on the method
of framing a constitution and to assist him in the formation of
a new Executive Council, representative of the main Indian
political parties, for carrying on the government while the
constitution was being hammered out. These two things were
at this stage more than ever interrelated, for without a broad
measure of agreement about the future constitutional set-up
it was impossible to bring Congress and the League together
in an effective Executive Council.

The task was sufficiently daunting. Since the original Congress-League rupture in 1937 all attempts to reconcile their conflicting aims had been unavailing, and these aims were now
more glaringly contradictory than ever before. Jinnah contended that there were two nations in India and that therefore
there must be two national States. The Congress maintained
the opposite. Between these opposing viewpoints there seemed
little room for compromise; equally there was little disposition
for it. Each side, being deeply distrustful of the other, preferred
to cling to its own perfect solution and unrealizable ideal rather
than risk yielding an advantage to the other by seeking for a
middle way. Moreover, if any compromise formula were to be
devised, each side knew that the other would stand on its letter
rather than its spirit, and instead of looking to its broad intention would seek later to twist its interpretation to suit their own
ends. There was, therefore, great wariness about agreeing to
anything.

One hopeful feature was the growing awareness in India
that the British Government really meant business. Though in
some quarters there was still distrust of British intentions, the
principal political leaders were becoming convinced of the
sincerity of the Labour Government's proclaimed resolve to
quit the scene and leave India to Indians. Power—and responsibility—were at last within their grasp, and this might be
expected to induce a more reasonable and realistic attitude;
for without agreement between the two major political parties,
transfer of power could only lead to chaos and civil war.

The main hope of such agreement lay in the possibility that
Jinnah would be persuaded to accept something less than he
apparently demanded. What was it he really wanted? Nobody

was quite sure. Ostensibly he claimed a sovereign independent Pakistan consisting of the whole of six provinces,[1] subject only to minor frontier adjustments. In 1944, at the instance of Rajagopalachari, Gandhi had offered him something less than this—a Pakistan consisting of those contiguous areas in the north-west and north-east of India in which Muslims were in a majority. On this principle Pakistan would be shorn of nearly all Assam and of large parts of the Punjab and Bengal. Jinnah, not content with a bundle of contiguous areas, had rejected outright this offer of what he called a 'moth-eaten' Pakistan. But how could he hope to get the Pakistan of his conception except by persuading the Sikhs and other sections of the non-Muslim population willingly to throw in their lot with Pakistan? Such persuasions were not necessarily foredoomed to failure. Yet he had so far made no attempt to conciliate or win them over.

All in all it seemed possible that he had not even now quite decided in his own mind what he wanted or how to get it, but believed that by uncompromisingly demanding a 'six province' Pakistan he would ultimately extort for the Muslims something which, if not Pakistan, would be better than a bundle of contiguous areas. A formula, therefore, had to be devised, which offered the semblance of a 'six province' Pakistan while preserving the essentials of unity.

The Cabinet Mission's arrival in Delhi coincided with the onset of the hot weather and the temperature steadily rose as they went through a round of preliminary interviews with representatives of the main political parties, the Indian States, the Sikhs, the scheduled castes, and, not least, with Gandhi. He established himself in considerable style and with due publicity in the 'harijan' quarter of New Delhi and, though claiming to speak only for himself, was available as a sort of universal counsellor to anyone who sought his advice. The Cabinet Mission specifically requested him to remain at hand and in touch with them during the whole progress of the negotiations.

Towards the end of April, after completing their round of interviews, the Mission took a short recess, expressing the hope that the main parties would themselves now come together and offer some agreed basis for framing a constitution. There was

[1] Punjab, Sind, Baluchistan, N.W.F.P., Bengal and Assam.

not the slightest prospect of any such thing occurring. Everyone knew that the Cabinet Mission would themselves have to
propound their own scheme, and herein lay the only hope of
finding a compromise. Several schemes had in fact been mooted
during the course of the preliminary interviews and conver-
sations. One of these, though not perhaps intrinsically the best,
when adumbrated by Sir Stafford to Jinnah informally, seemed
to awaken in that cold serpent-like figure a spark of interest, the
scintilla of a positive response. Seeing the chance, Sir Stafford
took it. The fundamental principles of this particular scheme
were set down in writing and communicated on April 27th to
both Congress and the League as a possible basis of agreement.
Each was invited to send four negotiators to discuss them in the
more temperate climate of Simla. These fundamental principles were as follows:

   (i) A Union Government to deal only with foreign affairs,
       defence and communications;
  (ii) two Groups of Provinces, one of the predominantly
       Hindu provinces and the other of the predominantly
       Muslim provinces, to deal with such of the remaining
       subjects as the provinces in the respective groups de-
       sired to be dealt with in common;
 (iii) the Provincial Governments to deal with all other sub-
       jects and to have all the residuary sovereign rights;
 (iv) the Indian States to take their appropriate place in
       this structure on terms to be negotiated with them.

Both sides accepted the invitation, but both made it clear
that this did not imply agreement with the fundamental principles. Jinnah merely reiterated his demand for a 'six province'
Pakistan and, as a corollary, the setting up of two separate
constitution-making bodies. Congress specified straight away
their main objection to the proposed scheme. 'We consider it
wrong', they wrote, 'to form Groups of Provinces under the
Federal Union and more so on religious or communal basis.
Any sub-federation within the Federal Union would weaken
the Federal Centre and would otherwise be wrong. . . . It would
result in creating three layers of executive and legislative bodies,
an arrangement which will be cumbrous, static and disjointed,
leading to continuous friction.'

It will be seen that they objected to just those features of the scheme which carried the faint impression of Pakistan. They stuck to this objection to the bitter end.

The discussions in Simla, though comparatively cordial, led to no agreement, and it was left, therefore, to the Cabinet Mission and the Viceroy to rehash and elaborate the scheme in the light of the views expressed and to put it forward publicly as offering the best arrangement for providing a new constitution for an independent India. This they did in a carefully drafted statement issued on May 16th.

In this statement the proposal for 'a separate and fully independent sovereign State of Pakistan as claimed by the Muslim League' was considered and decisively rejected. It was pointed out that a Pakistan of six provinces, as demanded by the League, would not solve the problem of communal minorities since twenty million Muslims would still remain in India and there would be non-Muslim minorities in Pakistan amounting to 38 per cent of the population in the western part and 48 per cent in the eastern part. 'Nor can we see any justification', the statement went on, 'for including within a sovereign Pakistan those districts of the Punjab and of Bengal and Assam in which the population is predominantly non-Muslim. Every argument that can be used in favour of Pakistan can equally, in our view, be used in favour of the exclusion of the non-Muslim areas from Pakistan. This point would particularly affect the position of the Sikhs.'

The possibility of a smaller 'truncated' Pakistan confined to the Muslim majority areas alone was also considered. The reasons advanced for rejecting this are of melancholy interest in view of what subsequently took place. 'Such a Pakistan', it was stated, 'is regarded by the Muslim League as quite impracticable. We ourselves are also convinced that any solution which involves a radical partition of the Punjab and Bengal, as this would do, would be contrary to the wishes and interests of a very large proportion of the inhabitants of these Provinces. . . . Moreover, any division of the Punjab would of necessity divide the Sikhs, leaving substantial bodies of Sikhs on both sides of the boundary.'

Having rejected Pakistan, the Mission proceeded to expand and commend the scheme which had been discussed at Simla.

In elaborating it they attempted to meet the views of both parties, but basically it remained the same. A three-tiered constitution was envisaged consisting of a Union limited to foreign affairs, defence and communications, Groups of Provinces dealing with such subjects as might later be determined, and the individual Provinces themselves in which all residuary powers would vest. After an initial period of ten years it was to be open to any Province, by a majority vote of its legislature, to call for a reconsideration of the constitution.

The Mission's statement then went on to propose that such a constitution should be brought into being by means of a Constituent Assembly to be elected by the members of the provincial legislatures,[1] and that the Constituent Assembly should follow a certain procedure designed to meet Jinnah's objection to a single constitution-making body. It was proposed that after an initial full meeting of a formal character, the Assembly should divide up into three sections—Section A consisting of the representatives of the five Hindu-majority provinces; Section B of the representatives of the Punjab, N.W.F.P. and Sind, and Section C of the representatives of Bengal and Assam. These Sections would draw up constitutions for the Provinces included in each of them and would also decide whether a Group should be formed and if so with what subjects; but a Province would have the right to opt out of a Group by a vote of its legislature *after* the new constitutional arrangements had come into operation. Finally the Constituent Assembly would meet again as a whole to settle the Union Constitution.

The statement referred to the need, while the constitution-making proceeded, for an Interim Government in which all the portfolios would be held by Indian leaders having the confidence of the people. It was mentioned that the Viceroy had already started discussions to this end.

The statement was well received. It was recognized at once

[1] Each Province was to be allocated representatives proportionate to its population and this provincial allocation was to be divided in turn between the main communities in each Province in proportion to their population. For this purpose only three main communities were recognized, Muslim, Sikh and General, the latter including all persons who were not Muslims or Sikhs.

as a genuine and ingenious attempt to reconcile conflicting aims and as unmistakable evidence of the British Government's sincere desire to bring British rule in India to a peaceful end. Gandhi speaking at a prayer meeting on May 17th said that the Cabinet Mission had brought forth something of which they had every reason to be proud; and even ten days later, when doubts had begun to assail him, he still considered it 'the best document the British Government could have produced in the circumstances'. In spite of these encomiums it soon became clear that Gandhi and the Working Committee of Congress would scrutinize every line and comma of the statement before committing themselves to an acceptance of the proposals.

Jinnah was less enthusiastic. The statement had flatly rejected the idea of a sovereign, independent Pakistan, and this he could hardly be expected to applaud. But though outwardly more critical of the statement, he was really, as it proved, less inclined to cavil at it than Congress.

The largest volume of vocal opposition came from various minority groups who felt that their interests were not adequately safeguarded—and not least from the Sikhs. The crushing defeat of the Unionist Party in the Punjab elections early in the year had come as a severe shock to them. As a result of the Sikander-Baldev Singh pact they had felt fairly secure while the Unionist Party still represented the bulk of the Punjab Muslims; and they had fully expected that the Unionists would be victorious at the elections. But to their utter dismay a rabid Muslim League Party had come to the front with whom they saw no prospect of reaching an understanding; and now, according to the Cabinet Mission proposals, the Punjab itself would be swallowed up entire in a group of predominantly Muslim provinces which, if not the equivalent of Pakistan, might ultimately turn into it or prove to be as bad.

It was pointed out to them that as the Muslims were a bare majority of the population in the Punjab they would find it impossible to rule the province without Sikh support—the Sikhs would, in fact, hold the balance of power. The Muslim League Party in the Punjab might for the time being seem very hostile to them, but ultimately, like the Unionists, they would be compelled to woo them. By these and similar arguments Major Short and the Cabinet Mission tried to reassure them;

but they would not be comforted. They had got it into their heads that the Muslims were out 'to crush them' and more and more their thoughts were turning to the idea of partitioning the Punjab so that they might escape altogether the threat of Muslim domination. Early in May the Akali leader with whom I had discussed this possibility as far back as 1942[1] came to see me in Delhi where I was at that time working. He had somewhat moderated his previous ambitions. He realized, he said, that there was no hope of the dividing line being so far west as the river Chenab, but would not the river Ravi be a very reasonable boundary? I pointed out some of the objections —such a boundary would deprive Pakistan of Lahore and of the overwhelmingly Muslim districts of Montgomery and Multan and yet leave many Sikhs on the wrong side. He said that he contemplated some exchange of population. I replied that this could only be accomplished by force and I counselled him not to think of the partition of the Punjab while there was a reasonable chance of preserving the unity both of it and of India as a whole. It was obvious, however, that he would continue to think of it; for now that the Punjab Muslims had gone over *en masse* to the League he despaired of reaching any accommodation with them.

Gandhi, who had hitherto shown little sympathy for the Sikhs—he objected to the Akali leaders as 'communalists'— began now, perhaps not very wisely, to draw public attention to their fears. Commenting in his paper *Harijan* on the Mission's statement he wrote: 'Are the Sikhs, for whom the Punjab is the only home in India, to consider themselves, against their will, as part of the Section which takes in Sind, Baluchistan and the Frontier Province?' Certainly it seemed hard that willy-nilly they should be lumped with predominantly Muslim areas, but this was dictated by the actual facts of their geographical distribution. There was at the moment nothing which could be done for them without upsetting the whole of the Mission's delicately poised scheme. Their fears, if not their interests, had necessarily to be overlooked.

Meanwhile both the two major parties were examining the scheme, apparently with some disposition to accept it. Hopes of a settlement were enormously raised when on June 6th Jinnah, abandoning his usual negative attitude, got the Muslim League

[1] See page 35.

to pass a resolution accepting the scheme and agreeing to join the constitution-making body. The acceptance, it is true, was stated to be 'in the hope that it would ultimately result in the establishment of complete sovereign Pakistan', which still remained the unalterable objective of the Muslims in India. But the Mission's scheme, whatever ultimate prospects and potentialities it might hold, was a definite rejection of 'sovereign Pakistan'. To have induced Jinnah at last publicly to accept something substantially less than what he had hitherto invariably demanded was a considerable success.

Jinnah's acceptance of the scheme had been fairly prompt and was certainly genuine; but it would be wrong to conclude that he agreed to it with enthusiasm. He had many misgivings and hesitated a good deal before recommending it to the Council of the League. Nevertheless from the Muslim point of view it offered solid advantages. All the six provinces[1] which the League claimed to be the Muslim 'home-lands' were included intact, without any division, in Sections B and C of the proposed Constituent Assembly; and since in these two Sections taken as a whole (though not in all the individual provinces composing them) the Muslims were in a clear majority, they could reasonably hope to ensure by majority vote[2] that in the constitution-making process these provinces would be formed into Groups or sub-federations. These Groups, though tied to an all-India Union, would be so powerful in themselves that no Hindu-dominated Union Government would be able to ride rough-shod over them; and there was always the possibility of secession after ten years. Thus over the short term, the scheme adequately protected essential Muslim interests and over the long term did not preclude the ultimate emergence of a 'sovereign independent Pakistan' embracing all the provinces which the Muslims claimed. All Jinnah's previous negations, more particularly his rejection of the 'moth-eaten' Pakistan offered by Gandhi in 1944, seemed justified now by results.

But the prospects of agreement still hung in the balance.

[1] Including British Baluchistan which was not constitutionally a 'Province' like the others, but would necessarily go into Section B.
[2] The Cabinet Mission had assured Jinnah that decisions in the Sections would be by a majority vote of the representatives of the Provinces within the Section and that the voting would not be by Provinces.

The Congress Working Committee had not yet given their verdict on the scheme and perhaps Jinnah's acceptance of it made them wish to scan it all the more closely. They tried hard to gain acceptance for an interpretation of the scheme which would make it optional for the individual provinces to join the Sections in which they had been placed. Since the Muslim League did not command a majority in the Punjab, the N.W.F.P. and Assam, it could be expected that these Provinces would elect not to enter B and C Sections and thus the grouping desired by the League would be frustrated. The Mission, however, firmly rejected the interpretation of the scheme suggested by Congress. The grouping of provinces, they said, was an essential feature of the scheme. A Province could opt out of a Group by the vote of its new legislature only *after* the constitution had come into force.

Days passed and the Congress Working Committee gave no decision but withdrew to Mussoori for recess, taking Gandhi with them. Meanwhile the Viceroy's attempts to bring about agreement between the two parties over the formation of an Interim Government had run up against the usual difficulties. The League claimed 'parity' with Congress and the exclusive right to nominate Muslims. Congress rejected both these claims. It became clear that, as in the case of the constitutional problem, there was no prospect of negotiating an agreement between the parties and that the only course was for the Viceroy and the Mission to put forward their own proposals and hope that they would be accepted by both parties as a reasonable compromise. The Mission was also getting impatient to return home and desired to bring matters to a head. Accordingly on June 16th—before Congress had pronounced on the constitutional scheme—the Viceroy, in consultation with the members of the Mission, announced that further negotiations were being abandoned and that he had issued invitations to a named list of fourteen persons to serve as members of an Interim Government. These consisted of six Hindu members of Congress (including one member of the scheduled castes), five members of the Muslim League, one Sikh, one Parsee and one Indian Christian. Thus Jinnah's claim to parity with Congress and with the Hindus was rejected, but his desire to veto non-League Muslims was respected.

The announcement stated that if the invitations were accepted by the two major parties it was hoped to inaugurate the new Government about June 26th. There then followed as paragraph 8 the following passage, designed perhaps to put pressure on Congress who were still hesitating over the constitutional scheme:

'In the event of the two parties or either of them proving unwilling to join in the setting up of a Coalition Government on the above lines, it is the intention of the Viceroy to proceed with the formation of an Interim Government which will be as representative as possible of those willing to accept the statement of May 16th.'

Since the League had already expressed its willingness to accept the May 16th statement whereas Congress had not, this seemed to imply that the possibility of forming a predominantly League Government without the inclusion of any representatives of Congress was not ruled out. Whether the Viceroy and Cabinet Mission really thought this to be a practical possibility or were merely bluffing is not very clear. It is somewhat difficult to believe that the British Government would have consented to the hazardous experiment of governing the whole of India with the aid of only Muslims, Christians and Parsees. Yet Jinnah seems to have thought that they might.

For a few days there was no public reaction to the announcement by either of the two major parties. The members of the Congress Working Committee had not all reassembled in Delhi and Gandhi also was temporarily absent. There was, however, a growing feeling of optimism. It was known that the proposals were acceptable to Jinnah; but he did not intend to intimate this until after Congress had spoken. In Congress circles there was some desire to substitute a Congress Muslim for one of the Congress Hindus, but it was hoped that they would not press the point in view of Jinnah's strong objection. Both Jawaharlal Nehru and Sardar Vallabhai Patel were believed to be in favour of acceptance and the rumour spread that the Congress Working Committee were going to express their readiness to work both the long-term and the short-term plan. All the labours of the past twelve weeks—the endless discussions in the

sweltering heat, the skilful and patient elaboration of a plan
to suit all parties, the drafting and redrafting of statements and
formulas—seemed on the point of being richly rewarded. For
nine years Congress and the League had been engaged in
barren controversy and non-co-operation. Now both were being
successfully shepherded into a Coalition Government and into
a Constituent Assembly which would frame a constitution on
an agreed basis. A cartoon appeared in the *Hindustan Times*
showing the Mission packing up to go home under the caption,
'All's well that ends well'.

It seemed too good to be true. And it was; for Gandhi had
not been reckoned with. Once again at the critical moment he
arrived on the scene and intervened with decisive and disastrous
effect. Those who were inclined to acquiesce in the omission of
a Congress Muslim from the Interim Government were overborne. Congress, being a national party with a Muslim president, could not, in Gandhi's view, agree to such an omission
even as a temporary expedient and on the Viceroy's assurance
that it would not be a precedent. It involved a principle which
Congress could not give up. It mattered not that the principle
had ceased to have practical significance now that Jinnah had
won almost all the Muslims to his side. It mattered not that
insistence on it would infuriate Jinnah, whose co-operation
in any unitary form of government was essential, and would
disrupt, with unpredictable consequences, the delicate web of
negotiations spun by the Cabinet Mission. Such mundane and
common-sense considerations did not appeal to Gandhi.

When the news spread that Congress were going to reject
the proposals for an Interim Government the dismay in Cabinet
Mission circles was intense, and intense too the indignation
against Gandhi. It was he who had wrecked the Cripps Mission
in 1942. Now he had done it again! Under the first shock of
disappointment deliberate maleficence was attributed to him.
This, of course, was mistaken. His influence may have been
baleful, but it was not intended to be so. His advice may have
been unwise, unstatesmanlike and, from the point of view of
preserving India's unity, absolutely calamitous, but it was given
in good faith and with the best of motives. If he could have been
shown all the grim consequences that were to flow from it he
would perhaps have said, as he had said on a previous occasion,

that he had not the remotest idea of any such catastrophe resulting from it. Following the promptings of an inner voice he was all too often careless of consequences—until they overtook him. In this case they were to overtake him with a vengeance!

With the rejection of the short-term proposals by Congress the last chance of an agreement which might have averted partition was thrown away. This is clear now; but it was not fully apparent at the time; for hope revived when it became known that Congress, while rejecting the proposals for an Interim Government, had at last made up their minds to accept the long-term constitutional proposals. Something, at least, seemed to have been secured.

The acceptance when it came was qualified and ambiguous. It was conveyed in a long letter dated June 25th from the President, Maulana Abul Kalam Azad, to the Viceroy. 'We have pointed out', the letter ran, 'what in our opinion were the defects of the proposals. We also gave our interpretation of some of the provisions of the statement'—which the Mission had firmly repudiated. 'While adhering to our views we accept your proposals and are prepared to work them with a view to achieve our objective.'

This might mean—and could always, if necessary, be claimed to mean—that they accepted the proposals only on *their* interpretation of them. But the Mission in their distress and disappointment were prepared to clutch at any convenient straws. This ambiguous acceptance, if not too closely scanned, gave ground for hope and also got them out of an embarrassing dilemma; for in default of acceptance by Congress of the constitutional plan they would have been plainly bound, in accordance with paragraph 8 of the announcement of June 16th, to form an Interim Government omitting Congress representatives altogether. But now they could find a way of wriggling out of any awkward obligation to go ahead with the League alone. Treating, therefore, the Congress's decision as a real acceptance, they came out with a statement on June 26th expressing their happiness that 'constitution-making can now proceed with the consent of the two major parties'. The failure to form an Interim Government was, they said, regrettable; but, after a short interval, renewed efforts would be made by the Viceroy to bring such a Government into being 'in accordance with paragraph eight of the statement of June 16th'. They themselves would leave India on June 29th.

The few days before their departure were filled with acrimonious controversy. Jinnah, as soon as he knew that Congress had rejected the proposals for an Interim Government, had quickly got the Working Committee of the League to accept them. He then claimed, with some apparent justification, that the Viceroy was bound by paragraph 8 of the statement of June 16th to ignore the Congress and proceed at once to form a government with representatives of the League and of such other parties as were willing to join. The plea that as both major parties had accepted the statement of May 16th, negotiations for an Interim Government had to be taken up *de novo*, had been dishonestly 'concocted by the legalistic talents of the Cabinet Mission'. He roundly charged the Viceroy and the Mission with breach of faith and cuttingly observed 'Statesmen should not eat their words'.

So the Mission ended in disappointment, tinged with resentment; for it was to the accompaniment of Jinnah's taunts and reproaches that the three Cabinet Ministers took their departure. This public controversy belied the hopes expressed that constitution-making would go forward speedily in a spirit of accommodation. The real situation was truly mirrored not in Sir Stafford's cheerful smiles but in the woebegone face of Lord Pethick Lawrence as he stood at the airport waiting to emplane. Three months in the heat of India seemed to have aged him ten years.

Within a fortnight of the Mission's departure all that remained of their precarious card-house had collapsed in irretrievable ruin. Gandhi, by persuading the Working Committee to reject the interim proposals, had already knocked down half of it. Nehru now proceeded to demolish the rest. At a press conference on July 10th he said that Congress, in accepting the Cabinet Mission's long-term plan, 'have agreed to go into the Constituent Assembly and have agreed to nothing else . . . we have committed ourselves to no single matter to anybody'. Thus the basic structure of the constitution, including the strict limitation of federal subjects, and the procedure to be followed by the Constituent Assembly, all of which formed part of the long-term proposals ostensibly accepted by Congress, had in reality not been accepted at all. In regard to Grouping, which the Mission had specifically stated to be an essential feature of their plan, Nehru expressed the view that 'the big probability is that . . . there will be no Grouping'. The reasons which he gave showed complete disregard for the Cabinet Mission's intentions as to the manner of voting in the Sections.[1] Contemptuously brushing the Mission aside he declared that what they thought or intended did not enter into the matter at all!

Jinnah retorted at once, and with some justice, that Nehru's interpretation of the acceptance as amounting to nothing more than an agreement to go into the Constituent Assembly was a 'complete repudiation of the basic form upon which the long-term scheme rests and all its fundamentals and terms and obligations'. It was clear, he said, that the Congress's so-called 'acceptance' of the long-term plan had been from the outset disingenuous—they had never intended to honour it. Since this was their attitude, since they did not really intend to abide by the plan or to work it in a spirit of compromise and co-operation, but rather to use their majority in the Constituent Assembly to enforce their own views, the Muslim League would have to reconsider the situation.

This they did at the end of the month. At a meeting held in Bombay they decided to withdraw their previous acceptance of the long-term plan and to prepare a programme of 'direct action' for the achievement of Pakistan to be launched as and when necessary. 'This day', Jinnah announced, 'we bid good-bye to constitutional methods.'

Nothing was now left of the Cabinet Mission's fragile edifice and, try as he might over the next six months, Lord Wavell was unable to reconstruct it. Congress could not be brought to declare unequivocally their acceptance of the long-term proposals in the sense that the League understood them and the Cabinet Mission had intended them; while Jinnah and the League would be content with nothing less. There was thus no agreed basis for constitution-making and hence no prospect of co-operation. There had never in reality been any agreement at all, but only the illusion of one.

The League's withdrawal of their acceptance of the long-

[1] See footnote on page 51.

term plan, though it meant that they would take no part in the Constituent Assembly, simplified in some ways the formation of an Interim Government. It was decided, though with a good deal of misgiving, to go ahead without them, and accordingly on August 6th the Viceroy wrote to Nehru—who had recently succeeded Azad as Congress President—inviting him to form a government. The invitation was accepted.

Before the new government had taken office or the names of its members had been announced, the first fruits of the Cabinet Mission's failure were being gathered. On August 16th, which the Muslim League celebrated as 'Direct Action Day', there was an appalling outbreak of rioting in Calcutta, lasting several days. According to official estimates about 5,000 persons were killed and 15,000 injured. Compared with what was to follow this holocaust was nothing extraordinary, but it made a deep impression at the time. People had not yet become hardened to mass slaughter.

There was widespread criticism of the Muslim League Government of Bengal and its Chief Minister, Mr. Suhrawardy. Against all advice they had declared 'Direct Action Day' a public holiday and, though warned of the likelihood of trouble, had apparently not taken adequate precautions. After the rioting had started, there was an unaccountable delay in imposing a curfew and calling in troops. The British Governor remained imperturbable but inactive. Charged under the Constitution of 1935 with a special responsibility for preventing any grave menace to the peace and tranquillity of the province, his duty seemed to require that he should intervene promptly to remedy the negligences of the Bengal Government and suppress these terrible disorders. He did not do so. During the next year this apparent example of supineness was to be copied by others in humbler stations.

In these riots the Muslims had been the aggressors; but after the first day or two the non-Muslim population, spear-headed by the Sikh taxi-drivers of Calcutta, retaliated vigorously, giving as good as they got, and in the end perhaps neither party could claim any very decided advantage. The disturbances, however, spread to East Bengal where the Muslims were in a considerable majority. Dacca was at first the centre of disorder, but in October there were serious outbreaks of Muslim hooliganism in the remoter districts of Noakhali and Tipperah. The killings were not on a vast scale, running into hundreds rather than thousands, but there was much destruction and pillage of Hindu property and abduction of Hindu women.

Numbers of Hindus, fleeing in terror from the affected areas, arrived in Bihar. Their tales of woe, luridly written up by the local press, so excited popular feeling that now in Bihar there was a massacre of Muslims by Hindus. Several thousands were killed, in many instances in peculiarly revolting and barbarous circumstances. There was no knowing where this chain reaction would end. 'We are not yet in the midst of civil war,' Gandhi declared, 'but we are nearing it.'

The Viceroy thought that the dangers of the situation would be lessened if the League could be brought into the Interim Government. He also had reason to believe that the League would once again accept the long-term proposals and enter the Constituent Assembly if Congress would unequivocally agree to grouping as contemplated in the statement of May 16th. He strove hard to bring the two parties to terms and his efforts seemed partially successful when in the middle of October Jinnah agreed that five nominees of the League should join the Government. They took office on October 26th.

Congress were not too satisfied with the new arrangements. They wanted to be assured that the League would rescind their Bombay resolution and enter the Constituent Assembly, and that the League representatives in the Interim Government would really co-operate with the other members and try to work as a team. On both points the Viceroy obtained from Jinnah qualified assurances, but the Congress felt that not much reliance could be placed on them.

The country at large, not fully aware of all the inner discords, hailed the League's entry into the Government with relief; and its immediate effects were tranquillizing. But it soon became apparent that Jinnah's assurances were of no value. The League had entered the Government not to co-operate with Congress but simply to prevent Congress from tightening its hold on the whole governmental machine at the League's expense. The Interim Government became in fact a dual government. There was, as Liaqat Ali Khan put it, 'a Congress bloc and a Muslim bloc, each functioning under separate leadership'. Each began to attract to itself its own supporters from among the civil servants and to build up its own separate and exclusive empire. As a Coalition Government it was a farce.

There was also no progress in regard to the League's entry into the Constituent Assembly. It was originally intended that this body should begin its work early in September but the Viceroy had postponed summoning it owing to the League's unwillingness to participate. Postponement could not, however, go on indefinitely and the Viceroy, under considerable pressure from Congress, fixed December 9th for the first meeting. Would the Muslim League delegates attend? Jinnah, despite his assurances to the Viceroy, took no steps to call a meeting of the Council of the League to reconsider the Bombay resolution and when urged to do so contended that such a course was futile so long as the Congress themselves declined to accept unequivocally the statement of May 16th. He strongly advised the Viceroy to postpone the Constituent Assembly *sine die*. Invitations were, however, issued for December 9th; whereupon Jinnah directed the Muslim League representatives not to attend.

In a desperate last-minute bid to bring about agreement before the Constituent Assembly met, the British Prime Minister now invited the leaders of Congress and the League, and Baldev Singh as representative of the Sikhs, to come to London for discussions. The field of disagreement had by this time been narrowed down, as Congress had reluctantly accepted that provinces could not *ab initio* refuse to take part in the work of the Sections in which they had been placed. The main point at issue was whether in the Sections the voting was to be by provinces, as Congress contended, or by simple majority vote of those present, as the League claimed and as the Cabinet Mission had intended. No agreement was reached, but the British Government issued a statement on December 6th upholding the latter interpretation and urging Congress to accept it 'in order that the way may be open for the Muslim League to reconsider their attitude'.

Congress responded. At the instance of Nehru and despite considerable opposition the All-India Congress Committee passed a resolution agreeing 'to advise action in accordance with the interpretation of the British Government in regard to the procedure to be followed in the sections'. There was a caveat to the effect that this must not involve any compulsion of a province and that the rights of the Sikhs in the Punjab would not be jeopardized. Nevertheless it was perhaps as near to a genuine acceptance of the original proposals of May 16th as could be expected.

Alas, second thoughts had come too late! If only Congress leaders had adopted this attitude in July instead of petulantly asserting that they had committed themselves to nothing and that the intentions of the Cabinet Mission and British Government were of no consequence, the Muslim League would have had no occasion to resile from their acceptance of the plan and all the discords, disorders and massacres of the past six months could have been avoided. But now the League had hardened their hearts. Convinced of Congress's fundamental insincerity, they were not prepared to swallow any caveats. Moreover, whatever the All-India Congress Committee might resolve, Gandhi had been talking in quite a different strain. Consulted by some Assam Congressmen on the subject of grouping he had said: 'I do not need a single minute to come to a decision. . . . If there is no clear guidance from the Congress Committee Assam should not go into Sections. It should lodge its protest and retire from the Constituent Assembly. . . . I have the same advice for the Sikhs.' With Gandhi tendering such advice the League could reasonably conclude that, on the strength of his authority, both the Hindus of Assam and the Sikhs of the Punjab would refuse to co-operate in the work of their respective Sections. In these circumstances the League decided that the qualifying clauses of the Congress resolution completely nullified their acceptance of the British Government's statement of December 6th. They therefore flatly declined to reconsider their own Bombay resolution.

A dangerous crisis was now approaching. The League representatives had been taken into the Interim Government on the understanding that the Bombay resolution would be rescinded and that the League delegates would attend the Constituent Assembly. It was now clear that the League would not carry out their part of the bargain. There was, therefore, a demand for the resignation of the League representatives from the Interim Government; and the Congress members soon made it plain that they would themselves resign if the League members were retained.

Either alternative was fraught with alarming possibilities. If the Congress members withdrew, the British, with League support, might have to hold down forcibly the whole of Hindu India. On the other hand the extrusion of the League representatives from the Central Government would be the signal for fresh communal disorders which might lead to a virtual state of civil war; for there was a danger now that the army and services would begin to take sides. The British Government would then be compelled either to restore order by British arms—and this would involve reassertion of British dominance for at least ten to fifteen years—or to scuttle ignominiously from an anarchic situation.

Physically the reassertion of British authority would not have been very difficult; but politically and psychologically it was quite impracticable—neither British opinion nor world opinion would have tolerated it or permitted the necessary measures to be taken. The Labour Government rightly ruled it out. But some fresh move had to be made. Drift and delay could only lead to chaos. So they took a bold decision. On February 20th the Prime Minister, Mr. Attlee, announced in the House of Commons that it was His Majesty's Government's 'definite intention to take the necessary steps to effect the transference of power to responsible Indian hands by a date not later than June 1948'. All parties were urged to sink their differences—it was no doubt hoped that the mere fixing of a date so close at hand would shock them into some kind of agreement—but lack of agreement would not cause any postponement of the date. If it appeared that by the date fixed a fully representative Constituent Assembly would not have worked out a constitution in accordance with the Cabinet Mission's proposals, His Majesty's Government would have to consider 'to whom the powers of the Central Government in British India should be handed over, on the due date, whether as a whole to some form of Central Government for British India, or in some areas to the existing Provincial Governments, or in such other way as may seem most reasonable and in the best interests of the Indian people'.

This announcement meant Partition, and Partition within

the next seventeen months. Whatever London might think, everyone in Delhi knew that the Cabinet Mission's proposals were as dead as mutton. No constitution would be framed on their basis; and owing to the Hindu-Muslim feud there would be no Central Government capable of exercising authority over the whole of British India to whom the powers of the existing Government of India could be transferred. The power which the British held would have to be divided in order to be demitted, as indeed Mr. Attlee's statement itself vaguely foreshadowed. The British Government and Gandhi might perhaps still delude themselves with the hope of a united independent India; but for others it had faded from sight. As Sir Syed Ahmad had foreseen years earlier, two nations—Muslim and Hindu—could not sit on the same throne.

Thus nine months of strenuous British endeavour to preserve unity had led only to the inevitability of Partition. This deplorable outcome is not attributable, as the foregoing account might suggest, simply or even mainly to Gandhi's ill-starred interventions or Nehru's fits of arrogant impatience. At critical moments they may have given an adverse turn to events and thereby occasioned a result which neither of them desired. But the reasons for the failure to agree on some form of united India lay deeper. The truth is that the aims and aspirations of the two communities, as expressed by those whom they acclaimed their leaders, were irreconcilable; and, as it turned out in the end, their professed aims were also their real ones. The Congress leaders wanted a strong united India; the League a divided or divisible one. The Congress aim had never been in doubt and accurately reflected the wishes of the Hindu community. The League's aim, only proclaimed in 1940, may not have reflected any real or rational wish of the Muslim multitude, but at least accorded with their blind impulses. Instinctively they had rallied to Jinnah, deserting other leaders; and Jinnah, whatever his original views, had by now, rightly or wrongly, come to regard 'a sovereign independent Pakistan', actual or at least permanently potential, as an indispensable Muslim need.

This deep difference of aim could not be bridged by a flimsy paper scheme, such as the Cabinet Mission had devised. Both parties, in so far as they accepted it at all, avowedly did so in order to achieve their own objectives—and these were contradictory. This being so, even if constitution-making had begun, it could hardly have got very far; and even if a constitution, such as the Cabinet Mission envisaged, had somehow come into being, it could hardly have worked for very long.

Jinnah at an early stage became convinced that the Congress would never tolerate the weak, easily divisible Union of India such as he desired. And it gradually dawned on the Congress leaders, especially after their experience of the attitude of the League representatives in the Interim Government, that the price which the League would exact for preserving unity would be too high. They would insist on strong States or groups of States with divergent interests and outlook and a weak Federal Centre which would be paralysed by its own internal communal divisions and quite incapable of tackling India's enormous problems of poverty, illiteracy and outmoded social customs. Rather than commit the whole country to this it would be better to lop some of the branches from the main trunk— to let Jinnah and the League take the areas which they could indisputably claim. This was the mood to which most of the Congress leaders had come by the beginning of 1947.

The labours of nine months were not, therefore, wholly in vain. They had at any rate brought home to everyone, except perhaps Gandhi, the necessity of Partition. But Partition was a major operation which, even if agreed to by the party leaders, was bound to entail much shedding of blood.

IV

The Mountbatten Plan

IN the course of his statement of February 20th, Mr. Attlee had announced that with 'the opening of a new and final phase in India' there would be a change of Viceroy. Lord Wavell, the silent, war-scarred, middle-class soldier, would give place to Lord Mountbatten, charming, brilliant, aristocratic, and a sailor. It was a change and a contrast and gave rise to some questioning. Lord Wavell had not resigned; he had been sacked. Why?

No clear answer was given. The rugged old veteran's honesty and straightforwardness had not always endeared him to Congress circles and some members of the Labour Government, ever more receptive of the Congress than the League point of view, considered, perhaps unfairly, that he had developed a League bias. In any case for this final phase qualities were needed different from and perhaps more glittering than the sterling virtues of Lord Wavell. In selecting Lord Mountbatten to wind up British rule the Labour Government could hardly have made a happier choice.

Lord Mountbatten reached Delhi on March 22nd. He had received instructions to work for a Unitary Government for India on the basis of the Cabinet Mission plan. Only if by October 1947 he found that there was no prospect of reaching a settlement on these lines was he expected to put forward alternative proposals for the transfer of power. Within a few days he grasped that these instructions were out of date and that all talk of a Unitary Government and the Cabinet Mission plan was now vain. Some alternative plan had to be devised and acted upon, not in leisurely fashion some six months later, but forthwith; otherwise anarchy might set in before power and authority could be transmitted to other hands.

The Central Government was by this time hopelessly divided against itself with League and Congress Ministers openly working against each other. Communal rioting of unprecedented severity had broken out early in March in the principal towns of the Punjab and had spread in some places to the rural areas. Soon the fires of frenzy were lapping over into the North-West Frontier Province. In parts of the country it seemed that law and order would break down altogether.

After one false start, which might have proved calamitous, Lord Mountbatten produced a plan for the partition of the country to which all the principal parties were willing to agree. He owed this plan to the knowledge and insight of his Reforms Secretary, Mr. V. P. Menon. His own tact and persuasiveness helped to secure its general acceptance. Its main outlines were communicated in strict secrecy to the party leaders in the middle of May and their concurrence in principle obtained. The British Government's approval was then sought and on June 3rd it was publicly announced and publicly accepted by Nehru, Jinnah and Baldev Singh.

In essence the plan was simple. The country was to be divided into two dominions, known as India and Pakistan; but Pakistan was to be of the truncated 'contiguous area' variety involving the partition of both the Punjab and Bengal, which Jinnah had hitherto always spurned. In order to give to this division of the country the seal of democratic approval diverse and somewhat complicated arrangements were to be made for recording the popular will in the Muslim-majority provinces. The issue to be put to them was whether they should join the existing Constituent Assembly or an altogether new Constituent Assembly which would frame a constitution for a separate dominion of Pakistan.[1]

[1] In Sind this issue was to be voted upon by the provincial legislature. In the North-West Frontier Province (where the pro-Congress 'Red Shirts' were in a majority in the legislature) it was to be decided by a referendum. In Bengal and the Punjab the Legislative Assemblies were first each to meet as a whole and vote on this issue on the assumption that the Province would not be divided. (It was expected that in each case the small Muslim majority would turn the scales in favour of joining a new Constituent Assembly.) Thereafter they were each to meet in two parts, one representing the Muslim-majority districts according to the 1941 census figures and the other the rest of the Province. These two parts would then vote separately on whether the Province should be partitioned. If either part by a simple majority voted for partition, then the Province would be divided. The two parts of the Legislative Assemblies would also decide on behalf of the areas which they represented whether to join India or Pakistan.

On the assumption that the voting in the Muslim-majority provinces would endorse the division of the country, arrangements were to be initiated as quickly as possible for dividing the armed forces and the administrative services and the assets and liabilities of the Central Government between the respective successor authorities and for carrying out a similar division in respect of the provinces of Bengal and the Punjab.

For the actual partition of these two provinces, in the event of Partition being decided upon, a Boundary Commission was to be set up. The Commission would be instructed to demarcate the boundaries of the two parts of Bengal and the Punjab on the basis of ascertaining the contiguous majority areas of Muslims and non-Muslims, and also *to take into account other factors*.

It was also proposed to anticipate the date for the transfer of power and to bring it forward from June 1948 to some date in 1947. At a press conference on June 4th Lord Mountbatten suggested that this might be August 15th.

The plan was acclaimed not only in India but throughout the world; and with all its defects and grim promise of bloodshed— the certainty of which those at the summit did not realize— it was perhaps the best that could be devised. Certainly no-one either then or later was able to suggest anything better. Yet only a year earlier the Cabinet Mission had given cogent arguments[1] against a settlement based on a 'truncated' Pakistan. They had pointed out that it was not in accord with Muslim wishes, that the radical partition of the Punjab and Bengal which it involved would be 'contrary to the wishes and interests of a very large proportion of the inhabitants of these Provinces' and that it would necessarily divide the Sikhs. No-one had controverted these arguments, but now all parties, including the Sikhs, acquiesced in this solution.

Of all the parties principally concerned the Congress perhaps had least difficulty in accepting the plan. Congress leaders realized that the mood of the Muslims was now so hostile that even if the British transferred the authority of the Centre to a purely Congress Government, their writ would simply not run in the extreme west and extreme east of the country where Muslims predominated. To gain control of those areas force

[1] See page 47.

would have to be supplied from the Centre and this would mean civil war. Thus at the very outset of independence they would be plunged into squalid, fratricidal strife which might see most of them into their graves. They would have to say good-bye to all their cherished ambitions of building up a strong, united, progressive India, free from the shackles of an outworn social system and capable of playing a part in the councils of the world. Rather than this it was better to sever completely from Mother India those stubborn Muslim areas that disowned her. They were willing to pay this price provided Jinnah and the League were not permitted to carry away too much. The plan by providing for the partition of Bengal and the Punjab satisfied them on this score.

For Jinnah the plan was a bitter pill. He had always rejected a truncated Pakistan and only a few weeks earlier had described the proposal for the partition of Bengal and the Punjab as 'a sinister move actuated by spite and bitterness'. But he had to bow to facts and logic. Logically the very principle on which he demanded the division of India justified the partition of these two Muslim-majority provinces. Bound by this logic the British Government, he knew, would never be party to coercing large unwilling minorities into joining Pakistan. And he and the League had not the strength to coerce them; physically he could not possess himself of East Punjab and West Bengal unless the majority of the inhabitants willingly attached themselves to Pakistan. But why should they? The League had done abso-lutely nothing to make Pakistan appear attractive to them. On the contrary in Calcutta Suhrawardy's League Government had quite failed to prevent an onslaught on the Hindus and subsequently in East Bengal Hindus had been plundered and terrorized. In the Punjab the story had been much the same. The League, after its success in the provincial elections, made no effort to conciliate and reassure the Sikhs and declined even to discuss their future. Throughout 1946 they were cold-shouldered or reviled and later—as will shortly be narrated—they were murderously assaulted and held up to ridicule.

So by their inexplicable acts and omissions Jinnah and the League were debarred from getting by agreement the Pakistan of their conception; and they were not strong enough to seize it by force. Once or twice Jinnah raised the question of an

exchange of population. If all the Muslims in India could be
concentrated he could legitimately obtain the whole area which
he coveted. But he did not press the suggestion and perhaps felt
that it was impracticable and might even lead to his own dis-
credit. For how would the populations be induced to move?
What except brute force or overwhelming fear would drive non-
Muslims to leave their ancestral homes in Bengal and the Punjab
to make room for incoming Muslims? And would the lure of Pakistan be sufficient to impel Muslims from all over India to migrate
to that doubtful El Dorado? Jinnah may have foreseen that his
own people would be liable to repudiate the promised land.

Whatever may have been his reasons, Jinnah never made the
planned exchange of population a live issue, and being by now
deeply committed to Pakistan in some form he had perforce to
accept it in such form as he could get it. As far back as November he had told Lord Wavell that the British should give the
Muslims their own bit of country, however small it might be,
and they would live there, if necessary on one meal a day! This
tallied with the views of his political henchmen and of the
ambitious Muslim civil servants who were secretly abetting
them. To these men, avid of power, even a small dunghill was
better than none at all.

For the Sikhs the plan meant division. They knew it, they
accepted it and privily they had their own plans for meeting it.
The hard choice before them had long been clear. They had to
submit either to inclusion as a whole in Pakistan or to division
between India and Pakistan through partition of the Punjab.
They had chosen the latter.[1] They had long been thinking in
terms of Partition and the recent conduct of the Muslims had
strengthened their preference for it. Inevitably by such Partition they would be split and if the 'contiguous area' principle
were to be rigidly applied all the canal colonies and about two
million Sikhs would fall to Pakistan. But the Boundary Commission was also to take into account 'other factors' and the
Sikhs clung to the hope that on the strength of these 'other

[1] Some of the Akalis had been canvassing the idea of an entirely separate
Sikh State of 'Khalistan'. Since they were not in an absolute majority in
even a single district no one could take this idea seriously; but in one guise or
another it had some influence on Sikh thinking both in the coming months
and in the coming years.

factors' the boundary might be shifted westwards so that they would not be split so badly. They were encouraged in this false hope by the ill-advised utterances of some British politicians.

For the British Government, as for everyone else, the plan was very much of a *pis aller*; but they could not dissent from what Congress, the League and the Sikhs were all ready to accept. They recognized that since agreement on the Cabinet Mission plan had proved unattainable, Partition was the inevitable alternative. Churchill on behalf of the Opposition gave assurances of support.

So with a quite unprecedented unanimity all set forth together on a path leading straight to mass slaughter. In Bengal this end was a dangerous[1] possibility, in the Punjab an absolute certainty. Fortunately for the peace of mind of those who led the way none of them, except Baldev Singh, knew much about the Punjab and so they did not realize what was coming. British officials of the Punjab were not in that happy position. They were aware of an impending calamity which they were powerless to avert.

[1] Disaster was averted in Bengal largely through the influence of Gandhi. The Muslim leaguer, Mr. Suhrawardy, also fell temporarily under his spell and became a peacemaker.

V

The Punjab and Partition

To understand the menacing situation in the Punjab and how it had arisen it is necessary to go back a little. It will be recalled that at the elections at the beginning of 1946 Khizar and the Unionist Party suffered a crushing defeat and the Muslim League emerged as the strongest single party with seventy-nine seats in a house of 175. But not having an absolute majority the League alone could not form a Ministry, and the extreme, uncompromising attitude which they had adopted during the elections precluded them for the time being from obtaining support from elsewhere. In the circumstances it was expected that the Governor would temporarily take over the administration under Section 93 of the Government of India Act until a stable Ministry could be formed. With time, patience and discreet promises of loaves and fishes the League would probably have succeeded in winning over a sufficient number of members to secure a majority. But a cardinal error was now made. Baldev Singh induced Khizar to head a Coalition Ministry supported by Congress Hindus, Akali Sikhs and his own nine Muslim followers. Khizar, by all accounts reluctantly and after much persuasion, agreed and the Governor, Sir Bertrand Glancy, passively accepted the arrangement.

From the public point of view it was a disaster; and for Khizar personally it was political suicide. In every Punjab Ministry since the first beginnings of provincial self-government the Muslims had played the leading part, as their numbers entitled them to do. Now for the first time, on the eve of independence, a predominantly non-Muslim Government was being installed in power. The Muslim League, fresh from their triumph at the elections and fully expecting to form a Ministry themselves, found themselves totally excluded by an undreamed of combination of Congress banias, Khizar and the Sikhs. Not only the League but the whole Muslim community felt outraged

71

and affronted. This unnatural and unholy alliance seemed to have been designed, with the connivance of the British Governor, simply to keep them from power. It was an example of just the thing that Jinnah always feared and that had prompted the demand for Pakistan. In a united India the wily Hindus would always succeed in this manner in attaching to themselves a section of the Muslims and using them to defeat the larger interests of the community. Khizar, despite his past record and reputation, was now represented as a traitor, clinging to power and office without regard for Muslim interests.

Sore and resentful the Muslim League now had a real grievance with which to inflame Muslim feeling. Communal relations in the province, already bad, became still further embittered and the mere existence of the Coalition Government made any sort of reconciliation impossible. If it had not been formed and the League leaders had been left with some hope of office, they would have been compelled, just in order to gain it, to adopt a more conciliatory attitude to the minorities; and once installed in power and made responsible for the peace and well-being of the whole province, they would have been less tempted than they were now deliberately to stir up strife. As it was, there was no inducement to them to seek the path of peace and come to terms with parties which, they felt, had combined to defraud them of their just claim to office.

It was amazing that the Governor acquiesced without the slightest struggle in the formation of a Ministry so harmful to the public interests. But it had become easy and fashionable in these days to evade responsibility on the plea of constitutionalism. His apologists have certainly taken this plea and pointed out that since Khizar was willing and able to form a Ministry, he had no option, as a constitutional Governor, but to let him do so. True, yet utterly removed from the real truth. For Khizar was no stranger with whom it might be necessary for him to stand on ceremony. From the day when he assumed office as Governor in April 1941 he and Khizar had been in almost daily contact. Though as a constitutional Governor he was bound in the last resort to let Khizar form a Ministry if he so insisted, there was nothing to preclude him from talking to

Khizar as man to man and throwing all the weight of his influence and advice against such a course. In view of Khizar's own hesitations a few words of discouragement from the Governor, who was known to be his well-wisher, must have turned the scale against it. But the words were not spoken. The Governor took the easy, strictly constitutional line of least resistance and left his successor, who took office a few weeks later, and the province at large to reap the consequences.

Ironically enough the Sikander-Baldev Singh pact, designed to bring the Sikh and Muslim communities closer together, was indirectly responsible for this lamentable political arrangement which was bound to drive them apart; for it was Baldev Singh's association with Khizar as a colleague in the Punjab Ministry that enabled this new ill-starred coalition to be formed. An alliance between the Akalis and Khizar was a boon to the Province so long as he stood at the head of a Unionist party which commanded the allegiance of most of the Muslims; but it could only be a curse when he had become a renegade at the head of a rump. Thus in the end the pact proved a snare.

Several of Khizar's friends, too late to prevent him from putting himself in a false position, were anxious that he should withdraw from it as quickly as possible. A senior British official urged him, soon after he had taken office, to resign straight away before he had hopelessly compromised himself in the eyes of his own community. I argued to the same effect with two of his henchmen, who visited Delhi in April, and the discussion went on until the small hours of the morning. I dwelt not only on the embitterment of communal feeling, but also on the irreparable damage to Khizar's own reputation which must result from his continuance in office. The Muslim community, I said, would never forgive him if he appeared to cling to power in defiance of Muslim interests and wishes. His party had been decisively defeated at the elections. However regrettable that might be from the point of view of the real interests both of the Muslims and the Punjab, the best course was to accept the defeat with patience and dignity and lie low for the time being. The ambitious and inexperienced young men who had come to the front as leaders of the League in the Punjab were bound to make a mess of things. After a few years the Muslim masses would turn back to Khizar with relief as a tried elder statesman,

c*

provided he did not now brand himself as a traitor in their eyes
and so permanently antagonize them.

My arguments seemed to make some impression on his two
supporters but did not convince them. They felt that the reins
of power—one of them was a Minister in Khizar's new Government—should not be voluntarily surrendered. 'We have a
"danda"[1] in our hand,' they kept repeating, 'and mustn't
give it up'; and it was with these words that they finally parted
from me.

But the 'danda' was in reality only a broken reed; for the
Punjab police force was about 75 per cent Muslim and in the
hands of a predominantly non-Muslim Government, confronted with a mass Muslim movement, could not be fully
relied upon. Here was another fatal defect in the political
arrangement that had been made in the Punjab. In times of
stress and communal tension any Punjab Government not
enjoying substantial Muslim backing was liable to find itself
in a precarious position. Khizar's Government not only had
no such backing but, relying largely on the support of Hindu
banias, was itself a standing offence to the Muslims of the
Punjab. In any show-down with the Muslim League Khizar's
Government, so far from being able to wield a 'danda', would
be impotent, unless it called in outside military aid and proclaimed martial law.

During the period of acute tension that followed the failure
of the Cabinet Mission, Khizar's Government remained uneasily
in the saddle. Though there were isolated communal incidents,
there was no widespread outbreak of violence in the Punjab
such as occurred in Bengal and Bihar. But this outward tranquillity deceived no-one. All the three major communities—
Muslims, Hindus and Sikhs—were collecting arms and getting
ready for open war. As the prospects of a Congress-League
agreement for a united India receded, the certainty of violence
in the Punjab increased. Towards the end of December the
Executive Officer[2] of the Amritsar municipality was to be
found busily repairing the municipal hose-pipes. When questioned on this unwonted activity he replied: 'The city will soon
be in flames. I'm making such preparations as I can.' His fore-

[1] Stick.
[2] The late P. C. Bhandari.

sight was unerring, but the hose-pipes, even when repaired, were insufficient.

On 24th January 1947 Khizar's Government took a decisive but fatal step. Alarmed at the collection of arms by various private volunteer bodies, operating under the direction of political parties, they declared the Muslim League National Guards and the Rashtriya Swayam Sewak Sangh—an extreme and militant Hindu organization—unlawful bodies under the Criminal Law Amendment Act. Simultaneously the police raided the headquarters of the National Guards in Lahore and began a search of the premises.

The Muslim League leaders were quick to see their chance. About half a dozen of them hurried to the National Guards headquarters while the search was in progress and courted arrest by obstructing the police. They were taken into custody.

The fat was now in the fire. The Punjab Government had inadvertently offered a challenge to the League without the strength to go through with it. News of the arrest of the League leaders spread through the city like wild-fire. There were demonstrations by Muslim mobs and meetings in mosques to condemn the action of the Punjab Government. Most unwisely the Punjab Government had at an earlier date issued general orders prohibiting meetings and processions in all the principal towns of the province. Such general orders usually lead to trouble. Their enforcement often unnecessarily precipitates the very disturbances they are designed to avert, while their non-enforcement brings government into contempt. The Punjab Government had developed the bad habit of promulgating these general bans. The Muslim League took advantage of the mistake. On the day of the arrest of the League leaders Muslim demonstrations in Lahore had been half-heartedly broken up by the police. The next day the League decided systematically to defy the bans. The authorities, not daring to interfere and break up meetings and processions by force, contented themselves with making a few arrests and sought to ease the situation by appeasement. On the 26th the League leaders who had been arrested in Lahore were released and on the 28th the orders declaring the Muslim National Guards and the Rashtriya Swayam Sewak Sangh unlawful were rescinded. But for some inexplicable reason the Punjab Government, instead of com-

pleting their climb down by withdrawing the bans on meetings
and processions, continued them in force and continued not to
enforce them. So for the next few weeks Muslim mobs and
gangs of Muslim students amused themselves, much to the
exasperation of the other communities, with 'non-violent'
defiance of the bans; while the police looked on and tried to
mitigate this open flouting of authority by occasional arrests.
The hooligan Muslim elements in the big cities perceived all
too clearly the weakness of the Government; the forces of law
and order, not too staunch in any case, became puzzled and
doubtful of what was expected of them.

This dangerous farce went on till February 26th when the
Punjab Government climbed down further and came to a
compromise with the Muslim League. The ban on processions
continued in force, but the ban on meetings was withdrawn
and all those arrested in connection with the agitation were
released. The League, on their side, agreed to discontinue the
agitation. Thus with loss of prestige and grave weakening of the
whole fabric of administration, Khizar's Government extricated
itself from its contest with the League. The half-hearted
attempt to promote communal peace by strong measures had
primed the province for an explosion.

Perhaps Khizar guessed what was in store. In any case by
this time he had had enough. The impotence of his Government
had been starkly revealed, and on February 20th Mr. Attlee's
announcement of the forthcoming withdrawal of British power
had introduced a new factor. Now at last and too late Khizar
realized that the onus of managing the affairs of the Punjab
should be thrown on the party representing the majority community—the Muslim League. On March 3rd he submitted
the resignation of his Cabinet.

The reasons which he gave to the public for resigning are
instructive. He said that the decision announced by Mr.
Attlee required that parties in the province 'should be brought
face to face with realities'. He went on:

'It is now incumbent on me to leave the field clear for the
Muslim League to come to such arrangements *vis-à-vis* the
other parties as it might consider in the best interests of the
Muslims and the Province. If I were now to continue to lead

a Coalition in which the Muslim League is not represented, this might put in serious jeopardy such chances as might otherwise exist of a settlement being arrived at between the communities in the Province.'

But already all chances of a settlement had been not merely jeopardized but destroyed. If only he had grasped a year earlier the truth of what he now said the realities would not have been quite so grim and the League would have had more time to face them. He himself might even have been able to exercise a moderating and conciliatory influence, if he had not cut himself adrift from the main body of Muslims by his leadership of a non-Muslim coalition. As it was, he was nothing now to his own community. His very life was in danger from its members and he had to be heavily guarded.

With Khizar's resignation the pent-up excitement of the past weeks broke loose. Though there was little or no chance now of the League being able to form a Ministry, the Governor had to go through the motions of asking them to do so before himself assuming control of the administration. The mere rumour of a League Ministry was sufficient to evoke demonstrations by the minority communities. The ban on processions was still in force, but in spite of this on March 4th Bhim Sen Sachar, the Finance Minister in the outgoing Khizar Government, feeling perhaps that non-Muslims should have as much liberty to defy law as the Muslims had enjoyed in the past weeks, led a procession to the Assembly Chamber in Lahore where he proclaimed to a vast assembled multitude: 'I, as a member of the Government, hereby declare that you have every right to take out processions.' The Sikh leader, Master Tara Singh, raised the slogan 'Pakistan Murdabad'[1] and brandishing a sword shouted, 'Raj karega Khalsa, aqi rahe na koi'.[2]

This foolhardy bravado brought at once its own nemesis. It touched off violent communal rioting throughout the province in which Hindus and Sikhs were far the worst sufferers. The first outbreak took place in Lahore on March 4th immediately after Master Tara Singh's ill-timed vauntings. It was

[1] Down with (death to) Pakistan.
[2] The pure (Sikhs) will rule; no resister will remain. (A well-known saying of Guru Gobind Singh, the tenth and last Sikh Guru.)

followed in the next couple of days by rioting in Multan,
Rawalpindi and Amritsar and minor disturbances in other
towns. The Muslim mobs, after their weeks of 'non-violent'
agitation, suddenly, as though on a preconcerted signal, came
out in their true colours and with weapons in their hands and,
in some places, steel helmets on their heads, indulged in murder,
loot and arson on a scale never witnessed before in the Punjab
during a hundred years of British rule. The minority communities fought back vigorously wherever they could.

The conflagration in Amritsar was particularly terrific.
The two principal bazaars were burnt to the ground and several
others partially destroyed. There was looting in practically
every part of the city. So far as I have been able to ascertain,
not a shot was fired by the police while this destruction was in
progress. In Multan many private houses of Hindus were set on
fire and the inmates had the choice of perishing in the flames
or running the gauntlet of a murderous mob awaiting them
below. Caught in this predicament a prominent Congress
Muslim, who was staying with a Hindu friend, narrowly
escaped with his life by exposing his person as evidence of his
religion. His host was duly done to death.

In the north-west of the province (in the Rawalpindi and
Attock districts) and in the Multan district in the south-west
the trouble spread to the rural areas. Here the Muslims were in
an overwhelming majority and the minority communities
practically helpless. The Multan authorities acted vigorously
and by arranging prompt dispatch of military forces to the
affected areas brought the situation under control before more
than about a hundred casualties had occurred. But in the
Rawalpindi and Attock districts many villages and small towns
were raided by armed gangs of Muslims with heavy loss of life
and property, and it was more than a week before large-scale use
of troops began to effect an improvement. The Sikhs[1] were
especial targets of attack, their houses and their beards alike
being set on fire. Many were killed, many fled, and refugees
began to flock into Rawalpindi for temporary shelter.

[1] In this area the Sikhs were for the most part Hindus of the money-
lending and shopkeeping classes, who had embraced Sikhism and grown
beards, rather than peasant cultivators like the majority of the Sikhs in
Central Punjab.

This foretaste of the blessings of Pakistan was hardly encouraging to the minority communities in West Punjab. Some of them, especially the Sikhs in the north-west districts, began to think that they were not wanted and had better seek homes elsewhere. But the exodus of Hindus and Sikhs at this time from West to East Punjab was surprisingly small. They were reluctant to read the signs of an impending revolution.

Many people have supposed that this outburst of communal rioting in the Punjab followed as a sort of chain reaction from the disturbances in Bihar in the previous autumn which themselves had been provoked by the earlier trouble in East Bengal. This is a mistaken impression. The Punjab had long been brewing its own explosive mixture which had now blown up spontaneously. It required no outside fuse for its detonation.

The explosion had long been apprehended, but its severity[1] and the failure in several places to deal with it promptly and effectively came as a shock. Congress, and Hindus generally, were loud in their criticism. It was pointed out, as though of sinister significance, that British officers were in charge in the very places where the riots were worst—the implication being that they had themselves stirred up the trouble or were indifferent to its suppression. The first charge is absurd, and since it was the Punjab practice to post British officers at the likely communal storm-centres, it was only natural that when the riots broke they should be in the thick of them. The charge of indifference may have more substance. Of several British officers the story was told that when appealed to by panic-stricken Hindus for help and protection they referred the petitioners to Gandhi, Nehru or Patel. Nor can it be denied that in a number of places the handling of the trouble was irresolute—in one or two deplorably so. There were several factors accounting for this. The one of most general application was the reluctance of the Muslim police to take really strong measures against Muslim mobs. Under vigorous leadership, as in Multan,

[1] The casualties, as officially announced by the Punjab Government on March 20th, had been 2,049 killed and 1,103 seriously injured. No less than 1,538 of the killed were said to be in rural areas. These figures were certainly underestimates. A later estimate put the casualties from March up till the beginning of August at 5,000 killed and 3,000 seriously injured. Most of these casualties must have taken place in March when the disorders were at their worst.

they might do their duty well, but for the most part they were half-hearted and occasionally even recalcitrant. This was not surprising. Communal feeling had risen so high in the province that the police were necessarily affected by it. Throughout February they had seen that the Government were themselves hesitant to order firm action against defiant Muslims. How could they now be expected to lay about them vigorously with lathis or shoot straight with rifles to break up riotous parties of their own co-religionists? Above all, if they did so, who would appreciate or reward their services? Certainly not the British, who were about to leave the country, still less the Muslim leaguers who would soon be masters of at least half the province.

Another factor was the depletion of the services by war-time demands and the grant of leave after the war. As a result the Punjab had been left with insufficient British officials of first-class quality to man all the key districts. At the critical moment men were holding posts for which they were not well-fitted either by temperament or experience. Many of them too were tired after long years of service without a break and dispirited at the prospect of their careers in India coming abruptly to an end. The suppression of a communal riot calls for a good deal of determination and energy from those at the head of the forces of law and order. Tired and dispirited men were not able to rise to the occasion.

One of the worst failures of the civil authorities was in Amritsar—that place of ill-omen for the British name. A generation earlier, when there had been a wave of lawlessness in the Punjab directed against the British, Brigadier-General Dyer had poured 1,650 rounds into a mob in Amritsar, killing 600–700 and wounding over 1,000; he had ceased firing only when his ammunition was exhausted. The episode had become the classic example of barbarous and excessive use of force. Now exactly the opposite mistake was made. For over twenty-four hours riotous mobs were allowed to rage through this great commercial city unchallenged and unchecked. The finest bazaars were burnt to the ground without a shot being fired to disperse the incendiaries. The young and comparatively inexperienced District Magistrate had available, besides the police, 144 men of the Inniskilling Fusiliers; but, like the Grand Old Duke of York,

'Who had ten thousand men
He marched them up to the top of a hill
And marched them down again',

he marched this force into the city and marched it out again
without making any effective use of it at all. Apparently he
thought that it was too weak and would be overpowered. He
could perhaps hardly be expected to know that Dyer performed
his exploit and cowed the city into abject submission with a
force of ninety men.[1] Indians living in Amritsar, who had witnessed both events, noted the contrast and drew adverse con-
clusions. In defence of themselves and their own Raj the British
had used unlimited force, but in defence of one Indian community against another they had appeared content to stand
aside and do nothing. The Amritsar district was to be the
scene of fearful bloodshed later in the year. The complete
breakdown of authority in the city at this time prepared the
way for it.

By the third week in March the disorders were beginning to
subside, but they continued sporadically, especially in Amritsar
and Lahore, for the remaining few months of British rule.
Punjab society, interwoven of three distinct communities,
had been rent from end to end and the whole system of ordered
government shaken to its foundations. Doubtless it was this
alarming situation in the Punjab that convinced Lord Mountbatten of the need for speed. In Bengal Gandhi's presence had
to some extent allayed the passions that had been aroused;
but he could perform no such miracle in the Punjab. With
Muslims he had no influence and even with Sikhs not much,
and his voice would not have been heeded. He rightly directed
his attention to Bengal.

This then was the position in the Punjab when the plan for its
partition was formulated. At the best of times, involving as it
did the division of the Sikhs, it would have been fraught with
danger. But when passions had been so furiously aroused, how
could it be carried through peacefully? Even if Muslim attacks
on minorities in West Punjab were not repeated, they were
certain to be revenged. The Sikhs in particular were blazing
with anger, and in their case insult had been added to injury.

[1] Fifty armed with rifles and forty with kukris.

It was customary in the Punjab to laugh at the Sikhs, more or less good-humouredly, for their supposed incapacity for much cerebration; but now their valour was also impugned and their complete discomfiture in the recent disturbances—they had been beaten up by the Muslims not only in north-west Punjab but also in the city of Amritsar—was widely commented upon in a satirical vein. Forgetting that in the actual city of Amritsar the Muslims were the largest single community and the Sikhs only a small minority, overlooking too the fact that in no place had the Muslim gangs come up against the hard core of the Sikh community—the peasant cultivators of central Punjab —officials who should have known better began to talk knowingly of the degeneracy of the Sikhs. They had grown rich and fat, it was said, in the Punjab colonies and had lost their former martial vigour. They could not now stand up to the hardier Muslims who had not been debauched by excessive prosperity. With the partition of the province they would be divided and that would probably be the end of them as a distinct community—and a good thing too. These were the sort of sentiments that were being freely expressed.

The Muslim League leaders did little even now to reassure the Sikhs or assuage their wounded feelings. Jinnah kept harping on the fact that by the partition of the Punjab they would be the worst sufferers. The Sikhs were themselves only too conscious of this, but partition seemed to them preferable to blind submission to Muslim rule, and Jinnah had not made the slightest effort to persuade them to the contrary. He had not even expressed regret for recent events in West Punjab, though they were hardly calculated to enhance the attractions of Pakistan for the minority communities. One of the Punjab League leaders, Shaukat Hyat-Khan (Sikander's son), seems to have felt the need for a more positive approach and in April made a statement assuring the Sikhs that under a Muslim League Coalition Government their legitimate rights would be fully considered and 'justice meted out to all freely and equally'. But generalities of this kind were quite insufficient to heal the gaping wounds or inspire confidence in Muslim intentions. How could they carry conviction when in north-west Punjab Sikhs had been murdered and pillaged and their beards set on fire by Muslim gangs with little interference from the Muslim police and little or no expression of regret by Muslim leaguers?

No-one who knew the Sikhs could believe for one moment that they would take lying down all the insults and injuries that they had received. They were bound to strike back when and where they felt themselves to be in the ascendancy and that too with a violence and ferocity which would far eclipse the Muslim outrages. What had been seen in the Punjab in March was only a curtain-raiser. The main tragedy was still to come.

After the March outbreaks I was deeply conscious of impending calamity. There seemed to me to be only one faint possibility of averting it and that was if an agreement could be reached between the League and the Akali leaders whereby the Sikhs would voluntarily take their place in Pakistan on defined terms acceptable and favourable to themselves. Although it was really *ab initio* futile, I now made an attempt to bring this about. I was at this time in Bahawalpur State, having moved there from Delhi early in April. An old Punjab friend, Mushtaq Ahmad Gurmani, had been selected by the Nawab of Bahawalpur to be his Prime Minister and at Gurmani's request I accompanied him there as Revenue and Public Works Minister. When we took over in Bahawalpur Lord Mountbatten's plan for the division of India had not yet been announced, but it was already obvious that some form of Pakistan would have to emerge and that in the process there was every prospect of a holocaust in the Punjab. We discussed the whole position many times. Gurmani had spent most of his life in Punjab politics and knew the conditions of the province intimately. Originally a Unionist, his sympathies had in recent years inclined towards the League, with some of whose leaders he was in close contact; but he was essentially a man of moderate balanced views and had no illusions about the fearful dangers now threatening the Punjab as the result of League policies. He bitterly complained that these dangers had never been properly brought home to Jinnah by the young politicians who instructed him on Punjab affairs. I expressed the view that, as things now stood, terrific bloodshed in the Punjab could only be averted if somehow the Sikhs were made to feel that they would be safe and secure in Pakistan and that there would be an honourable place for them there. After all that had passed it might be very difficult to convince them of this, but division between two separate national States would be so ruinous to them that they could hardly afford to reject out of hand any reasonable Muslim approaches. The question was whether the Muslims really wanted to have the Sikhs in Pakistan and were prepared to pay the necessary price. The Sikhs were, no doubt, a turbulent troublesome set of people, always making a nuisance of themselves; but with all their faults they were one of the finest stocks in India. Pakistan would be enormously strengthened if it embraced the whole of the Punjab and enjoyed the support of the whole Sikh community; and all the unknown hazards of dividing the Punjab between India and Pakistan would be avoided. It was worth making considerable concessions to the Sikhs to gain these advantages.

After several discussions with Gurmani on these lines I suggested to him that I should try to discover from the Akalis what guarantees and concessions they wanted for the Sikhs—I had a pretty good idea of what they would be—and that he should sound Jinnah and the League. He agreed to do so.

I wrote accordingly early in June, immediately after the Mountbatten Plan had been announced, to an Akali friend; and a few days later, at the suggestion of Major Short who was in England at the time, I followed it up with a letter to a mutual friend of ours—a Sikh who was not himself a politician or an Akali but who was in close touch with Baldev Singh. I put it to them that the Sikhs should now definitely decide to throw in their lot with their Muslim brethren in the Punjab and take their place in the new Dominion of Pakistan. Though this might be quite contrary to recent Sikh policy it was in accord with the real interests of the Sikh community which lay with north-west India rather than with Hindustan, and would also avert the terrible strife and bloodshed threatening in the Punjab. This was the time, I wrote, to reach a 'samjhota'[1] with the Muslims, for they knew the disadvantages of a 'truncated' Pakistan. There was no reason why the Sikhs should not secure from them:

(1) a separate unit of Eastern Punjab with a position in Pakistan equal to that of any other unit, e.g. Sind or Western Punjab;

[1] Agreement.

(2) special privileges for the Sikh minority in Western Punjab;

(3) special privileges for the Sikhs in Pakistan as a whole.

If the Sikhs took the course I suggested they would become the most important minority in Pakistan and it would be in the Muslims' own interests to make them happy, secure and contented.

The initial replies which I received were not encouraging. Both of my friends said that while they personally agreed with what I had written matters had gone too far and there was too much distrust of the Muslims for an agreement to be reached. They very rightly pointed out that the Muslim League had never themselves made any constructive approach and that there was no real indication that they would be willing to do so now. One of them also observed that there could be no guarantee that the Muslims, once they had got Pakistan, would abide by any agreement they might have made earlier.

I did not immediately give up hope and about ten days later, after some further interchange of correspondence, Major Short's friend wrote that Baldev Singh, who at first had been reported unresponsive, was now more favourably disposed to my suggestions.

Though I had no inkling of it at the time, I subsequently surmised that this change of attitude was occasioned by the failure of the Sikhs to get all they wanted from the Congress. They were really hankering after a quasi-autonomous East Punjab, shorn of the four Hindu districts in the south-east so that it would have more of a Sikh complexion. Congress were not at all agreeable to this; hence an inclination to try to get it from the Muslims. Short's friend gave me his own suggestions as to the possible basis of negotiations. He said that he was communicating them to Baldev Singh and thought that they would be acceptable to him. They were briefly as follows:

(1) There should be a separate unit of East Punjab from which the four south-eastern and predominantly Hindu districts would be excluded. (The four districts would have gone to India.)

(2) The East Punjab unit should have the right to secede from Pakistan.

(3) The authority of the Central Pakistan Government should be confined to defence, foreign affairs, communications, currency and economic planning and all other powers should vest in the provincial units.

(4) A three-fourths majority of Sikh legislators should be essential for any change in the constitution.

(5) The Sikhs should have at least a one-third share in the armed forces of Pakistan.

These were stiff terms, but except for the provision for secession Gurmani and I did not think them impossible as a basis for negotiation. At this stage—it was now nearing the end of June—I felt that it was worth writing to Lord Ismay, the Viceroy's Chief of Staff, and consulting him on the possibilities of a settlement on these lines. He replied that Baldev Singh had recently seen the Viceroy and told him that there was no sign of either of the major parties making any concession to the Sikhs. While he agreed that 'from the point of view of avoiding a row[1] in the Central Punjab' the best course was to promote a settlement between the Muslim League and the Sikhs, he very much doubted whether such a settlement would come about.

He was absolutely right, and in the next few days this amateurish attempt to produce a settlement collapsed ignominiously. It had been arranged that I should meet a prominent Akali leader in Lahore to discuss the suggestions which had been put forward as a basis for negotiations. I duly went to Lahore; but the Akali leader failed to turn up at the appointed rendezvous! It was obvious that he was not interested and had other policies in mind. Since he was, in my view, more influential in the determination of Sikh policy than even Baldev Singh, I considered his attitude decisive. But the Sikh friend who was in touch with Baldev Singh continued to entertain hopes and on July 9th wrote to me that Baldev Singh had sent a cable to Short asking him 'to come out and help smooth matters'.

I was glad that Short was coming to India, but I knew that it was too late 'to smooth matters' and that the whole position was utterly hopeless. If the Sikhs were lukewarm about a settlement, the Muslims were icy cold. A few days after my

[1] This rather mild expression perhaps indicated an unawareness of the magnitude of the disorders that were impending, *vide* page 94.

rebuff in Lahore I met Gurmani who had been away from
Bahawalpur for some time. He told me that there was nothing
doing for the Sikhs so far as Jinnah was concerned. He was resigned to a 'truncated' Pakistan and had said in effect to Gurmani that the Sikhs could go to the devil in their own way. It
was they who had demanded the partition of the Punjab.
They could now take the consequences.

This was quite consistent with his past attitude. At no stage
had he attempted to placate the Sikhs and secure their acquiescence in Pakistan. He had given them veiled threats, but no
promises. He had warned them that division of the Punjab
would be injurious to them, but he had not encouraged them to
believe that Pakistan would be pleasant. There were some
British officials who considered that in this he was very wise.
In their view the Sikhs, wherever they were, whether in India or
Pakistan, would be a 'bloody nuisance'. Jinnah was well advised
'to steer clear of the bastards so far as he could'. With a 'truncated' Pakistan he was likely to get about two million of them.
This was at any rate better than having the whole hornets' nest.

It is debatable whether this view was really in accord with
the long-term interests of Pakistan; but since it tended to
prevail in League circles a settlement with the Sikhs such as I
had envisaged was out of the question. The whole idea was in a
sense utopian. Possibly if such a settlement had been consistently worked for during the preceding year, it might have
been achieved; but it could not be achieved at the last minute,
especially after the March disturbances. Yet though at this
late stage a settlement was impossible, I was convinced that
nothing else could avert the horrors that were threatening the
Punjab. Early in July, therefore, when my attempt had pal-
pably failed, I resigned myself fatalistically to the coming disaster. At the beginning of the month the Punjab legislators had
duly met, duly followed all the procedure laid down in the
Mountbatten plan, and duly cast their votes so as to doom the
Punjab to division, thousands of its inhabitants to death and
millions of them to misery and ruin. The voice of the people
had become a judgement of God.

It was easy to predict disaster but what was the exact form
that it would take? The earliest forecast known to me, which
roughly corresponded with the event, was made by the Senior

Superintendent of Police, Delhi, at the end of March. Asked
for his opinion as to what would happen if, as already seemed
probable, the Punjab was partitioned, he replied crudely but
tersely:

'Once a line of division is drawn in the Punjab all Sikhs to the
west of it and all Muslims to the east of it will have their
– – – chopped off.'

This, though couched in general and figurative terms, conveyed a correct idea of what to expect. A more precise warning
came to me in the second half of June from a humbler but more
reliable source. This formed part of an episode which requires
to be recorded at some length.

At the end of June a meeting was arranged in Lahore to
consider what stand should be taken before the Boundary
Commission on behalf of Pakistan and the West Punjab.
Sir Mohammad Zafrullah Khan, who had held many high positions under the British but was at this time more or less a free-
lance, had been engaged as counsel by Pakistan and West
Punjab interests. Bahawalpur State had also retained his services. We had put forward and established a claim to be heard
by the Commission since we were vitally interested in the future
control of the canal headworks at Ferozepur and Suleimanke
both of which, according to the population figures, were likely
to fall very near the dividing line.

Zafrullah came up by train from Karachi to Lahore, Gurmani and I joining him at Bahawalpur. It was a delicious sen-
sation to step from the blazing afternoon heat of the Bahawalpur
platform into the quiet cool of Zafrullah's air-conditioned compartment. We were living in exciting times and so naturally there
was a good deal of lively conversation and speculation about
the future. One remark of Zafrullah's particularly stuck in my
mind. We were talking about the division of the Punjab and I
had said that the instruction to the Boundary Commission to
take into account 'other factors' was perhaps designed to
soothe the Sikhs and lead them to think that in fixing the
boundary weight would be given to their large interests in the
colony lands of West Punjab. But if any real concession was to
be made to them on this account, the boundary would have to be
drawn west of Lahore instead of between Lahore and Amritsar.
We must, therefore, I argued, seriously contemplate the possi-

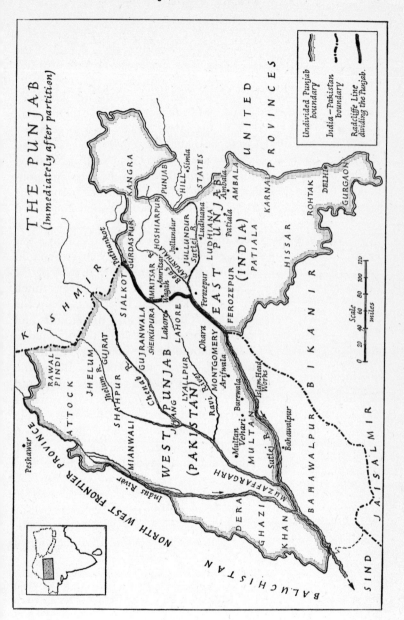

THE PUNJAB
(Immediately after partition)

bility that Lahore would fall to India instead of to Pakistan.[1] Zafrullah was considerably roused by this line of reasoning. He warmly refuted the Sikh claims and said finally: 'Moon, if the British give Lahore to India the Muslims will never forgive them.'

We reached Lahore the next morning and after breakfast were collected by the Nawab of Mamdot and other members of the shadow Cabinet of West Punjab and taken to a large house where the meeting was to be held. We entered a good-sized room and found twenty to twenty-five persons already assembled there—nearly all of them prominent Muslim lawyers and politicians. On the floor and on a big table a number of maps of the Punjab were strewn about, variously coloured and chequered so as to show the distribution of the population by communities. We all fell to poring over these maps. It became plain in a few minutes that no-one had any very definite idea where we should claim that the dividing line should run—indeed, except for Gurmani and myself, no-one seemed to have given much thought to the matter or even to know the basic facts about the distribution of the population. The Sikhs and the Hindus had for some time been putting forward publicly the untenable claim that the river Chenab should be the boundary. Someone suggested that as a counterblast we should claim the line of the Sutlej. This claim was equally if not more untenable and Zafrullah in particular was averse to putting it forward. I think he felt that it would be unwise for us to suggest any wide departure from the line which would be given by consideration of the population figures, for if weight was given to 'other factors' they would tend to tell in favour of the Sikhs and Hindus.

The line of the river Beas was then discussed as a possible boundary. I pointed out that this would give Pakistan the whole of the Amritsar district, which was quite unjustified on a population basis. Moreover it was hardly credible that the city of

[1] It is of interest to recall that almost right up till August 15th there was a widespread belief in Hindu circles, based on what seemed to be good authority, that Lahore would fall to East Punjab and India. This mistaken belief was the cause of considerable pecuniary loss to Hindu families of Lahore, who wrongly supposed that all their movable property in that city would be quite safe.

Amritsar, the main centre of Sikh pilgrimage, would be handed over to Pakistan. I suggested that our best course was to press for a boundary based on Muslim- and non-Muslim-majority areas with such minor adjustments as might be to our advantage and which we could reasonably claim. I mentioned particularly the importance of getting control of the Ferozepur headworks and the headworks at Madhopur near Pathankot.[1] It was not quite clear whether on a population basis they would come to us or not.

I believe a decision was ultimately taken more or less on these lines, but at this point a dispute arose whether the distribution of the population had been correctly shown in the maps. A desultory discussion ensued and my interest and attention wandered. Glancing round the room, I was astonished to notice standing in a group of people near the window a young Muslim naib-tahsildar[2] who had served under me in Amritsar four years earlier. He was looking towards me, smiling rather shyly as though uncertain whether I would recognize and remember him. I may have shown some momentary hesitation as I could hardly believe that this very junior official would be present in this somewhat august gathering. He was a bright intelligent young man and had been rather a favourite of mine. I went up and greeted him with enthusiasm and the following dialogue ensued:

'What on earth are you doing here, Mohammad Ali?'

'Sir, a friend told me there might be quite an interesting meeting here, so I thought I'd come and see what was going on.'

'But how did you get in?'

'My friend brought me along and we just walked in. Nobody stopped us.'

I was rather staggered to find that what purported to be a high-level conference was being treated as an open public meeting. I had certainly never expected that a naib-tahsildar would be watching or assisting our deliberations. However I concluded that this casualness was just one of the signs of the changing times and turned to other topics.

[1] Both these headworks were assigned by the Radcliffe award to India. There was a strong rumour that the award in respect of the areas adjoining these headworks was altered at the last moment. A later age will perhaps learn what foundation, if any, there was for this report.

[2] A subordinate revenue official.

'Where are you posted nowadays?' I asked.

'In Amritsar, sir. I'm here in Lahore on a few days' casual leave.'

'Still in Amritsar! You've been there a very long time. Well, how's Amritsar?'

'Sir, it is awful. I can't tell you how awful it is.' He was almost quivering with suppressed excitement.

'Why, what's the matter? I thought that things had quietened down there now.'

'No doubt everything is quiet at the moment. But I tell you, sir, *the Sikhs are getting ready to kill us and drive us away.*'

'What do you mean?'

'Sir, the Sikhs are determined to kill or drive out all the Muslims from Amritsar district. They won't spare any of us.'

'When are they going to do this?'

'When they think the coast is clear. They're just awaiting their opportunity. I think myself, sir, that as soon as the line is drawn and the British leave, they'll attack us.'

I was not at all surprised at this information. I said: 'I can well believe that what you say is all quite true—indeed I suspected that the Sikhs were planning something of this kind. But I don't think there is anything that can be done about it.'

He agreed that nothing could be done. I told him that I was trying to arrange a 'samjhota' between the Akalis and the League leaders but that the chances of success were very slender, so in all probability the Sikhs of Amritsar would carry out their murderous plan. 'I hope you'll take care to get away in good time,' I said, 'and won't allow yourself to be killed!' He replied, 'Sir, it all depends on God.'

I have never seen or heard of him again, but the warning which he gave and the tense excitement with which he uttered it have remained imprinted on my memory. There was no-one better placed than he to judge the temper and intentions of the Sikhs of the Amritsar district. He had been there for five years, constantly touring round from village to village in the course of his ordinary duties. He knew the people through and through. I accepted what he said as correct.

With this definite warning about Amritsar it should have been possible to deduce fairly accurately what would happen in the Punjab a few weeks hence. I cannot claim that I did so.

I foresaw, of course, a terrific upheaval in the central districts which would have repercussions in the farthest corner of the province; but I quite failed to grasp the speed with which disturbances and displacements of population in the centre of the province would resolve themselves into a vast movement of mass migration, affecting not only the whole Punjab but adjoining areas as well. I envisaged a slower, more prolonged, more confused and chaotic agony.

Punjabis in general were strangely unprepared for what was coming. During May and June, I, like several other British officials, wrote to Hindu friends in West Punjab, pointing out that in Pakistan they could hardly expect the same secure enjoyment of life and property as they had been used to in the past and hinting that they should consider some rearrangement of their affairs. One of them took the hint and expressed gratitude to me afterwards. The rest clung obstinately to their ancestral homes and in the end escaped with little more than their lives. In this they were encouraged by official policy and by statements made by the leaders of Congress and the League and even by Master Tara Singh. Everywhere it was being preached that people should stay where they were and should not leave their homes.

The possibility of mass migrations did, however, cross some people's minds. At a conference on June 4th Lord Mountbatten was specifically asked whether he foresaw any mass transfer of population as a result of Partition. His reply was tantamount to a negative. A measure of transfer would come about, he said, 'in a natural way, that is to say people would just cross the boundary or the Government may take steps to transfer population'. Such minor marginal shifts near the boundary or planned transfer by government were very different from the uncontrollable mass migrations which were shortly destined to take place.

In furtherance of the advice to people not to leave their homes, assurances of protection to minority communities were freely given. Apart from the promises made by individual leaders a joint statement was issued on July 22nd by the spokesmen of the prospective Governments of India and Pakistan solemnly guaranteeing protection to all citizens. This guarantee, it was stated, 'implies that in no circumstances will violence be tolerated in any form in either territory. The two Governments wish to emphasize that they are united in this determination.' These assurances were accepted at their face value with an amazing and pathetic credulity. In spite of all that had happened in March and the disturbed conditions which had prevailed thereafter in the cities of Lahore and Amritsar, most Punjabis allowed themselves to be lulled into a false sense of security. Disregarding their own inner forebodings they acted on the advice of the political leaders and the Government and remained where they were.

If Punjabis themselves were unduly sanguine about the future, it is not surprising that in official and political circles in Delhi there was no conception of the violence of the outbreak that was imminent. Their unawareness of what to expect has been candidly confessed by Mr. V. P. Menon.

'We had anticipated', he had written,[1] 'that there might be trouble in the border districts directly affected by the Partition, but we felt that the Boundary Force of mixed composition under Major-General Rees, an enormous and carefully picked body, would be able to cope with the situation. As for the rest, we had no reason to believe that the Governments concerned would not themselves be able to control any sporadic outbursts that might occur in their respective Dominions. We had the guarantee of the political leaders as set out in their joint statement of 22 July, as also the specific assurances in regard to the protection of minorities given by Jinnah in his address to the Constituent Assembly and in his broadcast to the people of Pakistan. It is true that the situation was full of fear and foreboding; but we had not expected to be so quickly and so thoroughly disillusioned.'

This passage reflects very faithfully the sentiments prevalent in Delhi at that time. Gurmani and I were both there for about a week during the last ten days of July—mainly in connection with the question of Bahawalpur's accession to Pakistan—and I had several talks with Menon himself and with other members of the Viceroy's staff. Cassandra-like I cried 'woe', but not too often or too loudly, since I could suggest no remedy and was convinced that nothing could now prevent catastrophe. It was no use therefore harping on it. I did however express my cer-

[1] *The Transfer of Power in India*, p. 417.

tainty that the Sikhs would turn upon the Muslims in East
Punjab and take a fearful revenge for the March happenings.
But in Delhi as elsewhere the idea had spread that the Sikhs
were shadows of their former selves and that their comparative
quiescence during the past few months in spite of so much provocation was evidence of their want of spirit. I could make little
headway against these deep-seated delusions.

There was, I found, a remarkable faith in the projected
Boundary Force. I could not share it. The Sikhs, I thought, were
bound to attack the Muslims when they saw the chance. If the
Boundary Force was really powerful and effective they would
wait till it was withdrawn. If it was ineffective they would disregard it. On my way back from Delhi to Bahawalpur I happened to hear some views about this force from a young Sikh
major who shared my compartment for part of the journey. He
was himself about to join it, but was utterly sceptical of its
capacity to maintain order. He thought that a large proportion
of the troops would be infected by the communal virus and
prove unreliable. He was also doubtful whether mechanized
infantry would be able to operate effectively in the rural areas
during the monsoon. I fully agreed with him in this. Cavalry
alone could, in my view, check or suppress the widespread disorders in the villages which were likely to occur, and there were
hardly any cavalry regiments in India which still had their
horses. I was also impressed by the total inadequacy of the
force in point of numbers. He told me that it would consist of
two to three divisions. I reckoned that, with the rural areas
ready to burst into flame and the prestige of government reduced to the lowest level by the failure to control the March
disorders, Amritsar district alone would require one division
and Lahore district, which is considerably larger, about two.
Thus the whole Boundary Force would barely suffice for these
two districts. Altogether there were twenty-nine districts in the
Punjab, of which about eight in the centre were likely to be
seriously affected and all the rest disturbed in a greater or lesser
degree. A force of two to three divisions—or even of 50,000
men, which appears to have been its actual strength—could not
possibly control the situation even if it were 100 per cent
reliable. By the time I got back to Bahawalpur I had written
off the Boundary Force completely.

During my stay in Delhi Major Short arrived from England in response to Baldev Singh's request to him to come out. He realized at once that the time had passed for thinking of a Sikh-Muslim rapprochement. All he could do for the Sikhs was to plead for drawing the dividing line in the Punjab sufficiently far to the west to bring some of the colony lands within India. With all my sympathy for the Sikhs I did not think that on merits this could be done. To include within India any of the Punjab colonies would mean shifting the line so far west that the city of Lahore and large tracts of country in which Muslims were in the majority would fall on the Indian side. The mere fact that the Sikhs had played a great part—as had also other communities—in developing the colonies could hardly justify such a material departure from the agreed principle for the partition of the country which was that it should be on the basis of contiguous Muslim-majority and non-Muslim-majority areas. On this basis the dividing line must necessarily fall between Lahore and Amritsar.

In various discussions in Delhi with Short and V. P. Menon I stuck to this view. Menon wanted to know whether by any juggling with the line the danger of disturbances in the Punjab could be diminished. I did not think so. I said that after all that had happened in March the Sikhs were bent on attacking the Muslims wherever they felt themselves to be superior and a shift of the line in their favour would not now deflect them. The Muslims, on the other hand, were not anxious to stir up fresh trouble, but if they were deprived of Lahore—and here I was probably influenced by what Zafrullah had said—they would be so incensed that without further provocation they would repeat the March outrages on a far bigger scale. The best course therefore and also the most just was to adhere strictly to the accepted principles for determining the boundary.

Short, who had to play an advocate's role, did not appear to be convinced; and when I left Delhi he was in a disconsolate mood, for there was really nothing he could do to help the Sikhs. Back in Bahawalpur I received about ten days later a laconic telegram from him: 'Your line has it.' This told me approximately where the line would run and gave the assurance that Lahore would come to Pakistan.

Bahawalpur State

AHAWALPUR, which was the seat allotted to me for witnessing the Punjab tragedy, was a Native State about the size of Denmark lying between the Punjab and Sind. On one side—the north-western—it was bounded continuously by rivers, first by the river Sutlej, then by the Panjnad (i.e. the combined waters of the five Punjab rivers) and finally by the Indus. The opposite, south-eastern boundary of the State ran for the most part through desert territory along the borders of the Rajputana States of Bikanir and Jaisalmir. At its south-western end the State marched with the Sukkur district of Sind and its extreme north-eastern tip just touched the Ferozepur district of what is now East Punjab.

Two-thirds of the State was desert and the remainder was only saved from being so by the rivers running along one side. The average annual rainfall being only about five inches, cultivation was impossible without irrigation which could only be provided by canals or by wells not far from the river banks where the subsoil water was fairly close to the surface. The inhabited agricultural zone of the State was, therefore, a narrow strip of territory, varying in width from five to thirty-five miles and running parallel to the rivers over a length of 300 miles. In the desert area only a sparse nomadic population of graziers was to be found.

The State, more or less in the form in which it existed in 1947, was founded by the ancestors of the present dynasty in the first half of the eighteenth century. They came from Sind but claimed descent ultimately from the Abbasid Caliphs of Baghdad. In 1833, in order to escape the attentions of Ranjit Singh, the Sikh ruler of the Punjab, the Nawab of Bahawalpur sought British protection and Bahawalpur joined the ranks of Native States over which the British exercised suzerainty. It was the only State of any consequence in India which had

D

both a Muslim ruler and a predominantly Muslim population.

The total population in 1947 was between one and a half and
two million, Muslims constituting about 83 per cent. In the
preceding twenty-five years it had nearly doubled. This was a
result of the Sutlej Valley Project which had extended irrigation and led to the immigration of colonists, principally from
the Punjab, to settle on the newly-reclaimed land. Most of the
colonists were Muslims but there was also among them a
sprinkling of Sikhs, settled for the most part near the north-
eastern border of the State. These Sikh colonists constituted the
bulk of the Sikh population of the State which was at this time
a little under 50,000. The Hindus numbered about 190,000.
The majority of them had been established in the State for
several generations, but among them also there were a good
many recent immigrants—bankers, merchants, shopkeepers—
who had bought sites in the new market towns that were spring-
ing up to serve an expanding agriculture. They were a somewhat floating population with their roots still elsewhere—
mainly in the Punjab and Rajputana.

These recent immigrants, whether Muslim, Sikh or Hindu,
tended to be more vigorous and enterprising than the indigenous
inhabitants and by their drive and energy were bringing the
State, which had previously been a rather stagnant backwater,
into the full stream of progress. Their influx had aroused envy
and apprehension in the minds of the original inhabitants. They
felt that they were outmatched by these thrusting energetic
stocks from the Punjab and would ultimately be outnumbered
by them. The strong rivalry between the original inhabitants—
the 'riasatis'[1] as they were called—and the 'non-riasatis' led to
some measure of discrimination against the latter who were not
treated in all respects as full citizens. The distinction cut across all
communal divisions and in the day-to-day administration was
a more obtrusive factor than they, since communal relations
in the State were normally harmonious. It was also to prove of
some significance in the ensuing disturbances. At the first sight
of danger the 'non-riasatis' among the Hindus and Sikhs could
slip away to their original homes, whereas for the 'riasatis'

[1] 'Riasat' was the word used to denote a 'Native State' and so 'riasati'
meant the inhabitant of such a State.

departure from the State meant pulling up much deeper roots.

The Sutlej Valley Project, which had brought into the State all these immigrants, had substituted weir-controlled irrigation for the old 'inundation' canals which only ran four to five months in the year and were dependent on the natural rise and fall of the river. With the construction of four weirs or 'head-works', from which the new canals took off, at Ferozepur, Suleimanke, Pallah and Panjnad, irrigation on both banks of the river could be extended and made more assured, and the low winter supplies of water could be utilized so as to give perennial irrigation to some areas.[1]

The Project, which had been commenced in 1922 and finally completed about ten years later, had not fulfilled all the hopes entertained of it and Bahawalpur State in particular had suffered from its comparative failure. This had given rise to a good deal of controversy and in Bahawalpur to some not unjustified bitterness. From the very outset the Bahawalpur authorities had pointed out that the water available in the rivers had been over-estimated and that this miscalculation vitiated the whole Project in the form in which it had been put forward. They protested against it being undertaken unless substantially modified. They protested in vain. The Nawab was at that time a minor and the representatives of the Paramount Power were, therefore, under a special obligation to see that the interests of his State were fully safeguarded. This obligation was not discharged. Disregarding the protests of the Regency Council, recklessly accepting palpable over-estimates of the water supplies and gross under-estimates of the costs, the Paramount Power forced Bahawalpur into the Project without removing its defects.

It soon became apparent that the Bahawalpur authorities had been right. The supplies of water, it was found, were insufficient for the designed capacity of the canals; at the Suleimanke and Islam (Pallah) weirs in particular the shortage at the critical seasons of the year was serious and chronic. In the end large

[1] The total area which it was planned should ultimately receive irrigation, either perennial or non-perennial, was 5,108,000 acres (or nearly 8,000 square miles) of which 2,825,000 acres were in Bahawalpur, 1,942,000 in the Punjab and 34,000 in Bikanir State. The total cost of the Project was Rs 34 crores of which Bahawalpur's share was Rs 14 crores.

areas of land which it had been intended to bring under irrigation had to be given up. Miles of canals dug through the deserts of Bahawalpur were later abandoned, and rest-houses, built for the accommodation of canal officers but never occupied, crumbled away forlornly in a barren wilderness.

Even worse than this unproductive expenditure was the terrific shortfall in the receipts which the Project had been expected to yield. The inadequacy of the supplies of water for the canals quickly became known and adversely affected the prices at which land could be auctioned. On top of this came the collapse of agricultural prices in the thirties. Colony land in Bahawalpur became practically unsaleable; even in the Punjab the auctioning of land had to be greatly reduced. The effect on Bahawalpur's finances was very serious. To meet its share of the capital cost of the Project, which turned out to be nearly two and a half times the original estimates, the State had to borrow Rs 12 crores from the Government of India. By 1936 it had not been possible to make any repayment; even the interest charges had not been met in full and the debt had swollen to about Rs 14 crores. An agreement was then entered into for its liquidation by annual instalments over a period of fifty years ending in 1986.

Ultimately the war came to the rescue of Bahawalpur. After 1942 with the steep rise in agricultural prices and consequently of land values the position and prospects vastly improved. The debt began to be repaid much faster than seemed possible in 1936 and by the end of 1945 had been reduced to Rs 5 crores. But the financial difficulties and transactions which have been described had a profound effect on the whole organization of the State and consequently also on the position of the Nawab. Born in 1904, he had lost his father in 1907 and there had been a long minority. When in 1924 he was invested with ruling powers he found that in consequence of the borrowings for the Sutlej Valley Project the administration of his State was half-mortgaged to the Government of India, and soon seemed destined to remain so for most of his lifetime. To safeguard their loan the Government of India had contrived to secure a tight control over the affairs of the State by the appointment of their own nominees to key posts, and they showed no sign of relaxing it so long as any substantial part of the debt remained outstanding.

It cannot be supposed that the Nawab felt happy about the position. It meant that in practice he lost both in power and in wealth. Owing to the State's financial difficulties the amounts which could be officially allotted to him for his personal expenditure, though considerable, fell far short of his requirements, and owing to the Government of India's grip on the main branches of the administration, he could not easily, like other rulers whose financial powers were unfettered, obtain for himself a larger share of the revenues of the State. The army was in fact the only large department where he had a comparatively free hand. There were therefore perpetual disputes about money. Moreover since real responsibility for the State was in effect assumed by the Government of India instead of being made to rest fairly and squarely on the shoulders of the Nawab, his own interest in the State's administration was not as keen as it otherwise might have been.

These were defects for which the Paramount Power, through its failure to safeguard the Nawab's interests during his minority, was partly responsible. A more determined or more ill-natured man might have made more than he did of his grievances. But the people at large were not adversely affected. The State was on the whole quite well administered. The Nawab himself was much of the time away in England or elsewhere; and even when he was in residence, the fact that his palace was at Dera Nawab, a place connected with Bahawalpur by the only metalled road in the State but over thirty miles distant from it, made him rather remote and the transaction of official business with him a little difficult. Nevertheless he was by no means unpopular; and if the army accounts were never audited and if there were leakages from various minor departments, the mass of the people were no wiser and felt no worse. 'The unwelcome novelties of education and hygiene' were not, as yet, universally desired; nor did the people at large think ill of a ruler for wishing to spend more of the State revenues on himself than a civil servant would approve. In a State with which I was later associated I found that an enlightened ruler, the founder of many schools and other useful institutions, highly eulogized by Lord Curzon himself, held no greater place in popular memory and esteem than his successor who had to be deposed for drunkenness and riotous living, having squandered the

State's resources on merrymaking, fireworks and colourful debauches. Circuses have more appeal than uplift.

When Gurmani and I went to Bahawalpur in April 1947 the control of the Government of India was still in force and had behind it the sanction of over twenty years. It was exercised mainly and most directly in respect of the departments of Revenue, Colonization and Public Works. For years the Revenue Minister who was in charge of these branches of the administration had been a nominee of the Government of India[1]—generally a retired official from the Punjab. The Chief Engineer and at least one of the Superintending Engineers had likewise been British officials drawn from outside the State. There had also been British officials, generally borrowed from the Punjab, employed as Colonization Officers, and a Government of India official acted as Accountant-General for Development Expenditure. Thus in practice, if not in theory, effective control of these departments had been vested in outsiders in-instead of in the Nawab and natives of the State.

However necessary and however welcome to the colonists this arrangement may have been, it was not popular with educated 'riasatis'. But they had to endure it; and it had one good result—the efficiency of the Revenue and Public Works departments had been raised to a high level and in their general working and in the quality of their personnel they fell little short of the standards prevalent in the adjoining Punjab. The same could not be said of the other departments of the State which, except for the army, were starved of money and comparatively neglected.

During the past twenty-five years the normal practice in Bahawalpur had been to have a Muslim as Prime Minister and an Englishman as Revenue Minister; but Gurmani's immediate predecessor was an Englishman, Sir Richard Crofton, and mine a retired Muslim official from the North-West Frontier Province. With our appointments there was a reversion to the usual pattern. I could not fail to detect that court and official circles in Bahawalpur were not sorry to say good-bye to Crofton nor over-pleased at having to welcome me—another Englishman. I sensed a vague hostility such as I had never

[1] My own appointment as Revenue and Public Works Minister had to receive the Government of India's approval.

experienced in the Punjab. In part this sprang from the pecu-
liar conditions of Bahawalpur which had long covertly nursed a
tradition of anti-western, obscurantist and reactionary Islam.
In part it was a manifestation of the general desire to see the
last of the British now that the time had come for them to
lay down their power.

Besides the Prime Minister and Revenue Minister there were
three or four other Ministers, drawn from the ranks of State
subjects, who held minor portfolios or Palace appointments.
All the Ministers together formed a State Council or *kabina*,
over meetings of which the Nawab himself occasionally presided. Since however all the important departments of the
State, except the Military Department, were in the hands of
the Prime Minister and Revenue Minister, the business trans-
acted by the *kabina* was mainly of a formal character.

The Chief Engineer of the State at this time was according
to established custom British—Mr. James Roy, a retired
engineer from the Punjab who in his younger days had built
the Panjnad headworks. One of the three Superintending
Engineers under him, Mr. Duncan, was also British and lent
to the State by the Punjab Government.

The Colonization Officers had been converted a few years
earlier into Deputy Commissioners and put in charge not only
of colony work but of all revenue work in the two districts
into which the State was administratively divided.[1] For a time
there had been two British officials holding these posts, but in
1947 only the Bahawalpur district was in charge of a Britisher
—Mr. Oliver, an I.C.S. officer from the Punjab—and the
Deputy Commissioner of the other district of Rahim Yar Khan
was a promoted revenue officer of the State, Maulvi Faiz Ahmad.

On the revenue side one other official drawn from outside
the State requires to be mentioned. This was the Settlement
Commissioner, Khan Bahadur Nur Mohammad, a retired
Deputy Commissioner from the Punjab and well-known both to
Gurmani and myself. After over twenty years of the new irriga-
tion system agriculture in the Bahawalpur district had become

---

[1] In the Punjab, Deputy Commissioners were also District Magistrates,
but to avoid arrogating to outsiders too large powers this arrangement was
not followed in Bahawalpur and revenue and magisterial functions were
kept more or less separate.

established and Nur Mohammad with a large 'settlement' staff had been appointed to reassess the land revenue. The work was very nearly complete and there was talk of terminating his appointment; but we kept him on and later at the end of July, when with the general exodus of British officers from India Oliver wanted to leave, he temporarily took over the work of Deputy Commissioner in addition to his own duties.

Bahawalpur had both an army and a police force. The latter was sadly neglected. Crofton had done something to raise its standards and had recently appointed to command it a retired Punjab police officer of good reputation named Nur Hussain Shah. But the neglect of years could not be made good in a few months. As in many Native States, the police were neglected for the army which was the special preserve and plaything of the Nawab and under his own direct control. It consisted of three infantry battalions and some miscellaneous units. A certain number of the troops were recruited from Bahawalpur State itself, but the bulk of them were drawn from the martial classes of northern India—mainly Pathans from the North-West Frontier Province, though there were a few platoons of Gurkhas.

State Forces in India were generally commanded by a regular officer of the Indian Army seconded for the purpose. The Political Department would have liked such an arrangement in the case of Bahawalpur, but the Nawab preferred to have a commander entirely of his own choice. The man selected was J. H. Marden. He had seen service in World War I, but was not an officer of the Indian Army. By 1947 he had attained the rank of brigadier and had been in command for a good many years.

One battalion of the Bahawalpur Army had served in Malaya during the war as line of communication troops, but even before the Japanese attack there was trouble owing to dissensions among the officers and the Nawab had to go to Malaya to help set matters right. On the fall of Singapore an influential officer named Gilani, along with a portion of the battalion, joined the Indian National Army[1] and attained considerable prominence therein. Another officer, named Durrani, his enemy and rival, stoutly resisted all Japanese blandishments and was subjected by

[1] The force formed by the Japanese to fight against the British from Indian prisoners captured in Malaya and at Singapore.

them to ill-treatment and torture. At the end of the war Gilani, of whom more will be heard, was cashiered and Durrani was awarded the George Cross.

Bahawalpur, being a Muslim State and situated between Sind and the Punjab, seemed destined to be linked in some way or other with Pakistan. Theoretically, of course, with the departure of the British and the lapse of Paramountcy it would become completely independent. But in practice complete independence would be difficult to maintain, and an endeavour to assert it might unnecessarily irritate the Pakistani leaders with unfortunate consequences. It was known that Jinnah, unlike the Congress leaders, was not hostile to the Ruling Princes and had no plans for sweeping them away or even for curtailing their powers. There seemed, therefore, every prospect of reaching some arrangement with Pakistan whereby Bahawalpur State would remain completely autonomous in regard to its internal affairs and cede sovereignty to Pakistan only in respect of defence and foreign relations.

When Gurmani and I accepted appointments in Bahawalpur nothing had been decided about this—even the creation of Pakistan had not been formally announced—but we assumed that some arrangement on these lines would eventually be worked out. It would mean for the Nawab, both in theory and practice, more real independence than he had ever enjoyed under the British, and naturally he himself desired as much independence as he could safely assert. We felt that Pakistan, beset with many pressing problems and with all the instability of a new State and a new untried democracy, would have little time or disposition to interfere with our affairs, provided we kept them running along quietly and did not have to go to Pakistan cap in hand for money to meet our expenses or armed forces to quell disturbances.

After all the financial difficulties of the past twenty years the State seemed to us at this time to be well set on a course of steadily increasing prosperity. Revenues had trebled in the past six years and the back of the debt had at last been broken. The State produced large quantities of surplus foodgrains which with skilful management could be passed on to less fortunate parts of the country with great profit to the exchequer. Irrigation from the Panjnad weir—the last to be

D*

constructed—was proving much more satisfactory than from the earlier Suleimanke and Islam weirs and was beginning to bring considerable wealth to the Rahim Yar Khan district. Altogether it seemed that the State, unless confronted with some unexpected crisis, was capable of standing on its own legs in a position of semi-independence. There was, of course, the ominous shadow of the great storm gathering in the Punjab, but we hoped that Bahawalpur would only catch the tail-end of it and would remain a comparatively sheltered haven.

It was a bit disconcerting to find that despite the uncertainty of the times the Nawab insisted on going off for the summer to England where he had a house near Farnham in Surrey. He promised, however, to return if any big issues regarding the future of the State had to be decided. With the announcement in June that the date for the transfer of power was to be put forward to August 15th these issues could no longer be postponed. Accordingly when towards the end of July Lord Mountbatten called the Ruling Princes to Delhi to talk to them about the future of their States the Nawab flew back to India to attend the meeting.

Lord Mountbatten's object was to persuade all the rulers to 'accede' to one or other of the two new Dominions in respect of defence, external affairs and communications—in other words to subordinate themselves in some measure to India or Pakistan. Some of the bigger States had other ideas; they thought that they could successfully assert independent sovereignty. A plan had also been mooted—and had received some backing from the Political Department—for combining the States, or a large number of them, into a kind of third Dominion. Gurmani occasionally seemed attracted by the idea. It was not, in my view, a practical proposition; but a few of the larger States forming compact areas, for example the Rajputana States, might have successfully stood aloof both from India and Pakistan, if they had acted together in unison. Herein lay the only real chance of the survival of any of the States. Accession, more particularly to India—and most States for geographical reasons were precluded from acceding to Pakistan—could only mean speedy extinction, since the Congress Party, which would hold the reins of power in India, was bent on their liquidation. Nevertheless Lord Mountbatten, with a brilliant persuasiveness which could hardly have been excelled, induced them all, with the unfortunate exceptions of Kashmir and Hyderabad, to sign what proved to be their own death warrants on the assurance that this afforded them the best chance of survival.

I had assumed that Bahawalpur would quietly accede to Pakistan. Our discussions with Muslim League leaders in Lahore and our engagement of Pakistan's counsel, Zafrullah, to represent our interests also before the Boundary Commission clearly implied that this was our intention. I was astounded, therefore, when Gurmani informed me that the Nawab was being advised in certain quarters to accede to India. Gurmani himself seemed hardly less astonished and perplexed. The reason for this perverse advice was not far to seek. The Muslim League leaders had been offering tempting concessions to some of the Hindu rulers in the hope of inducing them to join Pakistan. In the case of the Maharajah of Jodhpur they very nearly succeeded. Some people thought that the Nawab might extract similar concessions from India if he agreed to accede to India instead of to Pakistan. These calculations were quite unfounded. The Congress leaders were not interested in enticing Bahawalpur into the Indian Union. Moreover, since Bahawalpur was a Muslim State with a Muslim ruler and lay right astride the rail and road communications between Karachi and Lahore, its accession to India would be a deadly blow to Pakistan and must produce a violent Muslim reaction. I told Gurmani that I thought the Nawab would be promptly assassinated if he attempted such a course, and that Gurmani had better warn him of this contingency. I do not know whether he did so, but in any case after a day or two all talk of acceding to India ended as the Nawab decided that Bahawalpur should in due course accede to Pakistan.[1] After attending the celebrations in Karachi on the inauguration of Pakistan he flew back to England.

Like me the people of Bahawalpur had assumed that the State would accede to Pakistan; they knew nothing of any other possibility. The majority of them, being Muslims, were well content with the prospect, and throughout most of the State even the minority communities had accepted it philosophically and without undue alarm. During the March dis-

[1] The instrument of accession was not actually signed till October 3rd 1947.

turbances in the Punjab perfect tranquillity had prevailed in Bahawalpur and there was a general disposition to believe that this would continue. Only at the north-east end of the State in the colony areas around Bahawalnagar, where there were many recent Hindu and Sikh immigrants and contact with the Punjab was closest, were there signs of uneasiness. The replacement of Crofton by a Muslim Prime Minister known to have Muslim League sympathies was the subject of comment and questioning. Would non-Muslim interests be safe in his hands? A trickle of Hindus began to leave the State and there was some underground propaganda designed to stimulate a greater exodus; for extremist Hindu circles entertained the notion that they could ruin Pakistan by depriving it *ab initio* of all the banking and commercial facilities and expertise which the Hindu community had hitherto provided. In order to spread alarm and afford a colourable pretext for an exodus—since Bahawalpur had remained entirely peaceful—some Hindus started petty cases of arson in their own houses—singeing a sofa, charring the leg of a wooden bedstead or burning up an old bit of matting—and then made out that Muslims had done it, that their lives and property were in danger and that they must leave at once for some place of greater security. A few actually locked up their houses and went away with their goods and chattels and family cow to their original homes.

In order to allay this unrest Gurmani himself paid a visit to Bahawalnagar in May. His genial expansive personality, persuasive speech and benevolent smile made an excellent impression. He gave assurances to the minority communities of full protection and quite dispelled any notion there might be that he was a bloodthirsty, bigoted Muslim. To inspire confidence he ordered some detachments of the Bahawalpur army to be sent to Bahawalnagar, Harunabad and other towns in that area. I was not too happy about this arrangement as I distrusted the discipline of the Bahawalpur troops, but the minority communities themselves welcomed it.

During the month of June I toured through this part of the State and found that previous fears had to a great extent disappeared. The Hindus were no longer talking of leaving and appeared to be quite reassured. Only the Sikhs were worried. Two or three deputations of Sikh colonists came to see me and asked, in effect, whether they should leave the State or whether it would be safe for them to stay. I was obliged to hedge. I could not advise them to leave as that would have been totally contrary to the general policy that was being followed. Yet I could not promise that they would be safe if they stayed; for, apart from the fact that as Revenue Minister I was not directly responsible for law and order, I did not feel certain that we would be able to protect them. So I simply said that I could see no danger to them at the moment and that therefore I could not understand how Sikhs, who were supposed to be brave people, could be thinking of running away. It was, however, up to them to decide. If they really felt that they were in danger despite appearances to the contrary, there was nothing to prevent them leaving.

They went away dissatisfied and I got the impression that unless I personally guaranteed their safety—which I was not prepared to do—they would decide to leave.

Throughout July the State remained absolutely calm; but in the Punjab there was some fresh deterioration in the situation, especially in Lahore and Amritsar. One incident that occurred at this time afforded us a lurid glimpse of the fanatical hatreds that had been aroused in those cities. Gurmani and I had a mutual friend named Major Ashiq Hussain Qureshi, a wealthy Muslim landowner and a man of some prominence in the Punjab—he had been a Minister in Khizar's Government in 1944-6. Late on the night of July 31st my telephone rang. Gurmani was at the other end and said: 'Ashiq has been shot dead in Lahore by a police constable.'

We only learnt the details of the incident later. They were certainly remarkable. It appears that as Ashiq Hussain was driving from the city to his house in one of the suburbs, an armed police constable signalled to him to stop. He did not see, or did not immediately obey, the signal and when finally he brought his car to a standstill an altercation took place between him and the constable and they parted with mutual abuse. About twenty minutes later Ashiq had occasion to return to the city by the same route. The same constable, with whom there was now a sub-inspector, signalled to him to stop. He did so and the sub-inspector came up and asked him why he had not obeyed the constable's signal on the previous occasion. He

replied that he had done so as soon as possible and started com-
plaining of the constable's insolence; whereupon the constable lifted up the rifle which he was carrying and shot him
through the head. He was killed instantly and his brains
scattered over the seat of the car. The sub-inspector exclaimed:
'What a terrible thing you've done! Why, you might as well
have killed me! This is Ashiq Hussain.' The constable, who was
a Muslim, was taken aback at this and said in astonishment:
'Ashiq Hussain! I thought it was a Hindu.' He was arrested
and subsequently hanged.

This episode, confirming as tragically as it did how deeply
anti-Hindu Punjabi Muslims had by now become, came more
as a shock to me than anything that had previously occurred.

During the first half of August ripples from disturbances elsewhere began to reach Bahawalpur. Quite suddenly, without
notice or warning, 200–300 refugees arrived by train from Alwar
and Bharatpur—two small States south of Delhi—and deposited
themselves on a bit of open ground outside the city. They
claimed that they had been forcibly driven from their homes,
but there was no evidence of this and it appeared that they
had been impelled to leave more by fear of what might happen than by anything that had actually taken place. Their
arrival caused a mild stir in Bahawalpur city and various
Muslim organizations began to busy themselves with their
relief and to urge the Bahawalpur Government to make lavish
arrangements for their further entertainment. We were not at
all inclined to assume any responsibility for these uninvited
guests; and Gurmani told them that if they were seeking the
promised land of Pakistan they had come to the wrong place
and had better go on to Punjab or Sind. Gradually they drifted
away.

About the same time reports began to spread of renewed
disturbances in Lahore and Amritsar. No great notice was
taken of these reports in Bahawalpur, but a train outrage which
occurred on the evening of August 9th aroused a good deal of
excitement and indignation among sections of the Muslim
population. A number of the clerical staff of the new Pakistan
Government were due to pass through the State in a special
train carrying them from Delhi to Karachi, and preparations
had been made to cheer them on their way and offer them re-

freshments at Bahawalpur station. But before the train reached
the borders of the State, it was derailed in the adjoining district
of Ferozepur by the explosion of a bomb which Sikhs had
placed on the railway track. Two or three passengers were
killed and a number injured. A relief train had to be sent out
from Bahawalnagar. This was one of the first train outrages and
the first incident to make any noticeable impression on the
Muslims of Bahawalpur.

We were still awaiting the public announcement of the
Radcliffe award fixing the boundary line between East and
West Punjab. I had expected the announcement to be made a
day or two before August 15th and to be the signal for the storm
to break in the Punjab, but it was delayed till August 17th.
The Sikhs, however, did not wait for it. A few days earlier, as I
was soon to learn, they had begun their long-meditated revenge.

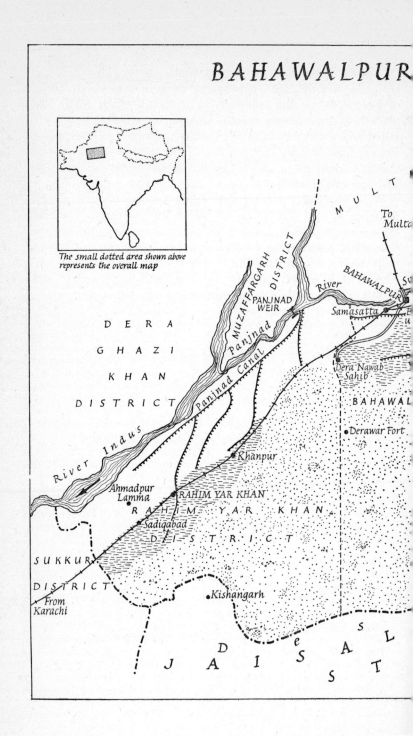

The small dotted area shown above represents the overall map

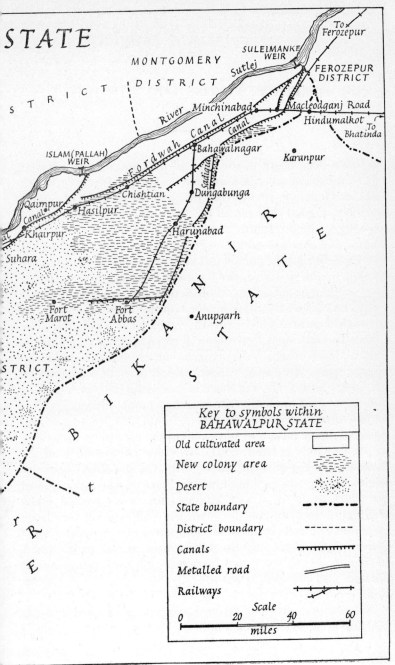

STATE

MONTGOMERY

DISTRICT

STRICT

SUTLEJ

SULEIMANKE
WEIR

To
Ferozepur

FEROZEPUR
DISTRICT

River Minchinabad

Macleodganj Road

Hindumalkot

To
Bhatinda

ISLAM (PALLAH)
WEIR

Fordwah Canal

Sadiqia Canal

Bahawalnagar

Karanpur

Qaimpur

Chishtian

Dungabunga

Hasilpur

Canal

Khairpur

Harunabad

B I K A N I R E   S T A T E

Suhara

Fort
Marot

Fort
Abbas

Anupgarh

STRICT

t

R E

Key to symbols within
BAHAWALPUR STATE

Old cultivated area	
New colony area	
Desert	
State boundary	
District boundary	
Canals	
Metalled road	
Railways	

Scale

0   20   40   60

miles

VII

Journey Across the Punjab

I HAD been down in the heat all the summer and felt that I must have a break sometime in August. It was arranged that Gurmani, who during July and the first half of August had been a good deal out of the State in Simla, Karachi and elsewhere, should return to Bahawalpur by the middle of August and that I should then go up to Simla for a fortnight. I had thought that the conflagration that was about to sweep the Punjab might possibly miss Bahawalpur altogether, or at any rate would not spread to it till September, by which time I would be back in the State to give Gurmani any assistance that he might require. This was rather a bad miscalculation. The flames spread much faster than I had expected and may be said to have reached the eastern border of Bahawalpur by August 22nd. But a week earlier, when I set out on my journey to Lahore and Simla, the State was peaceful and undisturbed; and so were the immediately adjoining Punjab districts.

This drive across the Punjab to Simla and back again ten days later gave me a bird's-eye view of the conditions prevailing in the Province at this time. I started for Lahore early on the morning of August 15th, taking with me my driver and my bearer. There was nothing abnormal *en route* save that around Burewala (a town in the Multan district) individual Sikhs walking or bicycling on the roads were all wearing very large kirpans.[1] Somewhere near the boundary between the Montgomery and Lahore districts there was a military picket and a barrier across the road, but apart from this everything seemed normal and tranquil right up to the outskirts of Lahore itself.

About four to five miles from Lahore, as we approached the built-up area, we overtook a military lorry in the back of which

[1] A kirpan is a form of dagger or sword which every Sikh is supposed to carry.

there was a soldier with a rifle and two or three bloodstained corpses bumping about on the floor. A little farther on five or six men were lined up along the side of the road with their hands up and a soldier covering them with his rifle. Two hundred yards beyond there was a corpse lying on a charpoy. It now became noticeable that the road and the houses on either side of it were entirely deserted. On the other hand, through the gaps between the houses, peasants could be seen with their bullocks ploughing the fields a few hundred yards away, as though nothing had happened.

The Lawrence Gardens were full of troops; the Mall empty, every shop shut, and as silent as the grave. I made for the railway station to find out about trains to Simla. As I passed down Empress Road a fire engine was coping with a burning house, and to the left, from the city proper, numerous dense columns of smoke were rising into the air.

The railway station was in the hands of the military and barricaded off by barbed wire. I forced my way past the sentry and found Colonel Walker (whom I had known on the hunting-field eight to nine years earlier) established in a room off the main hall and apparently in charge. There was no sign of any station staff except two clerks in the inquiry office who returned inane answers to my questions about trains. They finally referred me to the head office in Empress Road. I reached the conclusion that no train was likely to leave for Simla that evening, but if one did, there would be few competitors for a seat in it apart from myself!

I then drove to Faletti's Hotel for lunch. As I got out of my car, a hand was stretched out to me from another car moving off and there was Jack Bennett, the Inspector-General of Police, driving off to the airfield to catch a plane home. He told me that Jenkins[1] had left earlier in the morning. The departure of the Governor and the Inspector-General of Police was the outward and visible symbol of the end of British rule. I could not help reflecting that we were leaving Lahore in the same state of turmoil and disorder as we had found it almost exactly a century earlier.

After lunch I went and had a chat with John Eustace, an old friend and exact contemporary who during the last few

[1] Sir Evan Jenkins, Governor of the Punjab 1946–47.

months had been working as Deputy Commissioner, Lahore. He had handed over charge the day before to a Muslim officer and was staying in the Under-Secretary's house at the Residency out towards the cantonments. While we talked a house on the opposite side of the road, belonging to a Hindu, was broken into by a band of Muslims and plundered. Eustace said that the Muslim police in Lahore were now openly taking sides with the rioters. Muslim police constables had been giving covering fire from roof-tops while Muslim mobs below broke into Sikh Gurdwaras.[1] He thought that the military were probably also unreliable and already taking sides. The recent recrudescence of trouble in Lahore was due to events in Amritsar district where, for the last ten days, armed gangs of Sikhs had been setting fire to Muslim villages and butchering the inhabitants.

He strongly urged me not to attempt to motor through to Simla unarmed, but, except for a shotgun for sporting purposes, I had never kept or carried arms in India and did not intend to do so now. During the troubled weeks in Bahawalpur that were to follow, I remained throughout unarmed and was, no doubt, all the better for it.

At about 7.0 p.m. I went to the station again to make further inquiries about trains to Simla. Twenty Sikh police constables were gathered together in a corner of the main entrance hall behind a barbed-wire barricade. Walker told me that they had sought his protection from the alleged violence of a Muslim mob and he had admitted them within his station stronghold. I walked on to the platform which was practically deserted, and, seeing a man coming along in stationmaster's uniform, went up and asked him if any train was going to Simla.

'Sir,' he said, 'I have just escaped from Moghulpura on an engine with some of my staff. We were attacked by 8,000 Sikhs; they have killed several hundred. I have been telephoning for help for thirteen hours.'

I did not attempt to get at the real facts underlying this exaggerated story, but, as he seemed rather distraught, I just popped him in my car and sent him to his home somewhere near Kashmiri Gate. While waiting for my car to return, I found out from somebody who seemed to know, that only one

[1] Gurdwara = Sikh temple.

train would leave Lahore that night and that would be for Quetta!

I now gave up all hope of getting to Simla by train. Earlier in the afternoon I had learnt that some five or six British officials, all well-known to me, who were due to sail from Bombay in about a week and had grown doubtful of the prospect of getting out of Lahore by train, had obtained a military lorry and a military escort to take them and their kit to Delhi. They were due to leave the next day and were very keen that I should accompany them as far as Ambala (from where I would have to turn off for Simla) as this would mean seats for two or three of them in a comfortable car instead of in a lorry. There was obviously nothing better to do. My car rather badly needed repairs and my plan had been to leave it at a garage in Lahore while I went on by train to Simla, picking it up again on my return. But no garage was open and no trains were running.

We left Lahore on the morning of August 16th at 6.15 a.m. and took the route via Ferozepur so as to avoid Amritsar, which was thought to be particularly dangerous. Besides two military lorries, there were several cars in the convoy. All the British officials, except myself, were leaving Lahore and the Punjab for good. It was a dismal exodus from a Province which we had governed with great success for one hundred years and which, perhaps more than any other Province, had liked us. But that Province itself was no more. It had been cut in two and its life and culture, as we had known them, were in the process of being destroyed for ever.

Except for terrific storms of rain, which made driving difficult, our journey was entirely uneventful and the military escort (as I had surmised) quite superfluous. At both Ludhiana and Ambala a curfew was in force, but nothing very serious seemed yet to have occurred at either of these places. From Ambala up to Simla everything was entirely normal.

Simla also was normal and full of summer residents, but buzzing with stories of ghastly happenings in Amritsar and Lahore. It was destined a few weeks later to be itself the scene of some disgraceful atrocities, but for the moment life flowed along smoothly. I was surprised to find several Hindus, who had large stakes in the West Punjab, apparently unperturbed by all that was going on. I lunched one day with one of them and, despite the fact that almost all his property and business interests were now in Pakistan, he was delightfully cheerful and sprightly. He had, however, taken the precaution a couple of years earlier of getting to know Jinnah and asking him to lunch. That lunch proved a good investment; he managed to salvage most of his Pakistan assets.

Another Hindu business man, a bulky benevolent old fellow whom I had known since my earliest days in the Punjab, I met one day on the Mall. Knowing that he had extensive mining and other interests in Western Punjab, I asked him how he felt about them.

'I've left them all to God,' he said.

'So then you're quite unaffected by all these events?' I questioned.

'Well,' he replied, 'I cannot claim to be quite unaffected, but, thanks to moral rearmament, I'm fifty to sixty per cent un-affected.'

In a very different mood was poor old Sir Manohar Lal. He had for many years been Finance Minister in the Punjab and was reputed, when at Cambridge, to have been one of Alfred Marshall's favourite pupils. Though by no means devoid of nationalist feelings—he had been arrested during the troubles of 1919—he was deeply steeped in English culture and English habits of thought and action. He prided himself on his mastery of the English language; on files he recorded the most polished notes in an exquisite handwriting. I met him, as so often in earlier years, going along the Mall in a rickshaw—a bit shaky, but much the same as ever. He stopped his rickshaw and, grasping me warmly by the hand, said:

'Tell me, Moon, for you're an intelligent man, tell me, why are you British leaving us like this?'

I replied, 'I think mainly because we feel that you no longer want us.'

'But surely you know that it's only a handful of Congress people who think like that. Just see what awful things are now happening in the Punjab; and there's going to be worse.'

I did my best to reassure him, saying that we were witnessing the birth pangs of two new nations and that after a while all would be well. But he was not to be comforted. The world which he had known was collapsing before him. He did not live to see very much of the New Order.

Day by day news from the Punjab seemed to get worse. Owing to censorship, reports were vague, but the disorder was clearly growing and spreading. I decided to curtail my stay in Simla. I wrote to Gurmani saying that I hoped to be back in Bahawalpur by the evening of the 25th. Many people told me that driving across East Punjab would be dangerous, especially with two Muslim servants. But it was infinitely safer than going by train. There was, in fact, no danger at all except possibly if one had a breakdown, and even then military patrols on the Grand Trunk Road would have afforded protection. I am glad to say that my servants neither showed nor, I think, felt the slightest alarm—indeed my bearer insisted that we should go by Amritsar, which was considered the more risky route, in order that we might pass through Jullundur, his native town. He rightly foresaw that this would be his last opportunity of seeing it.

The rains had been particularly heavy and great pools and sheets of water were standing in the fields and village tracks. I could not imagine how, in these conditions, the Boundary Force could hope to move about and keep order in the country-side. With their wheeled transport they would get bogged down immediately. Cavalry was the only answer, and there was no cavalry. So far as I could make out, the villages of the Eastern Punjab were just being allowed to run amuck as they pleased. From the Grand Trunk Road, particularly on the stretch from Ambala to Ludhiana, murderous-looking gangs of Sikhs, armed with guns and spears, could be seen prowling about or standing under the trees, often within fifty yards of the road itself. Military patrols in jeeps and trucks were passing up and down the road, yet taking not the slightest notice of these gangs, as though they were natural and normal features of the country-side. This was not at all my idea of how things should be done. I felt that gangs such as these should not be tolerated for one instant, but mercilessly shot down wherever they were seen.

The towns were all under curfew and had a curiously dere-lict appearance. At Ludhiana not a soul was visible and there was no sign of life at all, except two donkeys copulating in the middle of the road just near the clock tower. At Jullundur a few people were stirring, but many of the houses looked as though they had been plundered and the streets were strewn with litter. I asked my bearer whether he would like us to turn aside to have a look at his house, but seeing the condition of the town he shook his head and said, 'No; it's all been destroyed.'

At Amritsar we had to stop for petrol, our tank being almost empty. I thought I might have to try to obtain some from the Deputy Commissioner as all the petrol pumps seemed to be closed. However, at last we found one that was functioning. The Sikh serving it recognized me and was very obliging, but also very talkative. He was full of some alleged massacre of Sikhs by a Muslim battalion on the border, just beyond Atari. When I asked him about the massacres of Muslims by Sikhs that had occurred in the Amritsar district, he disclaimed all knowledge of them.

At Wagah, midway between Amritsar and Lahore, we had to cross the newly established frontier between India and Pakistan, but there were as yet no formalities and we drove across without, I think, even being stopped. Lahore was not burning as briskly as it had been ten days earlier and seemed generally in rather better shape, but all the shops in the Mall were still closed.

We stopped the night in Lahore and pushed on the next morinng down the Multan road. There were no armed bands roaming about the countryside as there were on the Indian side of the frontier and we struck nothing unusual till we had gone about seventy miles and reached Okara. Stopping at the out-skirts of the town to get some petrol I was surprised to see Daultana, one of the Ministers of the newly formed West Punjab Government, sitting not far from the pump, sur-rounded by a group of men. It seemed a strange place to find a Minister. He came up to me and exchanged a few words and explained that there had been an 'incident' at Okara and he had come to inquire into it.

Ten miles farther on, as we rounded a bend in the road after crossing a canal, we almost ran into a bullock-cart, stranded in the middle of the road with the bullocks unyoked and standing to one side. We had to stop practically dead and then pull right over on to the side of the road, as the cart entirely blocked the metalled portion. As we did so, I noticed a man lying under the cart, and then two police constables suddenly appeared—they had been standing on the far side of the cart—and signalled us on. I felt a bit mystified and, looking back, saw one of the constables with his rifle raised to his shoulder aiming at the man under the cart. There was a crack —and the poor fellow was presumably finished off. This was to me a novel form of summary justice on the high road.

Along the outskirts of the town of Montgomery the road was completely blocked for about a mile by a string of bullock-carts laden with goods and chattels and paraphernalia of all kinds and halted under a fine avenue of trees. We had to get right off the road and drive along in the fields. Most of the men with the carts were Sikhs, but only low-caste Mazhabis or Labanas and not at all well-to-do. They were trekking towards India and had halted in the shade during the afternoon heat or perhaps even for the night. Some of them were pulling large chunks of bark off the trees to serve as fuel.[1] We were getting back again on to the road near the end of the column and I had alighted from the car to direct the driver over some rough ground, when someone recognized me as a former Deputy Commissioner of Multan and I was immediately surrounded by a throng of rather piteous-looking people clamouring for protection. I couldn't at first make out what from, as their column seemed in fairly good order; but they insisted that they were being looted and then, looking along the column on the side facing Montgomery, I saw that groups of men were helping themselves to bundles and packages from the carts and walking off across the fields towards the town carrying them on their heads. A few police constables were standing around, but doing nothing to prevent this. The Sikh refugees said that there were some military encamped on the other side of the town and begged me to go and ask them to give protection. I felt compelled to do so, but my efforts were entirely fruitless. I spent a long time searching for the military encampment, which was several miles away, only to find it empty except for one sepoy who said the troops had all gone out—he didn't know where.

I drove on again, making for the headworks at Pallah, where

[1] Great damage was done in this way to the trees along the routes followed by these columns of refugees. Rows of trees stripped of their bark became a common sight.

I would cross the river Sutlej into Bahawalpur State. I noticed that several chaks[1] near the roadside were deserted, but they didn't seem to have been plundered; the houses were quite intact and there were no signs of arson. Not far from Arifwala the road was again entirely blocked by bullock-carts evidently halted for the night, but the Sikhs with these were stalwart 'Jats' and evidently well-to-do. Their carts were large and well-built and the bullocks exceptionally fine. They had plenty of spears and I saw one or two guns. They seemed well able to look after themselves and to give as good as they got, if any-one dared to molest them. Altogether it was a much better organized and better equipped column than the one outside Montgomery.

It so happened that at this point there were quite deep ditches along either side of the road so I was unable to turn off into the fields to avoid the bullock-carts and was brought to a standstill. Almost immediately, however, a jathedar[2] came up, wearing the blue turban of an Akali, and ordered some of the men to fill up the ditch to enable me to cross into the fields. They did this quite quickly and also ran ahead and made a place for me to get back on to the road farther on. I asked the Jathedar why they were on the move like this. It was obvious, I said, that no-one had attacked them. They were all in fine fettle and apparently had been quite unmolested. Why then had they left their chaks and started on this trek? He replied, 'Hukum hai.' (It is an order.) I asked him, 'Whose order?' But to this he would give no clear reply, but just went on repeating, 'It is an order. We have received an order. We have to go to Hindustan.'

I had been somewhat delayed by these two road blocks and shortly afterwards I almost despaired of reaching Bahawalpur at all that night. There was a short stretch of unmetalled road which we had to traverse in order to get from the main road on to the canal bank leading to the Pallah headworks. A part of this had been flooded by a breach in a nearby distributary and here my car got hopelessly stuck when only about thirty yards from the canal bank. Though some villagers came to our help, no amount of pushing would move it and I thought that

[1] Colony villages.
[2] Leader of a 'Jatha' or band.

we were going to be marooned there for the night, when most opportunely a patrol of Mahratta Light Infantry belonging to the Boundary Force came along the canal bank in a jeep. They kindly gave me a tow and pulled my car out of the mud in no time. They said that there had been no disturbances in their area.

We reached Pallah at dusk and crossed the river to the Bahawalpur side. I asked the gatekeeper at the far end of the headworks if all was quiet. He said that there were reports of serious disturbances in Mailsi and Kahrore—two towns in the Multan district.

'But I suppose there's been no trouble this side?' I inquired hopefully.

'I believe, sir, there has been trouble in the State also,' he replied. 'A man came here a little while ago and said that Chishtian had been looted and several people killed.'

This was disquieting.

We had still more than sixty miles to do and drove on as fast as we could down the Bahawal Canal, reaching Bahawalpur at about 9.0 p.m. At my house there was a message to ring up the Prime Minister as soon as I arrived. I got through to him at once. He had been expecting me for some hours. He said that there were reports of disturbances at Bahawalnagar, but he had no details. Brigadier Marden was already there with a battalion of the Bahawalpur Army. He proposed himself to leave for Bahawalnagar the next morning and requested me to go with him. He thought that we might have to stay there several days.

I replied that I would gladly accompany him. I also told him that at Pallah I had heard a rumour of disturbances at Chishtian. Since this place lay on the route to Bahawalnagar we could look in there on our way.

My bearer and driver, without a murmur, got ready for an early start the next day.

VIII

Outbreak of Disturbances in Bahawalpur State

W E set out at about 7.0 a.m. while it was still fairly cool. I travelled with Gurmani in his car, my Buick following behind with his private secretary and with my personal assistant and our servants and chaprassis. In another car was the Commissioner of Police, Nur Hussain Shah, and a big burly Muslim in European clothes and a topi whom I had never seen before, but who turned out to be an ex-officer of the Bahawalpur State Forces. He was one of those who had joined the I.N.A.[1] Gurmani had apparently taken him under his wing in the last few days—whether to keep him out of mischief or because he thought he might genuinely be useful I was never quite able to determine. We also had with us a few other police officers, some police constables and a naik and several sepoys of the State Forces, and so altogether it was quite a procession of three to four big cars and a small truck which moved off along the main Bahawal Canal *en route* for Bahawalnagar.

The surface of most of the canal-bank roads in Bahawalpur was far from good, and the road along the Bahawal Canal was one of the worst. We could not, therefore, average more than 20–25 miles per hour. Still we travelled at a fair pace for the first twenty miles up to Lal Suhara where there is an important regulator and several branches take off from the main canal. Up to this point considerable stretches of the canal are lined with trees, which, besides affording shade, help to stabilize and compact the road. There is also fairly extensive cultivation on both banks, and so our route had been bounded by pleasant fields of ripening millets. But shortly after Lal Suhara the aspect of the country changes. A slight elevation of the land to the south

[1] The Indian National Army.

124

renders it uncommanded by the canal, and for about thirty miles cultivation and human habitations are almost entirely confined to the north bank—between the canal and the river Sutlej—and to the south one gazes out over a dreary grey desert, blotched with tibbas (sand-hills), and in places mottled with juniper and tamarisk scrub. The canal is practically tree-less and the road, which runs for the most part on the southern and desert bank, is correspondingly bad. We were proceeding slowly through this uninteresting terrain when, as we approached a bridge leading across the canal to a large village or townlet a little distance to the north, we suddenly saw on our right a group of about a dozen villagers bobbing up and down on a small sand-hill some thirty yards away. One of them in the middle was holding up a stick with a little green flag tied to the end. He seemed very pleased with the flag and was gazing up at it and shouting. The others were jiggering about round him. The whole thing gave the impression of being a very feeble and absurd pro-Pakistan or pro-Muslim demonstration staged for our benefit. Gurmani, with an expression of annoyance, told the driver to stop the car and we got out. In somewhat harsh terms we asked the villagers what the hell they thought they were doing. The man holding the flag grinned ingratiatingly and, pointing to the miserable bit of green cloth at the end of his stick, said, 'This is our flag. We now have Pakistan and Muslim Raj.' Gurmani was not very well pleased. He told the villagers that this sort of thing was not wanted and asked why they were fooling about at the edge of the desert instead of looking after their crops. By this time the Commissioner of Police had joined us and gone right up close to the knot of villagers and was eyeing them narrowly.

'These are Hindus,' he suddenly exclaimed, and, as we gaped astonishment, he grabbed hold of one of them saying, 'Look at this fellow; he's nothing but a Hindu shopkeeper. His ears are pierced. He's been wearing earrings.'

I was completely taken aback, and it was only after a few seconds that it dawned upon me that these were men who within the last day or two had accepted Islam, as it were, at the point of the sword. The new converts, to show their zeal for the Faith, started gabbling away at us bits of the Koran which they had hurriedly learnt up; but the Commissioner of Police quickly put a stop to this nonsense and began asking them how they had been driven to masquerade as Muslims. I was still somewhat incredulous and said, 'Surely they can't all be Hindus?'

Several of the villagers had by now unostentatiously separated themselves from the main group and were beginning to walk away. They were rounded up and brought back. The whole lot were then examined individually and it was found that three to four of them were Muslims and the rest Hindus. The Muslims were detained for further interrogation and put into the truck. I never discovered why they had brought their converts to demonstrate near the canal road and thus needlessly got themselves into trouble.

The Hindus, after being consoled and reassured and finally convinced that we did not mean to harm them, told us that they belonged to the large village on the other side of the canal and that it had been attacked and looted the previous day by large mobs of Muslim peasants from the surrounding countryside. They had been compelled to embrace Islam in order to save their lives. A good many Hindus had sought safety at the police station.

Taking one of them as a guide, we got into our cars, crossed the bridge and drove towards the village. The road was vile and we had to make several detours to avoid getting stuck in pools of water and mud. However, at last we reached the outskirts of the place, which turned out, in fact, to be a small town called Khairpur with 5,000–6,000 inhabitants. It served as a market-centre for a considerable tract of riverain country and so had quite a large population of Hindu merchants, bankers and shopkeepers, besides Muslim farmers and labourers. Skirting along the edge of it, we made for the police station which was situated outside to the west in a grove of trees.

A few Hindus were sitting about disconsolately under the trees. Someone went and called the thanedar[1] who came running out of the police station in a flurry. He was voluble and, I thought, rather jittery. He said that huge mobs from the nearby riverain villages had assembled the day before to loot the Hindu shops, but had been persuaded to disperse before much damage was done. So far as he knew, there had been no casualties. I

---

[1] The officer in charge of a police station (thana), usually a sub-inspector of police.

gathered that the Muslim inhabitants of Khairpur, so far from joining the looters, had been mainly instrumental in getting rid of them and protecting the Hindus. Possibly the conversion of some of them to Islam was one of the protective devices adopted for their benefit and to placate the raiders. The thanedar was, however, very much afraid that the place would be attacked again. He said that there was a party of Muslims within Khairpur who didn't like the pro-Hindu policy of the majority and wanted to call back the looters and join with them in the plunder. He requested very insistently to be supplied with arms. I asked where were the twelve rifles which ought to be available at the police station. He replied that they were no use and showed us some rusty old weapons of antique pattern, most of which had the bolt or some other essential part missing. Only two or three of them were capable of firing at all. In Bahawalpur, as in many other Indian States, the police were a depressed class, utterly neglected and despised, and all attention and funds were devoted to the army.

I soon found that Khairpur was typical of all the rural police stations in the State, and, indeed, that some of them had not a single rifle that would fire. The Commissioner of Police had done his best since joining the State service to improve the clothing and equipment of the force, but had not been able to get very far. The result was that the police, particularly in the rural areas, were quite unequipped to deal with the disturbed conditions that had now developed, even if they had the will to do so.

In view of the thanedar's apprehensions, which seemed not ill-founded, we decided to leave with him four of our escort of sepoys armed with modern rifles. Orders were also given for some rifles to be fetched from Bahawalpur for arming the police constables, though most of them had never been through their annual course of practice firing and could hardly be expected to use rifles effectively. Gurmani addressed some of the leading Muslim inhabitants in suitable terms, impressing on them their duty to help the thanedar and protect the lives and property of the Hindus—a duty which so far they seemed to have discharged quite well. The thanedar, in spite of the four armed sepoys and the hope of more rifles, still appeared rather worried, but we reassured him as best we could and got back

again into our cars. We were, on the whole, very pleased both
that nothing serious had so far occurred at Khairpur and also
that we had been able to make timely arrangements for rein-
forcing the sub-inspector. These were, in actual fact, wholly
inadequate.

We drove on along the canal bank for about ten miles till
we came to another market town, similar in general character
to Khairpur but a good deal smaller. Its name was Qaimpur.
It was situated, like Khairpur, to the north of the canal, but at
no very great distance from it—perhaps less than half a mile.
We thought that we had better go and have a look at it and so
once again we crossed over a bridge to the north bank of the
canal, intending to drive along a rough unmetalled road which
led to the place. But immediately beyond the far end of the
bridge there was a great deal of muddy water and so, thinking
that the cars would become bogged in it, we got out and began
to walk. Between us and the outskirts of the town there was a
stretch of open, flat, uncultivated ground. As we stepped on to it,
we saw advancing towards us from the other side and heading
for the bridge a party of twenty to thirty villagers, laden with
bundles of clothes, quilts, boxes and packages of all kinds.
I did not in the least tumble to the significance of what I saw,
but the Commissioner of Police alerted us all by saying, 'They're
probably looters!' When we met them we greeted them and
asked where they were going. They said they were going to
their homes.

'What is all this stuff you're carrying with you?'

'We've been shopping in the town.'

This was a palpable lie. The miscellaneous assortment of
articles they were carrying, including odd bits of furniture,
could not be the products of any normal shopping. They considerably outnumbered our party, but with the help of the
sepoys and our other staff we arrested them before they could
disembarrass themselves of their booty and run away. The
Commissioner of Police arranged for them to be marched up
under the guard of the sepoys to the police station at Qaimpur.

While all this was being put in train, some of us went on
ahead to the townlet. On reaching the outskirts, we saw several
people slipping out of the nearby houses and courtyards and
running away—some of them dropping in their hurry the loot

that they were carrying. I ran up a road after two of them, but the chase was hopeless and, after going about fifty yards, I had slackened pace, when a youth with a basket scooted out of a courtyard just ahead of me and made off up the road. I quickly overtook him and pounced upon him with great glee, quite delighted at my capture. I was, however, soon disappointed. The basket contained only some pots and pans and trumpery trinkets of little value and it was apparent that the lad was just a 'picker-up of unconsidered trifles' which others had left. An old man, who had also been scavenging in the wake of the main pillagers, now appeared and begged for mercy for his son. For the time being we put them both under arrest and took them with us to the police station. Later on we released them.

The police station was a ramshackle sort of building at the western edge of Qaimpur. Gurmani, whose weight and bulk unfitted him for our light-hearted diversions, had got there ahead of us in one of the cars which had found a way round the mud at the bridge. Near the police station there was a spacious mud-walled shed standing in an open compound and in this practically the whole Hindu population seemed to be crowded in a woeful condition of panic and lamentation. We learnt from the thanedar, who was remarkably cool and collected, that the town had been attacked early that morning by hordes of Muslims from the surrounding villages, and had been pretty thoroughly looted. We had just come in for the tail-end of the operation. Most of the looters had already left, laden with spoil, though there were still a few stragglers about. Since with his small force—most of the police rifles being as usual unserviceable—it had been impossible to ward off the attack, he had concentrated on saving the lives of the Hindus and, with the help of some Muslims of the place, had collected them in the large shed near the police station which had been placed at his disposal by its Muslim owner and became known to us as the 'Compound of Abdullah Shah'. He thought that he had been successful in saving most of them and that only one or two had been killed;[1] but their shops and houses had, no doubt, been broken into and plundered.

While we were still talking to him, there were loud shouts from close by. Some of our party had flushed several more

---

[1] The real number was seven.

looters who were to be seen making off as fast as they could across the fields. They were already 100–150 yards away, so there was no chance of catching them; but someone told two of the sepoys to open fire on them, whereupon they let off a number of rounds at quite a rapid rate, but without making the slightest attempt to take proper aim. This I soon found to be common form with the Bahawalpur troops, and on a later occasion some of them proudly claimed to have fired 657 rounds at a gang of Pathans without scoring a single hit, and expected me to applaud the performance. However, at this stage my knowledge of the Bahawalpur State Forces was derived mainly from hearsay rather than experience.

I was to learn a good deal more about them in the next few weeks.

The sepoys' futile fusillade was still in progress when there were more shouts from somewhere behind the police station and two more men were to be seen at no very great distance running away to the north. On the spur of the moment I dashed off in pursuit, followed by the Commissioner of Police (who must have been well over fifty), some constables and various others. Helter-skelter we went through the crops, scrambling over low mud walls, jumping watercourses and, I think, thoroughly enjoying ourselves, but without, perhaps, any very clear idea who we were pursuing and why. Our quarry at first ran straight on northwards as though they intended to leave Qaimpur altogether and were making for some village of their own elsewhere; but after a few hundred yards they bore round to the right in a semicircle parallel to the line of the town. I was steadily overhauling them when they turned sharply to the right down a track which crossed our path and led back into the town. I was afraid that in the maze of buildings I would lose them, but one of the constables behind had seen or anticipated their right turn and cut across to intercept them. Just where the track led into the town he suddenly appeared barring the way. One of them turned up an alley to the left and hid in a building where he was subsequently caught. The other, about fifteen yards ahead of me, ran full tilt into the arms of the constable. At exactly the same moment the Commissioner of Police from close behind me suddenly and for no ascertainable reason let off his revolver with a very loud bang—which surprised and startled me not a little. I never discovered what he was firing at or whether it was simply a *feu de joie*. Anyway, it made a very fitting end to the chase—like the huntsman blowing his horn over the kill.

It was past noon and, having stopped running, we at once became overwhelmingly conscious of the intense heat. We were all simply bathed in perspiration. As we sat panting and mopping our brows, we were opportunely relieved by a torrential shower of rain which, in a few seconds, drenched us to the skin but cooled us down. The rain fell so heavily for about ten minutes that it was with some difficulty that we picked our way with our two prisoners through the puddles and pools and slippery lanes of the town back to the police station.

The other prisoners, captured earlier near the bridge, had already arrived and were packed pretty tightly in the small police station lock-up. Gurmani was most indignant, indeed quite outraged, at the insolence of the villagers in attacking and looting Qaimpur, and loudly demanded that those we had caught should there and then, before any trial or investigation, be given a 'shoe-beating'—without prejudice, of course, to anything further that might be done to them later on. He was particularly insistent that the beating should be with shoes, presumably because this is attended as much with indignity as pain. I ought to have advised against such proceedings, for though it was appropriate and customary for a thanedar to give suspects a shoe-beating, it was hardly seemly for the Prime Minister and other high officers of the State to direct and supervise such operations. However, I kept silent and a batch of about ten of our prisoners were taken out of the lock-up and made to lie down prone in a line in the courtyard of the police station. A couple of constables then walked up and down the line whacking them in turn on the bottom with a shoe. Though they yowled and wriggled as if in great pain, the beating was really of a somewhat token character and could not, I thought, have any effect on these hardy yokels. If they were to be beaten at all, I should have liked it to be done much harder. Gurmani later on assured me that the moral effect of the indignity of a shoe-beating is very great, but I remained sceptical.

The Commissioner of Police very rightly disapproved of these proceedings and, not liking to speak to the Prime Minister himself, drew me aside, pointed out that they were not at all proper and urged me to request the Prime Minister to desist. I readily agreed, though I couldn't help wondering whether our steeplechase round the town, in which the Commissioner himself had taken such a lively part, had been altogether in order! Gurmani took the point as soon as I spoke to him. He announced tactfully that it was time for us to be getting along and directed that the men who were being shoe-beaten should be put back into the lock-up for the thanedar to deal with further at his leisure.

It was indeed high time for us to move, as we were still many miles from Bahawalnagar and the two new 'colony' towns of Hasilpur and Chishtian, which we would have to visit, lay ahead of us. The diversions to Khairpur and Qaimpur had been quite unexpected and had put us several hours behind our schedule.

The Qaimpur thanedar did not apprehend any further attack on the place as he thought the villagers had had their fill. He was rather anxious to get the Hindus off his hands and back into their own houses; but most of them were still so tearful and panic-stricken that we advised him not to press them to return just yet, but to let them remain on, as they wished, in the compound of Abdullah Shah under his immediate protection. We left with him two sepoys from our escort and said we would send him some more very soon.

It must be confessed that, as we journeyed on, Gurmani and I were in a mood of complacent self-congratulation. True, what we had seen and heard at Khairpur and Qaimpur was evidence of widespread lawlessness, but there had been few casualties—the number killed at Qaimpur was utterly insignificant compared to what we knew was going on in the East and West Punjab—and the prompt arrival on the spot of the highest officers of the State and our arrest at Qaimpur of a number of miscreants would, we flattered ourselves, have a very sobering effect. Moreover, more than half the State, from Bahawalpur south-west to the Sind border, was as yet absolutely tranquil and undisturbed. The trouble in the eastern part had only just begun and by vigorous action we should be able to nip the whole thing in the bud and show the Punjab, already the scene of a hideous holocaust, how to manage things! There were many advantages, we told ourselves, in a relatively small unit, such as Bahawalpur, in which it was possible for the members of the Government to get a direct personal grip of the whole situation.

Such were the consoling but deceptive thoughts that we exchanged as we drove on towards Hasilpur.

Our route required us to turn off from the Bahawal Canal some miles beyond Qaimpur and to travel for a little distance along a link road leading to the tail-end of the Fordwah Canal a few miles to the south. Once on this canal we could drive along it all the way to Bahawalnagar and beyond, if need be, to the headworks at Suleimanke at the extreme north-eastern corner of the State. This link road, which was maintained by the Irrigation Department, was of great administrative importance—and vital in the next few weeks—as it enabled one to go right from Bahawalpur city to the Bikanir border by canal bank—the only practicable way of covering the distance by car. These canal bank roads were kept for use by government officers and were not open to the general public or designed to carry heavy traffic.

The colony town of Hasilpur stands more or less at the edge of the desert near the tail of the Fordwah Canal. In the early days it had not prospered—indeed there was at one time an idea of abandoning it altogether—but in the last few years, with the agricultural prosperity and extension of cultivation brought by the war, it had come to life again. Excellent prices had been fetched for town sites at recent auctions and there was a demand for more. Altogether it was reckoned to be a growing and flourishing little market town with a bright future. It was, however, very far from being attractive in appearance. No trees or other vegetation had yet grown up; gaunt brick buildings rose starkly from the desert waste. The whole place was strewn with greyish sand and nasty heaps of sand lay scattered about even in the mandi[1] itself which had not yet been fully levelled and surfaced. In summer the burning heat was intense —I had stayed there myself in June—and there was not a scrap of shade. It says much for the hardiness and tenacity of the Hindu merchants of the Punjab that they were ready to settle down in these harsh surroundings and put their money into go-downs, shops and houses. They were now on the point of losing their whole investment.

[1] Market-place and hence used also of a town containing a market-place.

Being a colony town, Hasilpur was the headquarters of a number of revenue and colony officials, including two naib-tahsildars. There was also a police station with a sub-inspector in charge. We drove into the main bazaar, fully expecting some of these functionaries to be waiting to meet us. But there was not a soul to be seen. The bazaar was silent and deserted. We drove into the mandi and then out again and round the outside of the town, and at last we found someone who told us that the thanedar and all the Hindus had gone away to 'old' Hasilpur —a village lying about two miles to the north of the new town. I think neither of us had ever heard of its existence. We were shown the general direction in which it lay and were soon bumping along a sandy, sunken and twisty lane that was said to lead to it. I thought we were never going to reach it; and then, almost unexpectedly, we suddenly came upon it—a small but ancient village, rising up on a slight eminence, but concealed from view by big clumps of tall-growing reeds. Along its curving western side there was a belt, fifty to one hundred yards wide, of open sandy ground between the houses and the cultivated fields. Our road took us along this western side with the sandy belt on our left. As we drove along, I thought I saw well ahead of us some heaps of manure scattered about on this stretch of sand and nearer, though about seventy yards off and close to the edge of the fields, a couple of men seemed to be lying on the ground. I glanced towards Gurmani, murmuring, 'Why are those men lying over there?' and saw on his face a look of incredulous horror as he gazed out of the window of the car.

'They're corpses,' I exclaimed, answering my own question; and now, to my amazement, the heaps of manure took shape as heaps of human bodies. In twos and threes and sixes and tens, more and more came into view as we rounded the curve of the village, till at the north-western corner, close to the main entrance leading up into it, they lay 'Thick as autumnal leaves that strew the vale of Vallambrosa'. Men, women and children, there they were all jumbled up together, their arms and legs akimbo in all sorts of attitudes and postures, some of them so life-like that one could hardly believe that they were really dead. I was forcibly reminded of pictures that I had seen as a child of Napoleonic battlefields; and there was perhaps some reason for this in that all these people had in fact been shot down by rifle fire.

We got out of the car and walked slowly up into the village, too stunned to speak. We had heard reports of trouble at Bahawalnagar and Chishtian, but not a rumour of disturbances at Hasilpur, still less of such a massacre as this. It came, to me at least, as a staggering shock, sweeping away entirely, and for many days to come, the light-hearted and almost frivolous mood of the morning.

Near the top of the village, in a large two-storied building, we found the thanedar and a throng of women and children whose sobbing and whimpering swelled to a deafening crescendo of mingled grief and resentment as soon as they caught sight of us. It was hard to endure. In an open space outside there lay two or three wounded men under an ill-contrived awning of tattered sacking. One of them, almost stark naked, was literally covered with blood and an old woman was pathetically fanning his face and trying to keep the flies off him. We could do nothing to help.

Someone had noticed Brigadier Marden's car standing outside the village when we arrived, so we knew that he must be somewhere about the place. We were inquiring where he was when he himself appeared, dressed in uniform and carrying a tommy-gun. I did not at all like this last feature for in my opinion there was no reason for the commander of the troops to go about with anything more than a revolver. We commented on the hideous slaughter which Marden told us had only occurred that morning. He then said that at Bahawalnagar, from where he had just come, there had also been grave disturbances and heavy casualties. With a very serious face, he drew Gurmani aside and said he wanted to speak to him alone. I guessed at once what he was going to say and my guess was almost immediately confirmed for, in a few moments, Gurmani called me to where they were standing and said, 'Marden says the troops are unreliable.' This was a meiosis.

We did not stay very long at Hasilpur and I do not recall what, if anything, we did; I don't think anything useful. We were too dumbfounded. I tried cursorily to count the corpses as we left the village, but lost count at well over one hundred.[1] I was puzzled as to how such a terrific slaughter could have taken place, but I made no inquiries about it at this time— in fact I hardly spoke to the thanedar, though he was quite well known to me. Normally a bright, smart, cheerful little man, he was now subdued and seemingly overwhelmed by the disaster. Some days later, however, I did make inquiries and it will be convenient to set down at this point the outline of the story that was told to me subsequently. I cannot vouch for its accuracy as I never had leisure to probe into the matter deeply.

It appears that the thanedar suspected, or perhaps was warned, that the town of Hasilpur was going to be attacked. He decided that it would be impossible for him to defend the place and that his best course was to collect all the non-Muslim population in the small, compact and more easily defensible village of old Hasilpur. An additional reason for this course was that the police station was still located in the village. There were plans for a new one in the town, but it had not yet been constructed and only a makeshift office was maintained there. So the Hindus were evacuated from the town to the village. In due course, as at Khairpur and Qaimpur, bands of Muslim peasants began to gather round the place from all directions. The thanedar would have liked to parley with them and try to persuade them to go away; but among the population evacuated from the town was a fiery Sikh, armed with a rifle, who could not be restrained. Planting himself on the roof of a house, he opened fire on the marauders with considerable effect, killing or wounding several of them and dispersing the rest. Among those killed was one of their principal leaders, a well-known and popular badmash[2] of the locality.

The bands of rustics, though they may have had with them a few muzzle-loaders, were mostly armed only with lathis. They were not people of great courage or ferocity and, after meeting such a reception, they would probably not have dared to return by themselves and renew the attack. They were, however, much incensed at the loss of their leader and cast about for reinforcements. It so happened that there were encamped at the edge of the desert not far away a body of Pathans from the

---

[1] The actual number of Hindus and Sikhs killed at this place was about 350. A few Muslims, probably about six to twelve, were also killed.
[2] Bad character.

North-West Frontier. It was the regular custom for gangs of Pathans to come down into the Punjab, generally in the cold weather, to work on the roads and canals, returning after a few months to their own country with their earnings. They nearly always had with them unlicensed firearms which they kept concealed in bushes or buried in the earth somewhere near their camping-places. This gang near Hasilpur, who were either doing or expecting to do some work for the Irrigation Department, possessed several ·303 rifles. Their assistance was now invoked and was not refused. Pulling their weapons out of their hiding-places, the Pathans accompanied the peasants back to the village and, catching the people there unawares, mowed them down with rifle fire with the results already described.

This terrible incident at Hasilpur made us very anxious during the next few weeks to remove and keep away from the State all gangs of wandering Pathans.

We drove gloomily on to Chishtian—an important and well-established 'mandi' town—fearful of what we might find there. Several reports of disturbances had reached us, but Marden, who had passed the place in the morning, was comparatively reassuring. He proved correct. There had been a good deal of looting in the town and all the shops were shut, but the police, magistrates and revenue officials of the place seemed to be in quite good heart and assured us that their casualties had been few. Though they somewhat understated to us the numbers, subsequent inquiries showed that these did not in fact exceed a dozen. Compared with Hasilpur, Chishtian had got off very lightly.

I was rather pleased to notice among the crowd that met us a young Hindu tahsildar, named Gobind Baksh. He was employed on settlement work, and I had formed a high opinion of his ability. Somehow I had expected that, being a Hindu, he would be lying low at this time, as most of the Hindu officials were, but on the contrary he was well to the fore, seemed to be very little upset at what had taken place and not in the least alarmed for his own safety. He was wearing a fez—the common head-dress of urban Muslims in Bahawalpur[1]—which might be

---

[1] It was also the official head-dress in the State and I had to wear one when visiting the palace, and on ceremonial occasions. Many Hindus took to wearing a fez during those troubled times.

E*

supposed to offer him some protection. I was to learn later that he had more solid grounds for confidence.

We were still nearly thirty miles from Bahawalnagar and the day was drawing in. We did not therefore stay long at Chishtian but hurried on, reaching Bahawalnagar just after dark. We had been expected in the early afternoon and so were many hours late. There was a large group of officers awaiting us at the canal rest-house, morose and depressed.

Gurmani and I had settled in advance that immediately on arrival we would separately interview the principal officers one by one, and then meet together for dinner and compare notes. Dismissing therefore all but a few of the senior officers we sat down in different parts of the rest-house garden to hear what they had to say. I naturally gave most time to the Superintendent of Police and the Sub-Divisional Magistrate. The latter was in a very excited state, stuttering and spluttering so as to be almost incoherent. He was bitterly indignant with the military who, he said, had, without authority, forcibly interfered, yet had done nothing to stop the rioting in the town. He had been brushed aside by these armed men who had even threatened him! I sympathized with him and tried to calm him down. He had spent most of his service as a judge and had no experience of riots. He had done his best but clearly had been ineffective; and I did not blame him, for even Leghari, the Superintendent of Police, a much more weighty and experienced man, had not been able to make head against the military.

Leghari was not very communicative, but I was able to obtain from him a rather better idea of what had actually taken place. He was a large, solid man and quite calm, but, like the magistrate, indignant with the military and very depressed. He told me that since August 22nd there had been unrest and excitement in the town, caused by the arrival of refugees from India with alarming tales of atrocities; but there was at first no outbreak of violence. He suspected some undesirable elements among the staff at the railway station of fomenting trouble, but he had nothing definite against them on which he could take action. On August 25th a train had arrived at about 1.0 p.m. crammed with refugees, some of them badly wounded. Large numbers of Muslims from the town, tipped off, he thought, by the railway staff, had come up to the station to meet this train. When the wounded, some of them women, alighted from it, displaying torn limbs and lacerated breasts, the crowd at the station got worked up into a frenzy and with one accord rushed madly from the station into the town and began murdering the Hindus and looting their shops. Leghari with his small force of police tried to restore order, but meantime the military appeared on the scene and, he said, 'They wouldn't let us do anything.' He repeated this phrase several times. I asked what the military had themselves done. 'Well,' he replied laconically with a grim but rather attractive smile, 'they didn't stop the rioting.'

I then inquired about the casualties. He would not commit himself to any precise figure; there were still, he said, a lot of corpses which had not been picked up; but he thought that the number killed must run to several hundred.[1] I asked how many of these were Muslims, this being, of course, a point of vital significance; for since it was the Muslims who were murdering and looting, the armed forces, if they had seriously attempted to restore order, must have shot a few of them. Leghari thought that only one or two Muslims had been killed. This was what I had expected, but it was really quite ridiculous. Marden alone with his tommy-gun could surely have done better! Riotous mobs provide quite easy targets. I felt more than ever that his parading about with a tommy-gun was not the most helpful gesture in the circumstances.

This was my feeling at the time. But on later reflection it occurred to me that if Marden had used his weapon effectively against the rioters, his own troops, in the existing state of religious and political hysteria, would probably have turned upon him and killed him; and to get killed was not really helpful. Marden, like others, was in a very difficult position, and things were perhaps not so simple and straightforward as they appeared to me then.

It need hardly be said that the military officers were on their part very indignant with the civil officials, especially the Sub-Divisional Magistrate, who, they alleged, would never give any order. There may well have been some truth in this.

After my talk with Leghari the general situation was fairly clear to me. The better part of a battalion of State Forces was

[1] The numbers, as finally ascertained, were 409 Hindus and one Muslim.

encamped at Bahawalnagar; there had been ample armed forces on the spot to control a town three or four times its size. But the civil authorities had been unable to control the military and the military officers had been unable or unwilling to control their own men or direct them to any useful ends; indeed the implication was that the military had themselves become wolves and descended on the fold of helpless Hindu sheep. My worst fears and suspicions were confirmed.

Before joining Gurmani for dinner, I had a few words with the Commissioner of Police. He too had been talking to the various local officials, and I was anxious to get his estimate of the situation. I knew him to be a brilliant officer. He had risen from the rank of sub-inspector and had far more experience of quelling disorders than any of the rest of us. I set great store by his advice. I found him disappointingly negative and very pessimistic. He said that the situation was quite unparalleled in his experience. The military were out of hand and the police were negligible. He had not been used to this in the Punjab and felt quite at sea. He bewailed the miserable inadequacy of the police in personnel, training, equipment and everything. He told me—as he had told me some months before—that he would never have come to Bahawalpur as Commissioner of Police if he had realized the shocking state of the police force. He thought we *might* be able to restore law and order, but appeared quite doubtful about this and somehow implied that I should have to see about it and that it would not be his concern. Altogether he had little constructive to offer; but he did say one very valuable and encouraging thing. After deploring the inefficiency[1] of the Bahawalpur police, he said, 'But I think Leghari is a good man. You can rely on him.' He was right.

It was nearly 10.0 p.m. when Gurmani and I sat down to dinner on the chabutra[2] outside the rest-house. After we had compared notes and agreed that the civil administration had broken down and that the military were out of hand, he asked me what I thought should be done. I said that I could only offer one suggestion, and didn't know if he would like it, and that was that I should be given powers of District Magistrate

[1] I would by no means wholly endorse his condemnation of them, though, of course, they were not up to Punjab standards.

[2] Raised platform or dais (to avoid snakes, etc.).

and should try to restore order. He replied that he was just going to request me to undertake this and that he would give me not only powers of District Magistrate but full powers of Government over the whole of the eastern half of the State, i.e. the Bahawalpur district. He, for his part, would go back to Bahawalpur and endeavour to preserve peace in the rest of the State which was, as yet, unaffected.

I said that powers of Government were not really necessary and that powers of District Magistrate would suffice. It was however essential that the military should be made clearly to understand that, acting as they supposedly were in aid of the civil power, they had to take directions from the magistracy; and this, if I took over the functions of District Magistrate, would ordinarily mean from me. They couldn't just go about doing as they liked, brushing aside magistrates and police, as they had in the past few days. They should, indeed, keep away from the public altogether and confine themselves to their own military exercises, unless a magistrate asked for their assistance and assigned to them some specific task in the maintenance of order. In carrying out that task, once assigned to them, they were their own masters; but it was not for them to intervene, until a magistrate called upon them. These were the principles embodied in the Code of Criminal Procedure, which was in force in the State, and if the military officers didn't know them, they must be made aware of them now. In the past they had not been accustomed to taking orders from anybody except the Nawab, but in the past they had probably not been called upon to quell civil disturbances. Now that they were acting in aid of the civil power, they would have to take orders from the District Magistrate.

I requested Gurmani to impress all this on the military officers; they were not likely to take it from anyone but him. If they were brought under control and duly accepted the position assigned to them by law, then I was reasonably confident, with the powers of District Magistrate, of restoring order in the affected area; but otherwise there was likely to be worse havoc.

Gurmani promised that the very next morning he would give the military officers a most serious talking to. After he had done so, he would return to Bahawalpur and leave me alone to get on with the job. He would concentrate his own energies on preventing trouble spreading to the other parts of the State. He insisted that I should have full powers of Government as well as of District Magistrate in the Bahawalpur district. Though these proved useful, enabling me to make appointments and do many other things quickly, I think I would have been better without them. I did not, however, refuse them.

Having reached these decisions, we went to bed.

IX

Restoring Order—I

THE next morning Gurmani faithfully fulfilled his promise to speak to the military officers. I lay a good deal of stress on this, not only because for the ending of bloodshed and the restoration of order in the eastern part of the State it was of decisive importance, but also because it affords a refutation of allegations, made later by many Hindus, that Gurmani had engineered the attacks on them and 'conspired' to drive them from the State. These base calumnies had no foundation, except that Gurmani was a Muslim and a member of the Muslim League; yet, once set going, they were readily accepted and repeated as gospel truth. The facts are that Gurmani, with considerable moral courage, exerted himself to the utmost to protect the Hindus. In the prevailing temper he, as a Muslim, could have remained indifferent and allowed things to go their own way without injury, and even with credit, to his own reputation. Taking much pains to save Hindus was not popular. But Gurmani did not adopt the easy course. He showed throughout a determination to maintain in Bahawalpur the standards of a civilized government. Though he may have made some errors of judgement, as we all did during these times, he remained steadfastly loyal to the oath of office, which we had both taken and which he had himself prescribed, requiring us to treat with impartial fairness every class, creed and individual in the Nawab's dominions. At this critical moment the curbing of the licence of the military was the biggest service he could render to the non-Muslim sections of the Nawab's subjects.

India's past history afforded many examples of the miseries inflicted by armed men when freed from the shackles of discipline and let loose among an unarmed population. Less than a hundred and fifty years earlier, the Pindaris—broken remnants of Mogul and Mahratta armies—had been roaming at large through central India, pillaging and terrorizing peaceful village folk, and it had required elaborate military operations (ending in a regular war) to put a stop to their depredations. Later, though on a smaller scale, the chronic indiscipline of the troops of the Nawab of Oudh had been a reason for the annexation of that State. Similarly the excesses of Sikh soldiery in the Punjab, immediately after the death of Ranjit Singh, had been partly responsible for the eventual intervention of the British in that province. It had been the claim of the British Raj to have rescued India in the past from this type of anarchy; now in northern India we seemed to be on the brink of sinking into it once again. Past history was coming alive before my very eyes. There were already appalling tales afloat of the atrocities perpetrated by the Sikh troops of Patiala. Would the Pathan troops in the Bahawalpur Army be any milder? They had clearly shaken off the shackles of discipline and had wrought serious havoc in Bahawalnagar. How much further would they go? And how could we restrain them?

Gurmani and I had no physical force at our immediate disposal to set against them and no force which we could quickly summon to our aid from elsewhere. Under the British regime the troops of a Native State, if they got a little out of hand, could be instantly overawed by the Government of India. But the British regime had ended and, so far as we were concerned, the Government of India was now a foreign government. The successor government for us was the Government of Pakistan, and this had had only twelve days of existence and its very survival seemed far from certain. Amid enormous difficulties, it was trying to establish itself in Karachi; its hands were full with the troubles in the Punjab, and at this juncture it had no time to give any thought to Bahawalpur—in fact, its relations with us were still of the haziest character.[1] We stood therefore alone and had to do the best we could unaided. Somehow we had to gain a moral ascendancy over the Bahawalpur Army so that, even in these abnormal times, they would respect us as the lawful Government of the day from whom it was natural and right that they should take orders. There was every temptation for them to do otherwise. All around the usual moral sanctions were breaking down and the Nawab, away in England, was not present to reinforce them. Gurmani and I were newcomers

[1] Bahawalpur State did not formally accede to Pakistan till October 3rd.

to the State. In the adjoining Punjab, ordered government seemed on the verge of collapse.

Gurmani's talk to the military officers was, therefore, of crucial significance. I do not know exactly what he said to them, but he talked to them for a long time and, to judge by results, with considerable effect. Reluctantly, and with some grumblings amongst themselves both against Gurmani and me, they came to heel. There were to be one or two more bad incidents, which probably the officers could not prevent, but on the whole this battalion of the State Forces took no further party in harrying and pillaging the non-Muslim population and co-operated with me steadily, though not enthusiastically, in measures for their protection. The battalion commander came to see me during the day and told me that Gurmani had impressed on them that they must carry out my instructions. He assured me that they would do as the Prime Minister had ordered. He hoped, however, that I would not make any unreasonable demands upon the troops. I said that I did not expect to have to press them very hard and hoped to use the police for most duties, only calling upon the military when absolutely necessary. I would in any case consult him and take him into my confidence regarding any tasks which I might wish to entrust to his men.

The battalion commander was true to his word, though the duty of safeguarding the lives and property of Hindus and Sikhs can hardly have been congenial to him. Across the border in East Punjab Muslims were being mercilessly slaughtered. What easier than to take revenge on the innocent Hindus and Sikhs in Bahawalpur? While the ordinary Muslim may have had no desire actually to kill them, he was naturally inclined to handle them roughly or at best to look with indifference at their sufferings. This was the general feeling, and the particular circumstances of the battalion commander were not favourable to his rising above it. For his home was in the East Punjab; several of his relatives had already been murdered there; others, including his parents, were in grievous danger. Though in his talks with me he to a great extent suppressed his feelings, anger and anxiety were dominant. To co-operate, therefore, in the effective protection of the Hindus in the State required of him a strong effort of will. This effort, not without difficulty, he made. He was a steady, competent officer, of somewhat

phlegmatic temperament, and this was an advantage to him.
Many of the Hindus of Bahawalnagar did not bear their misfortunes with much fortitude, and certainly not in silence. The
noisy importunity with which they assailed those in authority
was often very trying to the nerves and must have been particularly harassing to the battalion commander. He bore it with
remarkably little irritation until Leghari and I were able to
deflect it all on to ourselves. I am glad to say that a little later
it was found possible to let him have a couple of military lorries
with which he succeeded in rescuing from his home in East
Punjab many of his relations and belongings.

While Gurmani was talking to the military officers, I went
down to the town with Leghari. Our activities there were of a
very prosaic nature, but it is perhaps worth giving a brief
account of them as they were typical of what, with minor
variations, we had to do in place after place and of what, no
doubt, many others had to do all over the Punjab.

The first thing was to ensure the protection of the surviving
Hindus. A large number of them were congregated in some
big buildings belonging to a wealthy Muslim, who out of pure
goodness of heart had given shelter to as many of them as he
could. His co-religionists had so much respect for him that they
had no inclination to molest those to whom he had given sanctuary. These, however, huddled together like roosting hens,
were still in a miserable state of panic and begged me to evacuate them to India as quickly as possible. This I promised to
do. Meanwhile I felt quite confident that they would be safe
in the care of their benevolent protector.

Other Hindus we gathered together in defined areas which
could easily be guarded. Leghari arranged for police guards
and the military were withdrawn. I authorized him straight
away to appoint special police constables, since the duties
falling upon the police were far greater than the existing
strength could cope with and we both wished to make the
minimum calls upon the military.

A considerable number of injured Hindus had been admitted
to the local hospital during the previous two days. The Muslim
doctor in charge, who earlier had had to tend the wounded Muslims arriving from India, scarcely concealed his delight at the
injuries to so many of the opposite community and openly

remarked that the sight had eased his mind. Though there was no complaint that he had positively neglected his Hindu patients, Leghari suggested that I should speak to him so as to make sure that he was kept up to the mark. I did so as tactfully as I could. He told me that he and his Muslim staff, whatever their feelings might be, were attending to all alike without the slightest discrimination. Despite his inward satisfaction at the sufferings of the Hindus I do not think there was any serious ground to complain of his treatment of them. If there were any shortcomings, they were certainly nothing compared to what was happening in a not so very distant district of East Punjab. There the Hindu civil surgeon refused to admit injured Muslims into the hospital and a number of them were left lying uncared for in the road. When compelled at last by an officer of another department to take them in, he deliberately neglected them and they all died.

The town of Bahawalnagar was in an indescribable mess. Many of the shops and houses had been ransacked and their less valuable contents thrown indiscriminately into the streets so that, apart from corpses, the whole place was littered with broken furniture, paper, burst sacks of grain, broken glass, garbage and rubbish of all kinds. The ordinary municipal services had entirely ceased to function and had to be started again. Many of the subordinate staff were either gorged with loot or stricken with fear. With some difficulty they were collected and, under a combination of threats and promises, they proceeded to clean up the town at a fairly good speed.

Casualties among the Hindus and the herding together of the rest in places of refuge had left many houses and shops deserted. Some of the revenue and colony staff were turned on to locking, numbering and registering these empty buildings and listing their contents, if any. Already at this stage we foresaw that we should soon be requiring them for allotment to incoming Muslim refugees. I gave some general directions for framing proposals for the assessment of their rent.

Another section of the revenue staff were deputed to the market-place to secure and list the bags of grain that had not been carried off by the looters. I attached great importance to laying hands on as much grain as possible as I surmised that in a few days' time we might have thousands of people to feed.

All this occupied me for the best part of the day.

Gurmani departed for Bahawalpur immediately after lunch, taking with him Marden and the Commissioner of Police. The ex-officer of the State Forces, who had joined the I.N.A., stayed behind for a few days. I think Gurmani's idea was that he would help to steady the troops. I had a long chat with him that evening. Although a Muslim, he had a liking for whisky and was prepared to consume it in considerable quantities. In an expansive moment he confided to me that he had been driven to join the I.N.A. simply by his craving for alcohol. I do not know whether this was really so, or was said to soften my judgement of his past conduct. But whatever may have been his conduct in the past, he was friendly and helpful now. He took a dim view of the behaviour of the Bahawalpur troops and, as a former officer of the State Army, was quite frank in his criticisms. He assured me, however, that Gurmani's talk to the officers had made a great impression on them, and that they would certainly now obey my orders. He also promised to assist me if I had any trouble with them.

There were quite a number of Hindu officials at Bahawalnagar in the Irrigation and Revenue Departments and I had to give up a good deal of time to their personal problems. I interviewed them—and many other people—during the afternoon and evening. Those in any sort of executive position— and these included two tahsildars and one executive engineer —were, through no fault of their own, wholly unable to carry on their duties; for they had lost all authority with their subordinates and with the public and could only move about under escort. The rest, who were mainly employed in clerical posts, were for the most part in such a state of trepidation as to be unfit for any sustained work. Thus, in effect, the whole Hindu staff in this area had to be written off and arrangements made to replace them. I told them not to worry about their official duties, but to take two weeks' leave and look after themselves and their families and that in the next few days I would try to send them under escort wherever they wanted to go. Many of them had their homes in the town of Bahawalpur and wished to get back there, but were justifiably afraid of travelling by train, alone and unguarded.

There was a marked contrast in the conduct of the two

tahsildars. The regular revenue tahsildar, in charge of the
tahsil at Bahawalnagar, was a small but efficient little man.
Though worried, he remained calm. He frankly admitted that
he had become completely ineffective and was much relieved
when I told him to take some leave and hand over to his
assistant. Thereafter he never bothered me at all, though as an
official of some consequence in the Revenue Department he was
certainly entitled to special consideration from me.

The other tahsildar was engaged in settlement work and was
very highly spoken of by the Settlement Officer, Nur Mohammad. Undoubtedly he was an able man, but the disorders
in Bahawalnagar had quite unnerved him and reduced him
to a quivering, but ubiquitous jelly. On the very evening of
our arrival he approached me with a moan about his personal
safety. Early the next morning, as I was setting out for the town,
he turned up again with loud and voluble lament. He wanted
to go back to Bahawalpur, to which I said there would be no
objection, and I gave him a time to see me in the afternoon. In
spite of this he kept on popping up during the morning with
sobs and tears and uncontrolled importunity until at last I told
him, as though he were a small child, that unless he went away,
pulled himself together and stopped crying, I would not give
him an interview at all. In the afternoon he came to see me in a
quietened mood, looking like a fat and melancholy seal. All
he wanted was an armed escort to take him back by train to
Bahawalpur. This is what many other Hindu officials wanted
and asked for in a decent and orderly manner. It was a reasonable request. But, of course, escorts could not ordinarily be
provided for single individuals; a whole party had to be arranged
and this necessarily took a little time. However, in a day or two
an armed escort for a party of Hindus wishing to go to Bahawalpur was duly organized. He then refused to go! On the evening
of the day on which he should have left and when I thought I
was rid of him he turned up again, saying that he thought the
escort might be unreliable and it was safer for him to remain in
Bahawalnagar. I was so disgusted with him that I promptly
suspended him for cowardice and left him to shift for himself.[1]

[1] Some time afterwards, at the request of Nur Mohammad, I reinstated
him so as to enable him to draw his leave salary and he was evacuated to
India along with other Hindus. It is perhaps of interest to record that

Besides the Hindu officials with their personal problems, there were many Muslim officials to be attended to. The officials of the Irrigation Department were in difficulty because heavy rains had breached several of the canal bank roads, severing *inter alia* our communications to the south with Harunabad, and labour gangs, on the plea of danger, were not forthcoming to repair them. The military had to be asked to provide escorts. Revenue officials reported that all the Sikh chaks, of which there were quite a number in this area, had been deserted. In the past few days the Sikh colonists, though for the most part quite unmolested, had gone across the border to Bikanir taking with them all that they could carry. But some stocks of grain and cattle had been left behind. What was to be done about them?

One of my most important visitors during the latter part of the day was the local thanedar. Under the guidance of Leghari, he had shown a good deal of initiative during the morning in shepherding the Hindus to convenient places of refuge and setting guards over them. He now told me that quite a lot of villagers from the neighbouring villages had taken part in the sack of Bahawalnagar and that, if he was given transport so that he could get to these villages quickly and carry out searches, he was sure that he could recover much stolen property and make a number of arrests. Other people would then voluntarily come forward and surrender part, at least, of their loot. I warmly welcomed the proposal and arrangements were made accordingly. I told the thanedar to arrest as many as he could and that I would try them summarily.

We had devoted the whole day (August 27th) to Bahawalnagar and it was urgently necessary for us to move around to other places which might be attacked at any moment and where the local authorities, unless stiffened physically and morally, would put up no effective resistance. So far as we knew, the wealthy colony town of Harunabad and the smaller town of Fort Abbas farther south were still intact. About Minchinabad, twenty-five miles away to the east—the abode of some very rich Hindus—and about Macleodganj Road, right on the

later, when I was in India, I was able to give both him and the other tahsildar good appointments in the newly-formed State of Himachal Pradesh, where they both did well.

frontier, there were conflicting stories. Some said that they had both been looted; others that they were safe. Chishtian, though already partially plundered, still had plenty to attract looters and might be attacked again. The Hindus at Khairpur and Qaimpur were in danger and there were other Hindus scattered about in villages whose position was even more precarious. All these places claimed our immediate attention. But we could not immediately reach them. Heavy rain had made all roads impassable a few miles from Bahawalnagar. To travel by rail was impracticable, unless we could arrange a special, as the regular services were so infrequent that we should get marooned at one place for a day and a night. A special could not be made available till the 29th, so we had to spend another whole day at Bahawalnagar. Though there was plenty to do there, the delay was unfortunate.

During the next ten days Leghari and I spent most of the hours of daylight touring up and down the eastern and most disturbed part of the State. For the first three days we travelled by special train; afterwards, when the roads had been re-opened, we went by car. Everywhere we had to do more or less the same, and so, before passing to any detailed account of individual scenes and incidents, I will give a general description of our tasks and of our daily routine and also of the main themes of our thoughts during these days.

Our principal tasks were:

(i) the collection and protection of the Hindus and the evacuation of those who wished to go to India,

(ii) the custody of their property, or whatever remained of it,

(iii) the recovery of stolen property and abducted women and the arrest of as many offenders as possible,

(iv) the collection and safeguarding of stocks of grain,

and

(v) —more and more as the days passed—the feeding and settlement of incoming Muslim refugees.

Besides this, along all the length of the frontier with Bikanir and to a depth of five to fifteen miles we had to devote much time to calming and reassuring the Muslim inhabitants who were, or professed to be, in mortal terror of attacks by Sikhs from across the border. They seemed to think that an international frontier, as our boundary with Bikanir had now become, must necessarily involve incursions by hostile armies. The villages right on the border had mostly been evacuated. The Sikhs, who had been in occupation of some of them, had crossed over into Bikanir, while the Muslims, fleeing from dangers largely but perhaps not wholly imaginary, had betaken themselves to the west of the big Sadiqia Canal. This canal runs for about fifty miles parallel to and a few miles inside the border. All the bridges over it had at this time military pickets and so no Muslim to the west of it had any solid ground for fear. Yet many appeared to be in a panic and clamoured for military protection. Much of this alarm was, I believe, feigned; the rumour of a Sikh attack could be an excuse or cloak for assailing and plundering the Hindus. But some of it was probably genuine. I had little sympathy with such absurd fears and could hardly conceal my contempt for them—which was not the right approach; so I generally left it to Leghari to calm them, which he did in the most admirable manner. I can hear him now repeating in Punjabi to group after group in slow measured tones without the slightest trace of irritation:

'There is no danger at present. No Sikhs are coming. So go to your homes and sit down quietly there and do your ordinary work. We are in touch with the Bikanir Government and have our own soldiers on the frontier. If any Sikhs come, we will stop them and also warn you in good time.'

These unnecessary fears were only gradually dissipated; and it took weeks and the lavish provision of military protection to induce the Muslim peasants to cross the canal and settle down once again to cultivation on the east bank.

The heat during the day was at this time still pretty intense and Leghari and I, as we moved around, were glad to take advantage of the shade of a tree or building for our confabulations with those who came to meet us, even if it meant walking for some little distance. Standing in the full blaze of the sun for any length of time was apt to be very trying; but, apart from this, the heat caused us no inconvenience. We ate little or nothing during the day, but drank water from time to time. It was a strenuous but healthy existence.

I was still holding charge as Revenue and Public Works

Minister for the whole State and the work of this office had to be disposed of at night. I had telegraphed for some of my staff to come and join me at Bahawalnagar, including my invaluable Clerk of Court, Mir Ajmal Hassan. He and my personal assistant went through all the papers during the day and reduced the work to simple potted form, so that I was able to dispose of it with the minimum of trouble and the routine of administration continued unimpeded. This is what my personal assistant liked to describe as 'the work of government running on quietly in the hands of petty clerks'. It was a common condition in Bahawalpur—and perhaps elsewhere also. As the work of settling incoming refugees developed, Ajmal Hassan, who had previously been a tahsildar, was of immense assistance in drafting detailed orders about the allotment of land to them and the assessment of the rent of houses, shops, etc.

I am a great believer in the written word and have never been able to understand those who boast of managing affairs by word of mouth—preferably down the telephone—and despise the man who uses his pen. Their affairs, I conclude, must be very simple, for an organization with the wide ramifications of government cannot be controlled by feats of memory and word of mouth. Apart from this, in India the giving of verbal orders is too often a method of evading responsibility; for, if anything goes wrong, the giving of the orders can be denied. Anyhow, I made a special point at this time of putting in writing all the numerous directions which I gave. I did this either immediately on the spot or, if not practicable, as soon after as possible. Every evening on my return to Bahawalnagar, I notified my personal assistant of all the orders I had issued during the day and dictated those which had been too long or complicated to record on the spot or required further elaboration. I found that this was greatly appreciated as everyone not only knew exactly what to do, but had my undoubted authority for doing it. It also helped me to keep a check on the actual execution of orders, for a written order, unlike a verbal one, cannot easily be denied, evaded or forgotten. In India the mere issue of orders is not necessarily equivalent to their execution.

Something must be said of the background of our thoughts at this time. Most prominent and persistent was our absolute uncertainty whether we should succeed in restoring and maintaining order. This gnawing anxiety amounted sometimes to the fear that not only Bahawalpur, but the whole of northern India, and with it Pakistan, might sink into utter and irretrievable chaos from which there might ultimately emerge some kind of war-lord administration on the Chinese model. Our sense of isolation aggravated this fear. I had no wireless with me and during the first twelve days of my stay in Bahawalnagar I received no letters (except from within the State) and no newspapers and so was effectually cut off from the outside world. Leghari used occasionally to gather some scraps of news from a privately owned wireless-set in the town; but the news was all bad and the rumours in circulation about what was happening in the Punjab still worse. It was impossible to get any coherent picture of the situation there; and perhaps ignorance was bliss; for whereas in Bahawalpur we were in these days steadily overcoming the disorders, in the Punjab they were reaching their climax of horror.

It was largely this dread of chaos that made us run about unceasingly from place to place and galvanize our subordinates into activity in all directions. We felt that, so far as we could, we must assert the authority of government in the most visible and unmistakable manner and, by vigorous and decisive action, show that we could stretch out our arm both fast and far. All the while the military had to be held in check and kept within their proper bounds; for potentially they were by far the most dangerous source of anarchy. Yet we could not at present dispense with their services. They were required to provide escorts for trains; to accompany labour parties who would not move without military protection; to patrol the frontier and to provide pickets at bridges over the Sadiqia Canal and at other places near the border—this was essential if only to allay Muslim fears and satisfy Muslim opinion—and, above all, to provide transport for the quick movement of police, prisoners and stocks of grain, since the transport available to the police was negligible.

As already mentioned, I had welcomed the proposal of the thanedar, Bahawalnagar, to start making searches for looted property in neighbouring villages. These were commenced on August 28th and met with immediate success. Many arrests were made and much stolen property recovered. A magistrate and troops and police were dispatched the next day in a lorry to search more distant villages and, though their movements were hampered by rain, they returned with a good haul. Searches were also taken up in Bahawalnagar itself and similar operations set going elsewhere. As the Bahawalnagar thanedar had forecast, a good deal of looted property was voluntarily surrendered in the hope of thereby securing lenient treatment. In the course of these searches considerable quantities of gold and silver ornaments, plundered from the Hindus, were recovered. These were listed and deposited in the sub-treasuries attached to the tahsils.

Some of the worst lawlessness had been shown by the riverain villages in the Khairpur-Qaimpur area. Gurmani arranged for troops from Bahawalpur to make a flag-march through this tract and a squad of police under an inspector was deputed to make searches, investigate offences and arrest all the known bad characters in these villages. On one village we clamped down punitive police. The main object of all these measures was to impress upon the rural population the continued existence of an effective government.

The fear of anarchy persisted for a considerable time. Right on in October, when everywhere the situation had greatly improved, one still wondered whether this might not be merely a lull before incursions of Pathans from the North-West Frontier or of Sikhs from the East Punjab produced a further storm and a final catastrophe. Another possible and alarming prospect was that Pakistan might be submerged altogether by an unmanageable flood of Mulism refugees from India. We could absorb, with perhaps not too much difficulty, the few millions of Muslims from East Punjab; but once the transfer of population had started where would it end? If all the Muslims not only from East Punjab but from the whole of Northern and Central India were driven into Pakistan, then Pakistan would be overwhelmed. Why should not India, out of sheer spite, deliberately hound her Muslim population across the frontier and so destroy the new-born State, the very existence of which was an offence to most Indians? These were apprehensions which had already crossed our minds by the end of August, and they did not diminish as week after week the tide of incoming refugees rose higher.

In the light of after-events these fears may appear foolish and perhaps were so even at the time; but they were very real and not wholly without basis.

Allied to the fear of chaos was the fear of financial breakdown. Bahawalpur had no independent currency of its own and so no possibility of resorting, in an emergency, to the printing-press. An empty treasury had a real and not merely a symbolic significance. It meant literally that salaries could not be paid and other expenses met. Under the British regime some of the Native States were occasionally confronted with just this situation—something very like it had occurred at an earlier date in Bahawalpur itself—but the Paramount Power had always been there to step in, make temporary advances, take control of the finances and set them in order. Now the Paramount Power had gone.

The financial position of Bahawalpur was not at this time critical. With the successful development of the 'colony' areas during the war, there had been substantial surpluses of revenue over expenditure. These might be expected to continue and so ordinarily we should be able to pay our way quite comfortably. But a sudden unexpected drain on our resources could quickly bankrupt us; for we had no reserves. Every rupee of the past surpluses had been used by Sir Richard Crofton for repayment of the debt to the Government of India. He had left the State practically without debt, but practically without balances. We would have preferred larger balances even if these meant a larger debt—which might never have to be repaid.

The upheaval that was now taking place, involving *inter alia* the loss of all our Sikh colonists, the dislocation of agricultural markets, and the paralysis or disappearance of the Hindu trading community, was calculated to reduce substantially our ordinary revenues, while expenses would rise by leaps and bounds. The cost of suppressing the disturbances would be only a small item in the account; it was the liabilities likely to be thrown upon us by the incoming refugees from India that were frightening. These might be enormous. Up to a certain limit, destitute Muslims flocking in from India could be accommodated in the houses and on the lands of the outgoing Hindus and Sikhs, but even these might have to be fed for six to eight months till the spring harvest came round, while others would be like a millstone round our necks. Unless we managed things carefully, we should be broken financially and our Government would collapse through sheer lack of ways and means.

We could, of course, if hard pressed, turn to the Pakistan Government; but their own plight seemed in those days to be precarious; we could not count on them with certainty. Furthermore, if we went cap in hand to Pakistan, we should put ourselves at their mercy and enable them to assert the Paramountcy of the old British-Indian Government. The Nawab and Gurmani were anxious to avoid this and considered it both possible and desirable that Bahawalpur should maintain a quasi-independent existence. The former had on August 15th taken the title of Amir in place of that of Nawab, which carried the suggestion that Bahawalpur was now almost comparable with Afghanistan! We had agreed to accede to Pakistan only in respect of defence, external affairs and communications. It was not the intention that we should subordinate ourselves further or admit the right of Pakistan to interfere in the internal affairs of the State. But to maintain this position it was essential to remain solvent.

The whole operation, therefore, of quelling the disturbances and handling incoming Muslim refugees had to be made substantially self-financing. Ultimately this would involve limiting strictly the number of refugees that we would take. As will be seen, this was a point which we kept constantly in view. Immediately, it required that we should secure possession of the movables, and particularly stocks of grain, left behind by Hindus and not let them fall into the hands of looters; and that we should settle incoming refugees promptly, so that land and other assets did not lie idle and unproductive of revenue and so that the refugees themselves would quickly become self-supporting. For the collection of stocks of grain, both from the mandis and the villages, the staff of the Civil Supplies and Co-operative departments were mobilized, and excellent progress was made with this work from the very start. We also bought up considerable quantities of grain at low prices of Rs 5–7 per maund. The first effect of the disturbances was to make grain prices tumble in the State, for there were large offerings by Hindus who were contemplating flight, and looted stocks also quickly found their way into the market. Later we were able to resell some of our purchases at a profit. The net result was that over the next four to five months we were able to feed thousands of refugees at practically no cost to the State.

As regards the settlement of refugees, we had one very great advantage. In addition to the ordinary revenue and colony staff, there was ready to hand all the extra settlement staff who were at that time engaged in the reassessment of land revenue in the eastern part of the State. This work was immediately suspended and the staff turned on to coping with refugees. The Settlement Officer, Nur Mohammad, was at Bahawalpur—where later he was to play an invaluable part—but the Assistant Settlement Officer, Rao Fazlur Rahman, and the rest of the staff were all scattered about the eastern tahsils—exactly where we wanted them. The outgoing Sikhs had left standing crops which would soon be ripe. If allowed to remain untended they would be carried off by neighbouring villagers or grazed by their cattle. We were anxious to make them over at once to refugees so that they could reap them in due course and thus support themselves through the cold weather. Still more important was it to get refugees settled on vacated lands and furnished where necessary with bullock-ploughs and seed in time to sow the 'rabi'[1] crop in October. If this were not done, there would be loss of production and of revenue and the refugees would have to be supported by us for a whole year.

All these matters filled my mind and seemed to press upon it with hardly less urgency than the task of restoring order and shepherding the Hindus to safety. I discussed them with Rao Fazlur Rahman and other revenue officers on the 28th and we reached certain decisions regarding the principles and terms on which temporary allotments were to be made. The main point of entry for refugees at this time was Macleodganj Road. It was resolved that Rao Fazlur Rahman should station himself at this place and, after preliminary screening, direct the incoming refugees from there to the various deserted 'chaks'. We could see at a glance from our records which were the Sikh 'chaks' and what was their cultivable area.

Rao Fazlur Rahman was a forceful officer and began the work the very next day with what proved to be an indefatigable zeal.

[1] There are two harvests in northern India, 'rabi' gathered about mid-April and 'kharif' gathered about mid-October.

X

Restoring Order—II

MOST of the Hindus in Bahawalnagar were in a fever to get away to India and I had promised to evacuate them as soon as possible. We planned to make a beginning on the afternoon of the 29th. Leghari arranged with the railway authorities for a special train and the military were asked to furnish an escort. The distance to be covered was not great. Macleodganj Road, the last station in the State, was only forty miles from Bahawalnagar, and Hindumalkot, the first station in India, situated in the State of Bikanir, only five to six miles farther on.

But an unexpected difficulty now arose. Owing to the disturbances the through train service running from Samasatta —a junction a few miles south-west of the town of Bahawalnagar—right across the State, then through a small strip of Bikanir (in which Hindumalkot is situated) and so on into the Ferozepur district and to the junction of Bhatinda (in Patiala State), had been altogether discontinued, and within the last few days the running of any trains across the frontier between Macleodganj Road and Hindumalkot had become irregular and intermittent, though it had not ceased altogether. The engine drivers at Bahawalnagar now announced that they could not take a train beyond Macleodganj Road. They said that to proceed farther across the border into India and up to Hindumalkot was dangerous; they were likely to be fired at by Indian troops and killed. We pointed out that the train would have a military escort and that, in any case, Indian troops would not be likely to attack a train carrying Hindu refugees. But they were not satisfied. They alleged that there were thousands of Indian troops at Hindumalkot, and one romancer even claimed that guns were in position there.

These unreal fears were, of course, a mere pretence, invented so as to avoid having to assist Hindu refugees. Communal feeling was particularly rife among the Muslim employees of the railways and they were only too keen to make things as unpleasant and uncomfortable as possible for members of the opposite community. But I was not going to be imposed upon and was quite determined that the train should be taken on from Macleodganj Road right up to Hindumalkot. Between the two stations there was nothing but desert, traversed by a rough sandy track. It was impossible to expect terrified Hindus, with all their women and children and luggage, to make their way on foot in the blazing heat from one station to the other. Moreover once to admit that there was danger in proceeding to Hindumalkot might lead to an absolute break in our rail communications with India, and this would be attended with enormous inconvenience—even greater than I at that time foresaw.

Failing to convince the engine crew that there really were no Indian troops lying in wait for them at Hindumalkot, Leghari and I then said that we would accompany the train ourselves and travel with them on the engine. We would inform the stationmaster at Hindumalkot in advance by railway telephone that we were coming; but if, in spite of this, they still felt nervous, they could halt the train at the distance signal and Leghari and I would go forward on foot to reconnoitre. Sensing that we were determined and were, perhaps, making fools of them, they agreed to these terms.

Since now we had in any case to go to Macleodganj Road on the 29th, Leghari and I arranged that we should leave in our own special train in the morning, stop a few hours at Minchinabad on the way and also spend some hours at Macleodganj Road itself, where we would pick up the 'refugee special' in the afternoon and take it on to Hindumalkot. Rao Fazlur Rahman would accompany us to Macleodganj Road and remain on there to cope with the incoming refugees and to be in general magisterial charge of the whole area.

We were, however, also very anxious to secure the safety of Harunabad which, so far as we knew, was still unravished, but an alluring prize. Since we could not go there immediately ourselves, we decided to send there an Assistant Commissioner, along with some influential non-official Muslims in the hope that by mere persuasion they would be able to prevent any

outbreak. There is a branch line from Bahawalnagar to Harunabad and on to Fort Abbas, but at the best of times a train ran
only about twice a week and no train was available at the
moment. So the Assistant Commissioner and his party had to
try to make their way there by road. Owing to the heavy
rains, we were uncertain whether they would be able to get
through.

Leghari and I reached Minchinabad early on the morning of
the 29th. We found the Hindus in a state of great alarm and the
two senior officials—a First-Class Magistrate and an Inspector
of Police—pleased with themselves but distinctly nervous.
They were pleased with themselves because so far they had
succeeded in saving the town from any serious looting. A few
shops in one of the bazaars had been knocked about a bit by
some local 'toughs' but the damage was slight and the miscreants had been locked up. They were nervous because early
that very morning large bands of villagers had been seen moving
about at some distance from the town as though gathering for an
attack. We endeavoured to put heart into them. Though they
had controlled more or less successfully the rowdy element
within the town and we applauded them, probably excessively,
for this, the police seemed to be somewhat lacking in firmness
and resolution. We found that, despite the fact that they were
fearing an attack from outside, they had not taken the precaution of arresting all the known badmashes within the town. We
gave orders for them to be secured and locked up immediately.
We also looked to the police rifles. About half a dozen were
serviceable—a large number for a Bahawalpur police station—
and Leghari directed some more to be sent for from Bahawalnagar. I was, however, certain in my own mind that even six
rifles, if properly handled, would be more than sufficient to
ward off any possible attack. I told the Magistrate and the
Inspector of Police that, if any band of villagers approached the
town, they must fire upon them without hesitation and must
shoot to kill. We also instructed them to send some men round
to the surrounding villages and put it about that the police in
Minchinabad meant business and would use their rifles with
effect. This was not what the Magistrate and Inspector, left
to themselves, intended. Their idea was to fire a few shots into
the air and hope that the villagers would be scared away. I told

F

them that they must on no account do this, but must resign themselves to the possibility of killing two or three people. They assented and assured me that they would carry out my orders, but I came away with no full confidence that they would do so. To them shooting at Muslims was like shooting at one's own side. Everywhere one was confronted with this strong disinclination to use effective force against the aggressors.

Having served for three years in the adjoining district of Multan, I knew something of the Muslim peasantry of this part of the country. They are not given to violent crime or noted for boldness and ferocity. They have none of the reckless daring of the Muslim tribes of north-west Punjab, or of the fierce, savage passions of the Sikhs. I knew that a mere handful of armed men, if properly led and made to open fire with effect, could easily disperse thousands of Bahawalpuri villagers. But I began to despair of finding any reliable, armed men.

However, in the event the Minchinabad authorities acquitted themselves quite creditably. Late that afternoon bands of villagers again approached the town. They were fired upon, two or three were wounded and the rest dispersed. There was no further trouble at Minchinabad; but in the course of the next few weeks all the Hindus evacuated the place and migrated to India.

Leghari and I left Minchinabad at about 11.0 a.m. and went on to Macleodganj Road. Here we found a scene of great disorder. The place, it turned out, had been completely looted several days earlier. A number of Hindu and Sikh shopkeepers had been killed; the rest had all fled across the nearby border. The shops in the bazaar were deserted, many of them half-burnt; there was nothing in them but rubbish and fragments of smashed goods. In the small mandi all the godowns had been broken open and hardly a bag of grain was left. The municipal staff had disintegrated and next to nothing had yet been done to clear up the mess. On top of this, in the last few days Muslim refugees from the Ferozepur district of East Punjab had begun to pour in. They were squatting in masses outside the railway station and along the railway line in a most miserable condition; the accumulating filth was appalling; and they could get no supplies—there was only one Muslim shop in the town still functioning.

At the station there was a platoon of Bahawalpur troops under Lt. Babar, an enterprising but rather headstrong officer, and not in any way qualified to deal with the situation. The only surviving civil official was the thanedar. It was fortunate that we had brought Rao Fazlur Rahman with us to take general charge. The thanedar, though he had some valid excuses to offer, had made no serious attempt to prevent the looting of the town or to clean it up afterwards. He prided himself on having preserved the old village of Macleodganj, situated some four to five miles away, which was largely inhabited by rich Hindus and contained a number of very substantial brick houses. There must have been plenty to loot and I never really discovered how the thanedar had kept it completely unharmed.[1] It may have been luck; more probably some bargain had been struck.

A large number of the colony chaks in the region of Macleodganj Road had been inhabited by Sikh colonists who had abandoned their lands and migrated to Bikanir a week or ten days earlier. The Muslims in this area had also abandoned their lands and retired to the interior, thinking it too dangerous to be so near the frontier. It took weeks to persuade them to return and reoccupy them and sections of troops had to be dotted about at strategic points to give confidence. There was, no doubt, some ground to fear tip-and-run raids across the frontier, but the extent of the panic was very hard to understand. The Sikhs, who had so lately run away to Bikanir, would have perhaps been surprised to learn the terror that they now inspired.

Rao Fazlur Rahman settled down at once to screen the masses of Muslim refugees and direct them to abandoned chaks, thus relieving the congestion at the railway station. We gave him all the help we could, restocking the place with grain from elsewhere, and getting Muslim shopkeepers to come and open shops and bring in provisions and goods for sale. Slowly the place came to life again, but owing to the enormous numbers of refugees that continued to deposit themselves on the outskirts of this derelict and devastated little town it remained a headache for many weeks.

While we were at Macleodganj Road, Leghari got wind of a

[1] I did not actually visit this village till September 1st.

rather horrible incident that was reported to have occurred there a few days earlier, and of which later we received confirmation. Some twenty to thirty Hindus, who wanted to go through to Bhatinda or to other places in India, had arrived at Macleodganj at a time when the through service had been interrupted. The railway officials, however, told them that if they did not mind waiting a little while, they would arrange for an engine to take them all on to Hindumalkot. Their carriage was then pulled out of the station and shunted on to a siding some distance away and close to a canal. Here they waited with growing impatience, as the day was getting on, but they were assured from time to time that the engine which would take them on to Hindumalkot was just coming and that they need not worry. No engine came at all. At nightfall they were attacked, robbed and slaughtered. But at least one of them managed to escape. He jumped out of the railway carriage into the canal, swam across it and made his way in the darkness over the border into India. I received a letter from him two or three weeks later telling this grisly tale, of which Leghari had already heard vague rumours.

We immediately set investigations on foot. The facts were generally confirmed, and the complicity of the railway staff in the outrage was quite manifest. We obtained sufficient evidence to arrest one of them on a charge of conspiracy to murder and I kept him incarcerated for a good many weeks. But it was impossible to complete the investigations and put a case into court owing to the difficulty of securing the attendance of the survivor(s), now in India, for interrogation and identification of the suspects. So ultimately we had to release him. Being a believer in retributive punishment, I hoped that he had had some uneasy moments and serious qualms of fear during the period of his incarceration.

I have several times had occasion to mention the misbehaviour of the railway staff, and there were to be more instances of it. The fact is that, just as Muslim feeling and the demand for Pakistan were strongest in provinces like the U.P., where the Muslims were in a minority, so too bitterness against the Hindus was most acute in the services of the Central Government, where the Muslims were hopelessly outnumbered and always felt themselves to be suppressed, frustrated and unjustly deprived or tricked out of promotion by the wily Hindus. In the Provincial Services of the Punjab, where the Muslims could easily hold their own both in point of numbers and otherwise, there was much less of this bitterness. Bigoted officials existed on both sides, but in general the relations between the two communities in the Punjab Services were friendly. Certainly the Muslims had no cause to feel aggrieved on account of lack of opportunity or unfair discrimination; during the past fifteen to twenty years the boot had been on the other leg. Conditions were substantially the same in the State Services of Bahawalpur. In the Central Services and in all-India institutions like the Imperial Bank they were different. The Muslims were, or felt themselves to be, a helpless and oppressed minority.

After August 15th the Muslim staff of the railways lost no time in exhibiting their feelings. With Partition there had been a good deal of reshuffling of railway personnel and many Muslims had come from India to man the railways in Bahawalpur, replacing Hindus. At once they began hoisting the Pakistan flag on all the stations—much to the annoyance of Gurmani, since Bahawalpur State had a flag of its own—and painting all the engines with Pakistani slogans. At more than one place they were the direct cause of serious outrages against the Hindus, and initially they were often far from co-operative about measures for their evacuation. At a later date I drew up a memorandum, setting forth all their misdeeds and delinquencies in Bahawalpur, which Gurmani forwarded to the Railway Administration with a strongly worded covering letter. Being a keen patriot, he hated to see a Pakistan Service falling to such low levels of conduct and efficiency. The Pakistan Railway Authorities took the criticisms very well and deputed a high-ranking official to look into the complaints and improve the tone of the railway staff. But this was all many weeks later.

To return to August 29th. The 'refugee special' from Baha-walnagar reached Macleodganj at about 4.0 p.m. The brigade and cannon supposed to be waiting to repulse us at Hindu-malkot had by now been quite forgotten. The driver of the train greeted us with a broad grin and, when reminded of the danger said to lie ahead of us, laughingly admitted that it was all humbug, for which a mischief-monger at Bahawalnagar had been responsible. There was no more talk of stopping to

reconnoitre at the distance signal; but, for convenience, Leghari and I did go on ahead of the refugee train in our own
special.

The young officer in charge of the Bahawalpur troops escorting the refugees had given deep thought to the military aspect
of our expedition. He produced a little sketch map, showing the
positions reported to have been taken up by the Indian forces
at Hindumalkot, and explained to me how he proposed to
deploy his own troops, if we met with a hostile reception. It was
difficult for me to take all this seriously, but I believe I offered
some criticisms of his proposed dispositions which he was good
enough to accept.

During the next few weeks Hindumalkot was to be for many
thousands of Hindus the goal of all their hopes, the gateway
from the hell of Bahawalpur to the longed-for paradise of India.
I trust that on reaching there they got some tranquillity of
spirit; for they can have got very little else. Imagine a signal
rising up from the desert, a small shed and a row of bare brick
buildings a quarter of a mile away, and you have about the
sum total of Hindumalkot. The Bikanir authorities certainly
did what they could for the reception of refugees, but by its very
nature Hindumalkot had little to offer in the way of creature
comforts. There could hardly be a worse place at which to be
decanted after a long, hot, exhausting journey in a tremendously
overcrowded train.

But this is to anticipate. Our first trainload of Hindu refugees
did not do badly. They had not had to travel far; they were
crowded, but not packed in the train like sardines; and on
arrival at Hindumalkot they were practically sole masters of
its exiguous resources, since only a handful of refugees had
come in previously on foot. Moreover arrangements had been
made for another train to take them on, if they wished, to
Bhatinda.

Indian troops were not much in evidence when we reached
Hindumalkot; there appeared to be only a small detachment,
perhaps two sections, posted there. Leghari and I were very
politely received by the stationmaster who had raked out some
subordinate official of the Bikanir State—probably a naib-
tahsildar—to meet us. The latter was aghast to see the huge
number of refugees we had brought with us and said he had

nowhere to put them as the few buildings were already occupied. We told him that most of them would want to go on to Bhatinda, but we also warned him that we would be sending more in the next few days and asked him to inform the Bikanir Government of this so that they could make the necessary preparations to receive them.

We told the stationmaster that we wanted to run trains through to Hindumalkot regularly every day and so prevent a complete break in rail communications with India. We hoped that India would put no impediments in the way of this and that the Muslim personnel bringing the trains would be quite safe. The stationmaster gave us every assurance and settled further details regarding the reopening of traffic with railway officials whom we had brought with us for this purpose.

While we were chatting, about half a dozen refugees, who had reached Hindumalkot a few days earlier, came up to us and salaamed. They were shopkeepers from Macleodganj Road and I recognized one of them, a venerable Sikh with a white beard, as a prominent citizen of that place whom I had met before. We had just begun to inquire how they were, when this patriarchal figure lifted up his voice and in ringing tones poured forth at Leghari a torrent of impassioned reproaches. He spoke with a vehemence of feeling and a volume of sound unimaginable perhaps to anyone not familiar with the Sikhs. Leghari, he said, had assured them of protection, told them to remain at Macleodganj and that no harm would come to them. They had trusted and obeyed him; they had carried out all his orders, as they always did. How could they imagine that he would fail them and break all his promises? But he had deserted and abandoned them—left them to be mercilessly slaughtered and plundered by bands of Muslim hooligans. Their shops had all been burnt and looted; hundreds of them had been killed; his own nephew and other close relations had been murdered before his eyes. What had Leghari's police been doing all this while? Where was the thanedar? Where was Leghari himself? He had never come near them or paid the slightest heed to their cries. He had deceived them with false promises of protection. If they had not trusted in him, they could have all quietly slipped away from the place several weeks before, taking their valuables with them. As it was they had had to fly for their lives, leaving everything behind them. He himself, a leading citizen and member of the Committee, possessed now nothing at all. Here he was in this desert, completely destitute, without a tent or shed to shelter in, hardly able to get even water. It would have been better to die like his nephew than to live to endure all these miseries. This is what he had been brought to by trusting Leghari; this is what came of being loyal to the Government and helping the police. How did Leghari now have the face to come among them? Why was he inquiring about them when he had ruined them all?

On and on flowed the ceaseless stream of words. If he paused for a few seconds to draw breath, it was only to begin again in the same loud, deafening tones. Nothing would persuade him to stop or to realize that we were standing a yard and not a mile away from him.

Though I was not insensible to the sting of his reproaches, they did not touch me so nearly as Leghari, to whom they were directly addressed; for I had been careful never to give anyone any assurance of protection. I was thankful for my comparative immunity and wondered what might be the feelings of poor Leghari. Whatever they were, he gave no indication of them, but stood silent and impassive, apparently unmoved by the flood of eloquence and impervious to reproaches. He made no attempt to answer or excuse himself; he showed no trace of irritation.

The only way of ending the painful scene was to quit it. We had finished our business and the refugees had by now detrained; so, hastily saying good-bye, we climbed back into our special to return to Bahawalnagar. All the while the white-bearded Sikh continued to pour out his sorrows at the top of his voice and as the train steamed away he ran along babbling beside it till finally it gathered pace and he was left behind, still hurling his denunciations at us. His sufferings had temporarily unhinged his mind.

When we were clear of him, Leghari suddenly became communicative. He said that he had never experienced anything so painful in his life and that he had not known how to endure it. I said that I thought he had borne it very well, and had admired the way in which he had listened to those bitter reproaches without saying a word. He replied that as he felt they were justified there was nothing he could say and so he thought it best to remain silent.

It was dark when we finally got back to Bahawalnagar. Mixed news awaited us. We learnt with relief that the Assistant Commissioner and his party had got through to Harunabad —though with considerable difficulty—and that there had been no outbreak of violence there. They reported that most of the Hindus were peacefully leaving the place and proceeding by road across the border into Bikanir State, which was not many miles distant. When Leghari and I visited Harunabad a few days later, there were only about fifty Hindus left. Large stocks of food-grains in the mandi passed into our hands intact.

Similarly the Hindus in the small outlying town of Fort Abbas and the Sikhs settled in a number of chaks in that area all went over peacefully at this time to Bikanir without any casualties or looting. In this distant outpost it was the Muslims who were, or pretended to be, in a panic, alleging that the Sikhs, who had left, were going to come back and spring upon them suddenly from the desert. We had to send some troops down to Fort Abbas to reassure them.

To offset this good news from the Harunabad area there were two bits of bad news. A Hindu railway official—a permanent way inspector—and his two nephews had been murdered at a place called Dunga Bunga about fifteen miles away; and a number of Hindus had been slaughtered in the train from Samasatta which had reached Bahawalnagar that afternoon. So the killing was still going on. The second incident was particularly disquieting, since hitherto we had been immune from the frightful train massacres which had been a feature of the disturbances in the Punjab.

In both incidents railway personnel were probably involved. The Dunga Bunga murderers remained untraced, despite vigorous investigations, but there was strong suspicion that members of the railway staff at that place had instigated, if not perpetrated, the crime. As regards the train murders, there was a conspiracy of silence. They took place somewhere between Khairpur and Qaimpur. The train had stopped ostensibly because a signal was against it, and the signal was against it ostensibly for some good reason. In reality it was all prearranged. While the train was halted it was beset by villagers

F*

and most of the few Hindus in it were robbed and murdered. It was reported that some of the Muslim passengers had joined in the slaughter, but the facts were never fully ascertained.

It was now plainly quite unsafe for Hindu passengers to travel by train without escort and we let it be known that those who ventured to do so without authority from the Government did so at their own risk. Most of the Hindus were only too keenly alive to the dangers, but a week or so after this incident a Hindu railway official of Bahawalpur, trusting to the assurances of Muslim friends who were perhaps treacherous, entrained without authority with his whole family—in all about a dozen persons—hoping to get through to Hindumalkot and Bhatinda. The whole party came to grief. They were attacked *en route*, robbed and murdered. Some months later a chance ray of light was shed on this incident. In December a British brigadier serving in India, whom I had known ten years earlier, sent me a letter saying that he had been asked by the station-master of Ludhiana to inquire whether I could trace his niece, a little girl of eight, who belonged to Bahawalpur. Her parents and other relations had all been killed in a train coming from Bahawalpur; but it was not known what had happened to her, and whether she was alive or dead. The quest seemed pretty hopeless, but I asked the tahsildar of Bahawalpur to see if he could hear anything of her in the villages between Khairpur and Qaimpur. Within two days he had found her and we were able to send her safely to her uncle at Ludhiana. It appears that when her parents and relations were attacked, the train was brought to a halt, they were dragged out of it and she tumbled out after them. While they were being done to death by the side of the line, she crept into a field near by and hid herself in the crops. After the noise and shouting had subsided and the train had gone on and all seemed quiet, she crept out again. Two villagers still lingering at the scene spotted her. Though they had probably both been parties to the massacre, they shrank from taking the child's life in cold blood. Not knowing what to do with her and fearing to incriminate themselves if they surrendered her to the authorities, one of them took her to his home, looked after her and treated her kindly. Her presence was revealed to the tahsildar and she was handed over to him only on the express understanding that no action would be taken against any of the villagers for hiding her such a long time. Outwardly she was quite unharmed, and we were able to send her safely to her uncle at Ludhiana.

Leghari and I had already decided that, on return from Macleodganj Road, we must go down the line in the opposite direction. The attack on the train, showing that there was still much lawlessness in the Khairpur-Qaimpur area, made this all the more necessary. We set out very early the next morning (August 30th). Heavy rain had again fallen, so we travelled by special train, and, fearing that there might be a good deal of disorder to contend with, we took with us about a platoon of troops.

At Chishtian all was still quiet. A number of Hindus from outlying villages had sought refuge here; they seemed fairly contented and only a few of them expressed a wish to be evacuated to India. Among the officials who met us was the settlement tahsildar, Gobind Baksh.

'Are you quite all right, Gobind Baksh?' I inquired.

'Nur Mohammad, not Gobind Baksh,' came a chorus from the bystanders.

'Nur Mohammad, sir, if you please,' said Gobind Baksh himself. 'My name is Nur Mohammad, I'm no longer Gobind Baksh.'

We had met him as a Hindu on the 26th. Now four days later he was a Muslim with a Muslim name. I inquired whether he had taken the name of 'Nur Mohammad' after his superior, the Settlement Officer, and he replied that he had. I was delighted, as there was no-one more worthy of honour and imitation than K. B. Nur Mohammad. I congratulated him warmly on his choice of a new name and expressed the hope that he would live up to the reputation of his namesake.

Since Gobind Baksh, alias Nur Mohammad, was now obviously immune from all danger and, having been fully accepted as a Muslim, could act with effective authority, I at once invested him with the powers of a first-class magistrate and packed him off to Hasilpur to take charge of affairs there.

During these times of trouble there were many Hindus in Bahawalpur, including about half a dozen officials, who sought safety by temporarily embracing Islam, but Gobind Baksh is the only Hindu known personally to me whose conversion was

genuine and permanent and who has remained in West Pakistan as a regular citizen of that State. The fact is that he was
enamoured of a Muslim girl and, under her influence, he had
for some time been contemplating the adoption of the Muslim
faith. The outbreak of the disturbances afforded the occasion
for him to take the final plunge.

There was much for the new Nur Mohammad to do at
Hasilpur. Travelling on there from Chishtian, we found that
the police and Hindus had all left the ill-omened village of
'old Hasilpur' and were now concentrated in the 'colony'
town. Most of the corpses had been disposed of, but, on taking
a tally of the dead and the living, it had come to light that a
great many Hindu girls were missing. We deputed special staff
to make searches in the neighbourhood and within a week
sixty had been recovered. The military were asked to round up
all gangs of Pathans and to send them across the Sutlej into the
Punjab—a task which they successfully accomplished within the
next few days. The Hindus at Hasilpur almost without exception wanted to go to India and arrangements were made for
their evacuation to Hindumalkot.

The small town of Qaimpur is about two miles distant from
the station. We did not visit it on this occasion, as the thanedar,
who came to the station to meet us, said that all was well there,
save that the Hindus were still clustering in the compound of
Abdullah Shah and would not return to their own houses. But he
said that there were reports of trouble at Khairpur so we hurried
on there. On reaching Khairpur station, we were informed that
the place had already been looted and the bazaar burnt. We got
onto some ponies and rode over to the town which was about a
mile away. There was the usual scene of devastation and a
small sprinkling of corpses, most of them lying in the shops
and houses beneath charred beams and rafters. The main
attack had taken place on the 28th when, according to the
thanedar, the assailants were so numerous that even with the
small reinforcements we had given him he was powerless to
resist them. The looters had returned in smaller numbers on
the 29th—the day before our arrival—and had been beaten off
with one or two casualties, and eighty of them had been arrested.
This was the thanedar's story and he had certainly got eighty
men in custody whom we presumed to be looters. Whether they

really were, I never ascertained. However, for the present we
sent them all off to Derawar Fort, an ancient fortress in the
desert, where we had decided to confine all those arrested in
this area in connection with the disturbances.

Our arrival at Khairpur forestalled a third attack on the
place. Bands of looters had been gathering during the morning
for further pillage, but on learning that Leghari and I were
present they drew off and Khairpur was not molested again.

The number of Hindus killed in Khairpur was only about
twenty-five. The survivors, perhaps not without reason, were
terrified out of their wits, but had as yet formed no firm resolution whether to stay or to leave. On the whole their preference
appeared to be for staying, and this was not surprising as
Khairpur was an old town and most of the Hindu families
living in it had been settled there for generations. They were
attached to the place and deeply rooted in it—unlike the Hindus
in the colony towns who had come in from outside in the past
twenty years and still had their roots elsewhere. We were at
this time not at all anxious that these old Hindu subjects of the
State should leave, unless they themselves positively wished to
be evacuated to India, and so we threw our weight in favour of
their staying. In the hope of encouraging them, we left behind
two sections of the troops we had brought with us. Arrangements had also been made, as already mentioned, for some
troops from Bahawalpur to make a flag-march through the
area in order to restore confidence. We said that we ourselves
would visit them again in two or three days and see how they
felt then about staying or leaving.

We returned to Bahawalnagar with the impression that on
the whole they had been reassured and were content to remain.
The following day, when Leghari and I went to Harunabad
and Fort Abbas, it was Muslims rather than Hindus that we
had to reassure. The latter had left, or were leaving, peacefully
and in good order, but all along the border the Muslims were
in fear of imminent attack, as already described. So far as we
could make out, petty raids were being made across the border
by both sides, though naturally we heard more of the raids
made against us than of the raids by our people into Bikanir.
One of our military patrols on the Sadiqia Canal had recently
shot seven Sikhs who were alleged to have been looting a

deserted village. Such drastic action was probably unjustified, but I was not inclined to question it.

When we got back to Bahawalnagar from Harunabad late on the evening of August 31st, there was a message waiting for me from Sardar K. M. Pannikar, Prime Minister of Bikanir, to the effect that he and some of the State officials, along with Mr. V. P. Menon of the Government of India and Major Short, proposed to come over to see me the next morning at Bahawalnagar. He requested me to ensure that they would not be held up by any military or police picket on the road by which they would come.

I gave the necessary orders. In view of the disturbed state of the border and the growing streams of refugees flowing across it in both directions, I felt that discussions with the Bikanir authorities were most timely and would be very useful. As regards Menon and Short, I surmised that the Government of India, having heard of disturbances in Bahawalpur State, had sent them to spy out the land and report how things stood. Since all that had occurred appeared to me very shocking and disgraceful, I was not too keen to have to reveal it to the Government of India who might make capital out of it, and if Menon and Short had not been good friends of mine, I should have been very uneasy. I hoped, however, that I should be able to give them in confidence a true picture of the situation without unduly compromising either Bahawalpur or Pakistan.

Menon had previously been Reforms Commissioner to the Government of India and had played a crucial part in the negotiations and evolving of formulas which had preceded Partition and Independence. I did not know the exact position[1] now held by him, but I had an idea that he was Sardar Patel's right-hand man and I regarded him as Patel's representative. Short, I assumed, was a kind of liaison officer and had been sent on this expedition because he was an Englishman who knew both Gurmani and me well.

When the party arrived the next morning, I was delighted to find among them another old friend, Rai Bahadur Chuni Lal. Ten years earlier he had been Superintendent of Police in a district of which I was District Magistrate and we had worked together in the closest harmony and friendship. He was now

[1] He had just become Secretary to the Ministry of States.

Inspector-General of Police, Bikanir. I had forgotten this and it came to me as a most pleasant surprise and a good augury for our future relations with Bikanir.

Sardar Pannikar and his officials expressed much concern at the number of refugees that had flooded into Bikanir from Bahawalpur and wanted to know how many more were coming. I was able to assure them that almost all our Sikh colonists had already moved across into their State and that no more need be expected. I told them that we were in the process of evacuating urban Hindus from some of our colony towns and that they should be prepared in the next few days to receive several hundreds of them at Hindumalkot; but most of them, I said, would probably want to go on into the East Punjab and would not stay in Bikanir, unless they had originally come from there.

Sardar Pannikar complained that the Sikh colonists were being driven across the border in a destitute condition and were arriving in Bikanir stripped to the bone. I had to point out that this was not true. Except perhaps for two or three chaks near Macleodganj, the Sikh colonists had gone out quite unmolested and had taken with them everything that they could load on to their carts. Our Muslim colonists, so far from attacking them, had been more inclined to run away from them. I am glad to say that one of the Bikanir officials had the courage to speak up and told Sardar Pannikar that the reports given to him about the robbing of refugees had been much exaggerated.

I then referred to the raids that were going on across the border. So long as these continued, I said, it was difficult for us to withdraw our troops and so bring things back to normal. It was agreed that there should be further meetings of military and police officers to discuss these frontier problems. The Bikanir officials complained that several of their people had been shot at without warning on the border and killed or wounded. I did not deny that this might have happened for though no orders had been issued to the Bahawalpur troops to shoot without warning, it was not easy to control small detachments strung out over long distances. In the present circumstances, I said, we must assume, and let it be generally known, that anyone who poked his nose over the frontier without due authority did so at his own peril and should not, therefore, be surprised or annoyed if he got killed or wounded. Sardar Pannikar objected to this. I admitted that it should not be the normal rule, but I said that at the present time it applied and that, in any case, I must give clear warning that any Sikh who ventured across the border into our territory without authority was very likely to be killed and there was nothing I could do to prevent it.

After these general discussions I had some talk with Menon and Short alone. I took the former down to the town, which had by now been cleaned up and presented a fairly good appearance. Though we had been evacuating Hindus to Hindumalkot for the last three days, there were still two to three hundred of them in Bahawalnagar, mostly concentrated in the buildings provided as a sanctuary for them by the wealthy Muslim. I thought Menon ought to have a talk to them and satisfy himself that they were all right; so I introduced him to some of them and began talking away myself in Hindustani till I realized that he wasn't following and remembered that, being a South Indian, he knew no Punjabi and hardly any Hindustani. Thus I found myself, an Englishman, in the curious position of acting as an interpreter between an Indian and his fellow countrymen.

I explained to Menon and Short the situation in Bahawalpur and the measures we were taking to suppress the disorders. I was mildly optimistic regarding the future. I said that I thought the worst was over, that we should probably be able to keep the Rahim Yar Khan district tranquil, and that we might hope to escape further mass slaughters. I then came to the question of casualties. Those which had already occurred were, of course, to me very shocking, as in the old days we had felt great concern if only half a dozen were killed in a communal riot. Still I decided that I must give the true facts. Disgraceful though they might seem to me, they were probably less bad than the exaggerated tales reaching India. So place by place I told Menon the exact casualties as known to me. At that time they amounted in all to about one thousand. I felt rather apologetic about these, to me, high figures and may have shown a little diffidence in disclosing them. I said to Menon that I had no objection to his passing them on to Sardar Patel—and wrote them all down on a bit of paper for him—but I requested him not to give publicity to them or to use them officially. He made light of my anxiety.

'Don't worry,' he said, 'these figures are not very bad. You don't realize what is going on elsewhere. This State is a paradise compared with East Punjab.'[1]

He was so encouraging that I was considerably heartened. I had wanted to reassure *him* and through him to convey to Sardar Patel that we were doing our best to steady things in Bahawalpur; but the net result of his visit was to reassure me. It may not have been very proper to draw comfort from the misfortunes of others, but I did so. To know definitely—what I had, of course, surmised—that our plight was nothing like so bad as that of others was a stimulating tonic.

I was also pleased to note that both Menon and Short were very well impressed by Leghari.

Menon gave me some account of the difficulties in the East Punjab and bewailed the lack of experienced officers to cope with the disorders and with the mounting tide of refugees. He asked why I was not there and, in his impulsive way, suggested that I should immediately come over and help them. I pointed out that my hands were full and that I could not at such a critical moment desert my post in Bahawalpur. He agreed, but asked me to consider the matter when Bahawalpur had grown calmer. This conversation was the germ of my subsequent service in India.

Our visitors left at about noon and immediately afterwards Leghari and I set out again for Minchinabad and Macleodganj, travelling this time by car. We wanted to be sure that Minchinabad was still intact, but our main object was to confer with Rao Fazlur Rahman. In the past forty-eight hours Muslim refugees had been pouring into the State at Macleodganj Road in quite overwhelming numbers. Some of them were wounded and in an absolutely helpless condition and this was once again inflaming communal feelings. Two or three cases of cholera had

---

[1] At a later date, when the Government of India put out a propagandist statement that 70,000 Hindus had been killed in Bahawalpur State, we issued a contradiction and in the course of it quoted this remark of Mr. Menon. He then denied having made it. He may well have forgotten it and, in any case, in the circumstances of those times, he could hardly be blamed for disclaiming words used on the spur of the moment in the course of private conversation. But he did in fact use these very words. They were uttered in the presence of Major Short and were recorded by me in a report sent to Gurmani the same day.

been reported. The medical staff was quite insufficient and no anti-cholera serum was immediately available. Rao Fazlur Rahman was at his wits' end and was finding Lt. Babar an irritant rather than a help.

Lt. Babar, who was in command of the detachment of troops at Macleodganj Road, deserves a short paragraph to himself. He had been, I subsequently discovered, a lawyer in Peshawar and, not finding that very profitable, had joined the Bahawalpur State Forces not long before this date. He was good company and during our association I had some enjoyable rides with him in his jeep along the Sadiqia Canal. But he was impetuous and on so many occasions did not see eye to eye with Rao Fazlur Rahman that I very soon had to ask for him to be removed. One of his most annoying habits was to arrest every Hindu he saw. It had been explained to him that he had no authority to make any arrest unless he was ordered to do so by a magistrate or saw someone actually committing an offence; but still he persisted and crowned his efforts by arresting a Hindu head constable of police who had been on leave and was trying to get back to duty at Jullundur. Lt. Babar seized him at the railway station, took away his belt, treated him in a humiliating manner and absolutely refused to release him until Leghari and I appeared on the scene and set him at liberty. I then told Lt. Babar that, if he did it again, I would arrest *him* and put him in the lock-up on charges of wrongful restraint and wrongful confinement. After this, he desisted.

On the whole Lt. Babar gave me more amusement than annoyance, but Rao Fazlur Rahman, manfully grappling from hour to hour with thousands of refugees, could not take his eccentricities quite so lightly. Strictly speaking there was no need for troops at Macleodganj, but we had to keep them there in deference to Muslim opinion and Muslim fears.

By midday on September 1st when Leghari and I started on our journey to Minchinabad and Macleodganj Road there was a long column of Muslim refugees strung out from the latter place almost up to Bahawalnagar. They were trudging slowly along the side of the Fordwah Canal (and making havoc of our canal road) with their bullock-carts, women and children and such of their simple chattels as they had been able to bring with them. We ran into the head of this column a few miles out of

Bahawalnagar. As we drove along, my heart sank at the vast numbers. We found that, besides those on the road, there was now a dense concentration of them at Minchinabad as well as at Macleodganj. Their condition varied. Some of them had sturdy bullocks and well-laden carts with plenty of bags of grain and did not themselves look at all done up by their march. Others seemed dead-beat and practically destitute. Most pathetic were those who had got stranded through their cart breaking down or one of their bullocks falling lame or dying. But at least now they were in a friendly country and could hope to obtain help. We stopped here and there, as we motored along, and tried to console them, advising them where they could best halt for the night and assuring them that we would allot them land. The great majority of them came from the Ferozepur district of the (East) Punjab. I was at a loss to understand why they had entered Bahawalpur instead of crossing the Sutlej into the (West) Punjab. They all said that Indian troops had scared them away from the road leading to the bridge over the river at Suleimanke and that they had therefore been compelled to turn aside into Bahawalpur. Some of them with connections in West Punjab still wanted to get there and were anxious to know where was the next crossing of the river. We had to direct them to the Pallah headworks—a good many miles distant.

I had scraped together all the revenue staff I could lay hands on and given them to Fazlur Rahman for refugee work, and we now had officers posted at all the principal centres both to allot land to cultivators and to allot shops and houses in the towns to urban refugees. But we were terribly short-handed, especially at Macleodganj itself. The only way in which we could supplement our resources was to recruit any trained revenue staff we could find among the incoming refugees. I authorized Fazlur Rahman to do this and we procured a few useful men, including one excellent naib-tahsildar.

A little cross-examination of the Medical Officer at Macleodganj showed that the reported cases of cholera at that place —more were reported from Minchinabad the next day—were likely to be false alarms. We sent for anti-cholera serum and staff from Bahawalpur and a large number of inoculations were carried out. But these were probably superfluous, and it is doubtful whether there had been any real case of cholera at all. Though there continued to be numerous alarms during the month of September, nothing came of any of them.

This huge wave of refugees from Ferozepur brought with it a man of some prominence in that district. He was a large landowner named Bagh Ali and had been a member of the Legislative Assembly of the old united Punjab. He arrived on foot at Macleodganj Road along with five thousand members of the Sakhera tribe, many of whom were his tenants. He had been trekking for a week and was clearly unaccustomed to such exertions. Clad in raiment by no means fine or clean, unshaven, pinched and haggard, he presented a distressful appearance. One could hardly imagine that he was a wealthy Muslim landowner and an M.L.A. I had not met him before, but he was well-known to me by repute, for earlier in the year he had been the central figure in quite a celebrated scene in the Punjab Assembly. He had been one of the handful of Unionists supporting Sir Khizar Hyat who had been returned in the elections of 1945; but the Muslim League tried hard to win him over to their side and thought they had succeeded. One day there was a regular struggle for his body on the floor of the House, each party claiming him as their own and trying to drag him over to their benches. Sir Khizar had won this tussle and Bagh Ali had remained with him instead of going over to the League.

I reminded Bagh Ali of this incident. He said at once that his present tribulations were a just punishment from God for his failure to support the Muslim League. He feared that there were many more in store for him for, having offended the League, he could not expect to receive a warm welcome in Pakistan. He was quite uncertain whether he would be allotted any land in exchange for what he held in Ferozepur. He then told me that, in view of his previous opposition to the demand for Pakistan, he had left Ferozepur very much against his will, but had been compelled to quit by the Sub-Divisional Officer at Fazilka. This bit of information astonished and disturbed me. I knew that for the past three weeks the Sikhs had been deliberately driving Muslims out of the East Punjab, but this was the first intimation that Government officials were aiding and abetting their expulsion. If the Sub-Divisional Officer was acting under orders, where was this all going to end? We might soon have the whole Muslim population of India thrust upon us. We should then perforce have to turn out all our Hindu population whom we were at that time still trying to retain unharmed within the State. I sent a telegram to the Governor of the East Punjab seeking clarification of his Government's attitude, but received no reply. Many months afterwards I learnt that a reply was sent, though it never got through to me, in which the Governor explained that an agreement had just been reached for an exchange of populations between East and West Punjab. The actual date of this agreement was September 2nd. Evidently the Sub-Divisional Officer, Fazilka, acted in anticipation of it. I did not come to know of it till some days later.

Bagh Ali also told me, like many others, that he and his people had intended to cross the Sutlej into the West Punjab, but had been forced aside into Bahawalpur because the road to the bridge at the Suleimanke headworks was unsafe for refugees. It was clear that unless this road was reopened we should continue to be inundated with refugees unable to pass over the river into West Punjab. So I instructed Fazlur Rahman and Lt. Babar to run up together to Suleimanke to reconnoitre and also to report generally on the condition of the headworks, about which I had begun to feel grave misgivings.

Bagh Ali was doubtful of the reception he would meet with in West Punjab; he was also doubtful what our attitude towards him would be. I guessed that, being quite worn out, he would be thankful to end his wanderings and stay on in Bahawalpur now that he had got there. But would we allot him land and permit him to take up the position of a landlord with the tenants he had brought with him cultivating under him? This was the question that was agitating his mind, though he did not like to put it to me directly. I decided that we were unlikely to get better cultivators than these Sakheras from Ferozepur and that from the State's point of view it would be a good bargain to take Bagh Ali and his tenants with him. They had almost all got their bullocks and implements with them, and since he was a man of position and education he would relieve us of a lot of trouble by himself looking after them and settling them on the land. The tenants themselves were quite satisfied, indeed delighted, with the idea. They felt for Bagh Ali a sort of feudal loyalty, which was enhanced by the fact that he had stood by them in their troubles and himself led them out on foot from Ferozepur. So, in consultation with Fazlur Rahman, I allotted a large block of vacated land in the vicinity of Bahawalnagar to Bagh Ali and his tenants for one year in the first instance.

Gurmani was not very enthusiastic about this arrangement. Though there were plenty of big landlords of the old feudal type in the non-colony area of Bahawalpur, he did not like the idea of introducing any more. He may have thought that there would soon have to be far-reaching changes, sweeping away the old landlord-tenant relationship. I had myself felt for some years that a new pattern of agricultural society was required in India, superseding both landlords and tenants and peasant proprietors and based on the co-operative organization of the village. Nowhere had seemed more suitable for experiments on these lines than the new colony area of the Punjab; but none had been made. The present upheaval, with the uprooting of large sections of the population, might seem to afford in some ways an opportunity for change and the introduction of new patterns of rural society; yet I was convinced that to attempt anything of the kind at this time of crisis was wholly impracticable.[1] My view was that all those who came in from India should, so far as possible, be given exactly the same rights and status as they had enjoyed there. If landlords were to be abolished or rights in land curtailed, this should be done uniformly for all alike. Such changes should not be arbitrarily applied only to those unlucky ones who had been driven out of India and Pakistan.

These views were favourable to Bagh Ali!

It will be remembered that Leghari and I had promised on the 30th to revisit Khairpur in two or three days; so we spent the whole of September 2nd motoring along the route Chishtian, Hasilpur, Qaimpur and Khairpur, and, having thus approached so near to Bahawalpur, I went on and stopped the night there. At all places there were manifest signs of returning confidence and restoration of order. The recovery of stolen property and abducted women, the arrest of offenders and the collection of food-grains were going on apace. At Chishtian

[1] Though experiments were contemplated in some quarters, on neither side of the frontier was it found practicable to carry them into effect.

shops had reopened. At Qaimpur the Hindus were at last persuaded to leave the compound of Abdullah Shah and return to
their own homes. At Khairpur there was no longer talk of
evacuation to India; the Hindus had decided to remain.

In view of this general improvement I was somewhat perplexed at being approached in Bahawalpur itself by a deputa-
tion of Hindus who said that they felt unsafe and asked to be
evacuated to India. No incident of any kind had yet occurred
in or near the town of Bahawalpur. A good number of Hindus
from the rural areas had sought safety in the capital, but serious
disorders had stopped short around Khairpur. I was at pains to
ascertain from the Hindus whether they had any specific
grounds for alarm; but I could discover nothing other than
general fears and a vague uneasiness. I was not disposed to
encourage their thoughts of flight. To start evacuating Hindus
from the capital would make nonsense of our efforts to retain
and protect Hindus in Khairpur, Qaimpur and other places
eastwards. It could hardly fail to lead to a general exodus of
Hindus from the whole of the Bahawalpur district, if not from
the whole of the State.

I talked the matter over with Gurmani. He was emphatically
opposed to the idea of evacuation and said that only a small
section of the Hindu population wanted to leave. They were
recent comers, not deeply rooted in the State, and were trying
to spread alarm and despondency among the rest. He somewhat pooh-poohed their fears. He said that most of the Hindus
of the town, who were old 'riasatis' long settled in the State,
were feeling quite reasonably secure and had no thoughts of
moving.

All this chimed with my own views.

Except for this uneasiness among some of the Hindus everything appeared absolutely tranquil in the town of Bahawalpur.
Nominally, as District Magistrate of the Bahawalpur district,
I was also responsible for law and order in the town; but since
I had to be away in Bahawalnagar and Gurmani himself and
the Commissioner of Police were present on the spot, I had
tacitly assumed that they, with the help of the ordinary magistrates, would look after things there and only call me in if a
crisis arose and the District Magistrate's presence was required.
Gurmani rightly felt that there ought to be someone in the

town of Bahawalpur with the powers of Additional District Magistrate, but that none of the ordinary magistrates was of sufficient weight and experience to be invested with these powers. He therefore proposed that one of the judges of the High Court, a Muslim named Gilani who belonged to Bahawalpur and was much respected by the Hindu population, should temporarily be made Additional District Magistrate. I hardly knew Gilani and would have preferred to have the Settlement Officer, Nur Mohammad, who, though elderly, was an experienced District Magistrate. But Gurmani wanted to have a local man and so I agreed to the proposal.

A few days later, when I was once more back in Bahawalnagar, Major Short passed through the place on his way to Bahawalpur to see Gurmani with some message from the Government of India. I felt sure that while he was there some of the Hindus would approach him about evacuation. I thought that he ought to be informed in advance of our attitude; so I told him that we did not at present favour evacuation and requested him not to give any encouragement or even countenance to the idea without first discussing the matter with Gurmani. Short said that his instinct was to let the Hindus go if they wanted to. I had considerable respect for his instinct or, as he put it, for what his antennae told him; and his antennae in this instance did not err. But I had to point out that it was not just a question of letting Hindus go, but of positively providing for them to do so; for, since railway travel was now unsafe, none of them could leave unless we furnished escorts. Yet if we began furnishing escorts for Hindus wishing to leave the town of Bahawalpur, it would imply that we did not consider them safe there, and all of them would then wish, or feel compelled, to leave. We were thus in a dilemma.

Short was not wholly convinced by my arguments, but undertook to be wary in any talk he might have with Hindus until he had ascertained Gurmani's views. On his return journey he had a brief conversation with me. I gathered that, as I had expected, some Hindus had approached him, but that, in the light of his talks with Gurmani, he had dissuaded them from thinking of evacuation. On the whole he seemed to be satisfied that, in view of the improving situation throughout the State, the line which we were adopting was correct.

Back again at Bahawalnagar my main concern during the next ten days was the settlement of incoming refugees and the stabilization of the border. Anxiety about fresh communal outbreaks gradually diminished as days passed without further incident. We had one or two narrow shaves in Bahawalnagar itself, when Hindus were being sent off to Hindumalkot, passions having again been aroused by the arrival of wounded refugees from India. But from about the 6th there was a pause in the influx of refugees, and feelings subsided. Some troops of the Bahawalpur Army were, however, guilty at this time of a shocking atrocity. Fourteen Sikhs had been captured near the border and were being held at one of the military posts on the Sadiqia Canal for transference to police custody. It is not clear whether they had actually committed any offence. Most probably they were some of our own Sikh colonists returning just to fetch some more of their property. In any case it was for the police to investigate the offences, if any, of which they had been guilty, and the military had rightly notified the police and asked them to take over their prisoners. The police sent a guard; but it arrived in time to take over only corpses. All fourteen had been shot. I was intensely angry and so was Leghari. I insisted on the military holding an inquiry and some sort of rather perfunctory inquiry was held, but nothing much came of it. There was no desire, much less determination, to probe the matter to the bottom and to punish the guilty. The story was put forward that the Sikhs had attempted to escape and was readily accepted, though it did not account for the facts. The killing of Sikhs had now become a more or less legitimate form of blood sport.

I received about this time a report from Fazlur Rahman and Lt. Babar about the visit which, at my direction, they had paid to Suleimanke. They stated that there were hardly any Pakistan troops there, but large numbers of Dogra troops of the Indian Army were posted quite close to the headworks on the south side of the river. These had clashed with a party of Pakistan police and there had been an exchange of fire. It was probably this incident, or rumours of it, that had frightened the incoming refugees and deflected them into Bahawalpur. In accordance with their suggestions we posted detachments of Bahawalpur troops at strategic points near the southern approaches to the headworks so as to give confidence to the

Muslim refugees, who tended to be overawed by the Dogra troops, and to shepherd them over the bridge into the Punjab.

Fazlur Rahman gave an alarming account of the position at the headworks themselves. Muslim irrigation officers had recently arrived to take over charge, but were without subordinate staff, without communications and in a state of panic and helplessness. These headworks were vital to us, so I decided to go there myself, taking with me one of our superintending engineers—a Muslim officer whose headquarters were at Bahawalnagar.

At Suleimanke we found an executive engineer, an assistant engineer and one clerk, all newly arrived, in charge of the headworks and all their protective works, with no subordinate staff to assist them. The power-house was not working and telegraph and telephone wires had been cut. A platoon of Pakistan troops and a small party of police were stationed there, but they had no transport.

If through any accident or sabotage a breach was made in the protective embankments twelve miles long, it would be difficult, if not impossible, to repair the damage.

I now learnt to my amazement that, while the headworks themselves were in Pakistan, the frontier had been so drawn by Lord Radcliffe that most of the protective embankments on the south side were in Indian territory and were at the moment in the hands of Dogra troops. It seemed extraordinary that there had been no-one to impress upon Lord Radcliffe the importance of including the principal protective works in the same territory as the headworks. This could very easily have been done, as the area involved was uninhabited and, for the most part, uncultivated. I fondly imagined that this absurd error[1] would quickly be rectified. But it never was. We were destined very soon to feel the inconvenience of it.

It was essential to strengthen the hands of the Executive Engineer and we agreed to lend him immediately some of our own technical staff, for which he was very grateful. I also, at his request, sent him two sections of Bahawalpur troops along

---

[1] An exactly similar error was made at Ferozepur, save that there the headworks are in Indian territory and some of the protective embankments in Pakistan. Presumably Lord Radcliffe was never apprised of the relevant facts.

with a truck to assist in the protection of the headworks and to
ensure the safe passage over the river of Muslim refugees.[1]
These measures were useful at the time, but in the end proved
inadequate.

By September 8th the general situation in the State had
vastly improved and I reported to Gurmani as follows:

'No particular incident has been reported and, provided
there are no alarms caused by marauding Sikhs from the
Bikanir border, this area should now settle down once again
after the recent disturbances. Minchinabad town has already
resumed a more or less normal appearance and there are
signs of some return of normal life at Hasilpur, Chishtian and
Bahawalnagar.

'There has been no large fresh influx of refugees, but a considerable number are shuttling aimlessly to and fro by train
from Macleodganj to Samasatta. . . .

'A meeting has been arranged for the 11th of September at
Karanpur (Bikanir State) between officers of this State and of
Bikanir to discuss repatriation of refugees and measures for
preservation of peace along the border.'

Repatriation of refugees! It is strange to recall that at this
time we were actually thinking in these terms. At Karanpur,
after the official meeting, I met large numbers of Bahawalpur
refugees who had collected there. While I made it clear to them
that I saw no prospect of taking back any Sikhs, I expressed the
hope that, if all went well, the Hindus would be able to return
in one or two weeks' time. I genuinely thought so. I would not
have been so optimistic if I had known fully what was going on
elsewhere; for in the Punjab the disaster was still deepening
and this was bound to affect us. But I could view only the Bahawalpur scene, and in Bahawalpur we seemed to be surmount-
ing our troubles. I foresaw, of course, difficulties in reintro-
ducing the Hindus when we had already taken in a good many
Muslim refugees. But the number of refugees settled in the
urban areas, to which the Hindus would mostly return, was as
yet comparatively small. I thought it would be possible, with
some temporary adjustments, to accommodate both them and

[1] The Bahawalpur troops were withdrawn about September 13th by
which date the Pakistan troops at the headworks had been considerably
reinforced.

the returning Hindus, while the Muslim cultivators settled in the lands vacated by the Sikhs could remain quite undisturbed. Within a week, these ideas had undergone a revolution.

The lull in the disturbances and in the arrival of refugees had enabled us to make good progress with the investigation of cases and the sorting out of offenders. The sub-jail at Bahawal-nagar had become so overcrowded with prisoners awaiting trial that I had to have a jail delivery—releasing most of those who had been confined there before the disturbances began. Not finding at first any suitable magistrate to invest with summary powers, I myself tried summarily during the first week of September more than a hundred persons, produced before me by the thanedar, Bahawalnagar, from whom looted property had been recovered. Most of them confessed and I fined them Rs 10–20; but a few were fined more heavily and, so as not to make things too easy, I sent about half a dozen to jail for a month. The method of selecting the latter was somewhat arbi-trary and would not have satisfied a High Court Judge! I was reminded of an incident recorded in the Hunter Commission's Report on the Punjab disturbances of 1919. The boys of some schools in the town of Kasur had taken part in the disorders and, at the suggestion of an English magistrate, the military officer who was administering martial law in the area had caused six of them to be flogged. Some members of the Com-mission were at pains to ascertain how the six boys subjected to flogging had been selected and the following passage occurs:

Q. Some schoolboys were flogged and you gave directions that the biggest six boys were to be selected for that purpose?
A. I said, generally speaking, take the six biggest.
Q. Do you think that a reasonable thing to do?
A. Yes, I think so, under certain conditions.
Q. It was a mere accident that a boy being big should invite on himself punishment.
A. It was his misfortune.
Q. His misfortune was that he was big?
A. Yes.

The conduct of the authorities, as revealed in this passage, had always struck me as a bit odd until in not dissimilar circumstances I found myself doing somewhat the same thing! The persons whom I sent to jail were selected on the strength of their appearance, demeanour and the advice of the thanedar.

Sometime on September 13th I received at Bahawalnagar a wire from Gurmani saying that some prisoners had attempted to break out of the jail at Bahawalpur and that they had not yet been brought under control. I deliberated whether I should straightaway go there. It looked a bit ugly that an attempted break-out of the jail had not been suppressed as soon as detected. But Gurmani had not asked me to come, he had got with him the Commissioner of Police, Gilani and various other officers, I was myself still fully occupied in the Bahawalnagar area and for me to run up to Bahawalpur, unasked, on the strength of an inconclusive report might seem rather meddlesome. I decided to wait. The next day there came a reassuring telegram—the disturbance in the jail had been quelled. On the 15th Leghari and I went first thing in the morning to Harunabad where cholera was reported to have broken out among the refugees. The Muslims of this place were, as usual, very fidgety about imaginary dangers from across the border. We were standing in the roadway about 11.0 a.m. talking to some of them about the precautions we had taken when someone remarked that there had now been trouble in Bahawalpur. I said that there had only been some disturbance in the jail and that this had been suppressed. But I was told that my information was out of date; there had been a recrudescence of the trouble and bloodshed in Bahawalpur; telegrams to this effect had reached Harunabad less than an hour earlier. Leghari sent for the thanedar who made inquiries at the post office and the canal office[1] and presently confirmed that such telegrams had been received and appeared to be authentic.

We at once got into the car and drove back to Bahawalnagar. Dropping Leghari there and picking up my personal assistant, I drove on to Bahawalpur, cursing myself for not having gone there on the 13th. Five minutes after I had left a wire was received from Gurmani asking me to come immediately.

---

[1] The Irrigation Department had a separate telegraphic system of their own.

Disturbances in Bahawalpur City

THERE was an ominous hush over Bahawalpur when I reached it that evening—a hush that I had now learnt to associate with towns in which disturbances had taken place. I did not have to go through the city or close up to its walls in order to get to my house, but even from a distance I missed the faint hum and stir of its normal life and knew that it was dead.

I rang up Gurmani and in the course of conversation learnt that he had wired for me to come and so was expecting me. He asked me to come round to his house as soon as possible, and said he would call some of the senior officers for a meeting. As I was walking over, I met in the road one of the assistant secretaries. I did not know him well as he worked mainly for Gurmani. He had always struck me as a rather bigoted Muslim. I nodded a greeting, whereupon, to my surprise, he burst out with apparently genuine pleasure.

'Thank God, you've come, sir! We've all been waiting for you.'

'Waiting for me?' I queried. 'Why have you been waiting for me? I'm afraid I shan't be able to do anything. I've only this moment arrived and know nothing about the situation.'

'The Prime Minister will tell you the whole position. You'll be able to suggest something, I know. I've been saying it all along.'

I was a bit puzzled. The time was hardly opportune for conventional flattery, but if his words were more than this, then I was apparently expected to retrieve the situation. I had no clear idea what it was, still less how to deal with it.

I walked on to the Prime Minister's house and had a few minutes with him alone before the arrival of the officers whom he had summoned. He greeted me with his usual geniality, but at once began inveighing against the police and military who, he said, had completely let us down. The former, after mustering all their forces, had proved unequal to dealing with a small outbreak in the jail. Disturbances had spread to the city. He had called in the Bahawalpur Army. They had made more noise than the police, but had done no better. There had been indiscriminate firing and widespread looting. Both the mob and the military were out of control. A number of Hindus had been killed—he could not say how many—and it had become very difficult to protect them.

I was far from pleased to learn that the military had been called in. If the police were ineffective, they were at least submissive. The military were armed and in a dangerous mood. It was Bahawalnagar over again. Having regard to our experience there, it was, in my view, a mistake to have turned to the military at all for help in maintaining order in the city. If more armed force was deemed essential, then at most a platoon should have been called in. They could have been kept under strict observation and control and would have been ample to check the Bahawalpur mob, if they were prepared to use their arms effectively. If they were not, then a larger force would be no better, but rather worse. As it was, a whole battalion had been brought to the city.

I think I expressed to Gurmani some misgiving at the military having been called in, but he replied that the police had been utterly useless, so what else could he do? There was no point in pursuing the matter since I was myself to blame for not having come to Bahawalpur as soon as I heard that there was trouble there. Normally it would have been the duty of the District Magistrate to do so.

With the Bahawalpur soldiery already dominating the scene, I felt that the best course might be to try to extricate all the Hindus from the city straight away and send them off by rail to India, as some of them had requested us to do a fortnight earlier. (How foolish we had been not to accede to their request!) I threw out this suggestion to Gurmani who seemed not unfavourable to it, but we had no time to discuss it, as by now the officers who had been summoned had assembled and were ushered into the room.

There were among them several military officers—including, I think, Brigadier Marden—Gilani (the High Court Judge who was acting as Additional District Magistrate), my whisky-drinking friend of the I.N.A. and another man in civilian clothes whom I had never met before. He turned out to be Gilani of I.N.A. fame, a younger brother of the Judge. I was at a loss to know in what capacity he was present as he had been kicked out of the Bahawalpur Army and had now no official position in the State. He was a smooth, slick and obviously able man and took quite a prominent part in the subsequent discussion. He spoke sensibly and to the point, but in view of his past history his presence at this juncture at our deliberations was, to me, not very welcome and seemed even rather sinister. However, Gurmani had apparently thought that, owing to his reputed influence with the troops, it would be as well to keep him under his thumb and that he might be genuinely useful as a sort of liaison officer. He himself was said to be anxious to earn Gurmani's good opinion so as to facilitate his reinstatement in the Bahawalpur Army.

The Commissioner of Police was conspicuous by his absence. He made some excuse, but, as I subsequently learnt, he was thoroughly disgruntled. He complained to me later that the military had been called in and the police entirely superseded without any reference to him. If he had been consulted, he told me, he would never have advised such a course. The police were holding the situation at the time and there was every hope of their getting the better of it; but the intervention of the military had aggravated it and made it quite unmanageable. Since he had been unceremoniously thrust aside, he considered that his advice was no longer wanted and washed his hands of the whole affair. Gurmani was annoyed at his absence and I very much missed him, for he was the only really experienced police officer we had.

After some brief talk on the general situation, Gurmani mentioned my suggestion that the entire Hindu population should be immediately removed from the city and then evacuated to India. The suggestion seemed to commend itself to everyone present. But I had put it forward without any deep consideration and was not yet sure whether it was practicable. The whole Hindu population of the city could not be moved to India in one day. They had to be collected together in one or two places which could be easily guarded, and then sent off to

[1] See pages 104–5.

India in batches. What place could serve as a temporary
'keep'? In the city itself there were several Hindu shrines to
which were attached extensive outbuildings and courts, acces-
sible only through one main entrance gate. These could accommodate several hundreds but not the fourteen to fifteen thousand at which the Hindu population was estimated. Various
alternatives were suggested, but it was quickly apparent that
only the new jail, at that time still under construction, would
serve the purpose. This was situated rather more than a mile
from the city and was reached by a rough track, in places deep
in sand. Only the outer wall had been completed. This enclosed
an extensive open space in which barracks, workshops and other
buildings would in due course be erected, but so far only a few
small sheds had been put up. Within the protection of this wall
the whole Hindu population could remain for a few days in
perfect safety and considerable, but not insupportable, dis-
comfort. It was still warm enough at night to sleep outdoors, so
from this point of view the absence of buildings did not matter.
The most unpleasant feature would be the fierce heat of the
sun by day, as there was scarcely any shade. But this would not
kill them. The area being extensive, sanitation presented no
great problem; some primitive latrines could easily be put up
for the more fastidious. But was there any water? Nobody was
sure whether the water supply had yet been installed: so someone was sent to ring up the Public Works Department and find
out. After some delay we received an affirmative answer.

I still had considerable apprehensions about the whole
operation. Not knowing the temper of the city mob and of the
Bahawalpur troops, I could not gauge the danger of the
Hindus being attacked as they moved out of their houses in the
city and made their way to the new jail. The I.N.A. Gilani
assured me that the danger of this was negligible, and I saw
myself the next day that my fears had been exaggerated. The
Muslims were out for loot, not for blood. They were not inclined to kill, unless wantonly provoked or baulked of their
plunder. But on that first evening of my arrival in Bahawalpur
I had not been able to size this all up properly.

Since the new jail was more than a mile distant from the
city, many of the Hindus—the old and infirm, women and
children—would have to be transported there by lorry. We

G

could only rake together about ten lorries, including military
vehicles, and some of them were doubtful starters; but we
reckoned that, if we started promptly at about 9.00 a.m. we
should just be able to complete the job by nightfall.

The Hindus would all have to be prepared for the move,
especially if it was to start the very next morning. It was necessary to inform some of their leaders straight away of what was
intended, so that word could be passed to all Hindu families
that night that they would be expected to leave the city the
next day. I was also anxious to get the reaction of Hindu representatives to our plan for their evacuation. Gurmani sent for
the Hindu Minister, Dewan Fateh Chand, a tall, thin, grey-
haired man whom I had always found a very pleasant colleague. He came in presently, very pale and nervous and with
a haunting look of anxiety on his face. We put before him our
plan and he seemed on the whole to approve of it. I specially
questioned him whether, as it was already late, it would be
possible to get the Hindus ready for a move—which would in
fact be a final departure from their hearths and homes—by the
next morning. He was hesitant about this and said that he
would like to consult other members of his community. Somehow or other he then contacted several leading Hindus. Most
of them were whole-heartedly in favour of the evacuation plan
and considered it feasible. It was decided to proceed with it.

I think this decision was right and it was fortunate that we
took it; but I myself certainly reached it on quite wrong premises. I was under the impression that the lives of the Hindus
were in far more imminent danger than I found the next day to
be the case. The city mob and the Bahawalpur Army were, as
already stated, out for loot rather than blood. The removal of
the Hindus from the city was, therefore, exactly what they
wanted. It opened the field for loot and did away with resistance
and obstruction. They had no special desire to wade through
blood to get their plunder. They were conveniently relieved of
this necessity. I had come to suspect this during the course
of this first evening and I became convinced of it in the
next two days. With fuller knowledge of all this (which
fortunately at the critical moment I did not possess) I would
probably not have advocated the drastic remedy of immediate
and wholesale evacuation, but would have been tempted to

try to restore order with the Hindus still in their houses. Such
a course would have been at best futile, at worst fatal. It could
have had no chance of success unless the Bahawalpur soldiery
were first removed; and that was impossible. The disturbed
state of the city afforded a plausible argument against any proposal for their immediate withdrawal, and in any case they had
no intention of releasing their hold until they had secured and
divided the spoils. The other battalion had sacked Bahawalnagar; Bahawalpur was their prize. Since the army wanted to
share the loot rather than stop the looting, an attempt by an
unarmed civil officer like myself to control the situation while
they were present was doomed to failure. Either his orders
would be unheeded, or, if he managed to cajole or dragoon a
small party of them to take effective action against Muslim
looters or himself seized a rifle and shot a few, then this, in
the temper of the times, would have been the signal (as at
Hasilpur) for a general massacre of Hindus in which he too
would probably have succumbed.

Hindsight, therefore, confirms the somewhat panicky decision that we took, though not the grounds on which I, at least,
at the time supported it.

The arrangements made or envisaged for the reception of the
Hindus the next day at the new jail were of the sketchiest.
There was nothing much that could be done that night, except
to make sure that the water supply was working. This was done.
I was hopefully counting on procuring grain from the mandi
in the town and left this over till the morning. But it was
essential to select at once someone to act as camp commandant
and remain continuously at the jail after the arrival of the Hindus to keep order and see to their needs. No-one could be more
fully relied upon to do this with efficiency and to the greatest
comfort and contentment of the Hindus than the Settlement
Officer, Nur Mohammad. But would he be willing to undertake
such a thankless task?

Nur Mohammad was a retired officer of the Punjab Civil
Service and a wonderful product of the Indo-British association.
He combined the best of both the East and the West—a type
all too little known to the outside world. To the charm, the
exquisite courtesy and the piety of a cultured Muslim gentleman were joined the regular, methodical habits of business and

the sense of duty and responsibility derived from British training. Added to these were a first-rate intellect, a delightful sense of humour and a natural benevolence—a combination of qualities which made him one of the best and best beloved officers of his day. Before retirement he had been a Deputy Commissioner in the Punjab for a considerable time. Twelve years earlier, when I was in Multan, he was in charge of an adjoining district. I had known him ever since then.

'All Deputy Commissioners,' he used to say, 'have some weakness. With some it is money, with others women, with others love of power. My own weakness,' he would continue with a chuckle, 'which I share with Mr. —— (naming a well-known English I.C.S. officer) is simply love of popularity. An amiable weakness, if you will, but a weakness none the less. It makes you too soft; you can't say "No" to anyone.'

I felt that this amiable weakness and a touch of softness would not come amiss in handling a mass of helpless, frightened, friendless Hindus, rudely thrust out of their homes into the rigours of a jail camp. He would pour balm and oil into their wounds, whereas the general disposition was, in his own words, to rub salt into them.

I requested him to take on the job. It was a good deal to ask of an elderly Muslim nearing sixty. It would involve a day-and-night vigil at the jail, roughing it in the open like the Hindus themselves, and the strain of bearing patiently the ceaseless outpouring of their woes. I could see at once that he was dismayed by my request and most reluctant to shoulder the responsibility. But his sense of duty prevailed and, to my great relief, he consented to do it.

He at once began questioning me about all our projected arrangements and clearly felt doubtful whether the operation was practicable. He was particularly concerned as to how we could safely dispatch them to India by rail in view of the fearful train massacres that were occurring almost daily in the Punjab. His fear was that, having moved them to the jail, we might then find it impossible to send them on by rail and would have them on our hands indefinitely in conditions which would lead to the death of many of them through disease, undernourishment and exposure. I told him that I had already safely dispatched large numbers of Hindus from Bahawalnagar and

Hasilpur to Hindumalkot and hoped to get them out from Bahawalpur along the same route. I reckoned that we should be able to send them all off in four to five days and that scratch arrangements for maintaining them in the jail would suffice for this short period. We had already verified that there was water installed there and I would requisition grain from the mandi. He said that the mandi had been looted and that he thought I would find nothing there. This was not encouraging, but I had plenty of stocks elsewhere and could, if necessary, bring them into Bahawalpur. There would be some delay, but a day's fast would not kill the Hindus.

He was not altogether satisfied with this for, as he pointed out, it would be very disgraceful to herd all the Hindus out of the city and into the jail and then for some time have nothing to give them to eat. He also drew attention to the absence of shade in the new jail and, during the next couple of days, complained about it repeatedly. There was no remedy for this and, having been continuously out in the sun for most of the past three weeks, I was perhaps not very sympathetic. I told him that the Hindus would get used to it and that, if necessary, they could get into the shade of the walls. The walls were burning hot and in the middle of the day cast no shade at all; so the latter suggestion was not very helpful. The former was more correct and the only real answer.

It was by now getting late. I ordered my bed to be made up just outside the main city gate so that I could be immediately available in case there was an uproar during the night. Marden also came and established himself there. The night was absolutely peaceful except for occasional stray rifle shots. I remarked to Marden on this casual unauthorized firing—a manifest symptom of indiscipline—but knew that in the circumstances it was not really possible for him to control his troops.

The evacuation of the Hindus from the city started the next morning, but by no means as early as we had intended. The lorries were late and the Hindus still later and it was not till about 11.0 a.m. that we got them moving out towards the jail in earnest. Until the lorries had blazed the trail, none of them would proceed to the jail on foot, but hung about just inside the main city gate at the bottom of the principal bazaar. Once, however, the lorries started plying there was soon a regular stream of pedestrians flowing out from the city gate to the new jail.

The city was in rather less disorder than I had been led to expect. Most of the Hindu shops in the main bazaar, running up from the city gate, and in the other principal bazaar which crossed it, had been wholly or partially looted, and there was the usual litter scattered about; but no sign of arson or wanton destruction of buildings. Farther on, the mandi had been thoroughly ransacked, as Nur Mohammed had warned me, and not much of value was left in it. There were some corpses lying about in the side streets and alleys, but in the main bazaars they had all been cleared away. Parties of Bahawalpur troops were stationed at cross roads and other focal points and a few were negligently patrolling the bazaars. Otherwise up till about 10.30 a.m. the streets were practically empty.

While waiting for the evacuation to begin, I did what I could to salvage some grain from the mandi and get it ground up and sent to the jail. There was a retired naib-tahsildar, a very honest, god-fearing but crusty old man, who, before the disturbances began, had been working under me in the Civil Supplies department. As soon as I could find him, I put him with some clerks in charge of the plundered mandi. He collected and guarded every grain like a dragon, scaring away would-be pilferers with flashing eyes, a fierce white beard and furious threatenings. But all that he could lay hands on fell far short of our needs.

Timidly and tardily the Hindus crept out of their houses and began gathering in the principal bazaars to board the lorries. There were no evident signs of danger and, as the day wore on, the bazaars became crowded with them waiting with bundles, suitcases and small trunks for places in the lorries, or making their way on foot towards the city gate. The evacuation was carried out fairly systematically, ward by ward. As soon as a ward was cleared, the looters quickly moved in and began ransacking the empty buildings. I surprised two sepoys in a deserted shop bending over some sacks and rummaging through their contents. They were so engrossed that they did not see or hear me approaching from behind until I gave one of them a hard kick up the bottom; whereupon they both snatched up their rifles and ran off clattering down the street.

But to stop this looting effectively was wholly impracticable, particularly as the officers of the Bahawalpur Army were conniving at it. A good many of them were to be seen lounging about a building just off one of the main bazaars which had been made a kind of advanced headquarters. Passing nearby this place in the middle of the afternoon, I saw a number of tin boxes and trunks strewn about the roadway. I asked a couple of military officers who were lolling at the door of their headquarters to get some of their men to clear these from the road and stack them all together on one side. (They were the property of Hindus and I intended later to have them carted to the jail so that they could be claimed by their owners.) The officers coolly replied that they could not do this without the orders of their C.O.! I did not stop to pick up a quarrel, but simply ignored their insolence. A little later I collected two or three of my own men to do the job but by that time the boxes had all disappeared. The Bahawalpur Army had carried off their booty.

The movables which the Hindus left behind, because they could not carry them away, were perhaps legitimate spoils. Anyway one could hardly blame the ordinary Muslim for picking up what was his for the taking, whatever one might think about the propriety of officers claiming a share. But naturally, once this game had begun, almost everyone from the highest to the lowest desired to take part in it. A certain number obtained a kind of title to their gains. Outgoing Hindus entrusted their property, sometimes by written deed, to Muslim friends and acquaintances. These documents usually had no legal validity and were not recognized in respect of immovable property; but they afforded good practical cover to claims to movables. Some valuable furniture and carpets changed hands in this way.

By and large the contents of houses had to be left to their own fate. More important was to prevent the Hindus being relieved of such hand luggage as they were trying to carry away with them and as soon as I saw that their lives were not in imminent danger I devoted myself mainly to this. Military pickets and military escorts travelling on the lorries, not to mention casual Muslims in the streets, all tried to take their toll. I shuttled to and fro in my car between the city and the jail, endeavouring to check these exactions, and Nur Mohammed at the jail end imposed some restraint. But they went on. A small incident will serve as an illustration. On one of my visits to the jail in the late afternoon, a young lad of sixteen to seventeen complained to me that as he passed the military picket at the main city gate they had snatched away his suitcase. I told him to get into my car and took him with me back to the city gate. There was about a section of troops posted there under a jamadar. As soon as we alighted from the car, the young man espied his suitcase in a room leading off from one side of the gate.

'There it is,' he said and pointed it out to me lying on the floor amid some of the soldiers' kit-bags. I pushed my way into the room, picked up the suitcase and brought it out. The jamadar now appeared on the scene. I did not deem it politic to be angry with him or reprimand him, so I simply said in Hindustani,

'Jamadar sahib, this suitcase seems to have got in here by mistake.'

The jamadar saluted—a gesture which most of the Bahawalpur troops had by this time forgotten—and replied, 'No doubt it has, sir, for it isn't ours.'

'Very good, then, I'll take it away.' The jamadar saluted again and I got into my car with the suitcase and its owner and drove back to the jail.

On my return to the city, the same jamadar stopped me at the gate. He said that they had captured some Sikhs, about half a dozen I understood, and wanted to know what to do with them. I imagined that he had got them there at the gate and, knowing from experience how unsafe it was to leave Sikhs in the hands of the troops, I said immediately that he could make them over to me and I would see about their further custody. I asked him how and why they had captured them. He replied that the Sikhs had had revolvers and had been firing out of the windows of a building and had been captured with much difficulty. Still thinking that he had got them confined in one of the rooms adjoining the gate, I told him to bring them out. But he then said that he had already sent them away. Once again I was apprehensive until he explained that he had sent them over to his superior officers and pointed to a big school building about two hundred and fifty yards away which had been made the battalion headquarters. I was much relieved. I told him that that was quite all right and I would see about them later.

I hurried on into the city. It was getting late and if we were to evacuate all the Hindus by nightfall, we should have to hustle. There were now crowds of them waiting in the main bazaar and it did not seem possible to move them all in the short remaining period of daylight. The I.N.A. Gilani met me in the street and said that, as it was now impossible to get them all out that day, those belonging to a certain area should be allowed to take refuge in the precincts of the biggest of the Hindu shrines. I immediately agreed. A well-known Gosain presided over the shrine, a big fat fellow who used to be present on all ceremonial occasions to do a kind of public obeisance to the Nawab on behalf of the Hindu community. He was very anxious not to have to go to the jail camp, and assured me that there were ample stocks of food at the shrine—which proved to be the case.

It was about now that I heard a report that Marden had been wounded. It was said that earlier in the day he had been fired at from a building somewhere in the city and hit in the knee. No-one seemed to have any exact information about the incident.

Dusk drew on and the last lorries to ply that day moved down to the city gate. Quite a number of Hindus who had not been able to get places in them were still standing in the bazaar, laden with luggage. They asked me whether they should go back to their homes. I advised them to do so, as I thought it would be dangerous for them to try to walk to the jail in the gathering darkness, and I told them that we would transport them there the next day. Some women in the group said that their houses were some way off and that they did not feel equal to returning to them with all their luggage. They pointed to an entrance nearby, leading to a shrine with a lot of rambling buildings attached, and asked whether they should go in there. It seemed safe enough, as there was only one narrow entrance, so I told them they might do so.

I now repaired to Gurmani's house to report progress and to find out what had happened to Marden. It turned out that he really had been wounded in the knee. Gurmani was trying to

G*

get a skilled surgeon from Multan to come and extract the
bullet. Marden was hopping about on one leg, remarkably
cheerful, though probably in considerable pain. I never ascertained the exact circumstances in which he received this wound.
He simply told me at the time that he had been fired at from
a building—I presumed by one of the Sikhs whose capture had
been reported to me by the jamadar. The Hindus believed,
and believe to this day, that he was shot at by one of his own
men, but I don't think this was the case. He bore his wound
with fortitude, but was out of action for some time. This episode
led to a rumour in East Punjab that both Gurmani and I had
been killed.

I had all along been anxious to get the military withdrawn from the city as soon as possible. While, therefore,
a number of us were gathered at Gurmani's house and were
discussing arrangements for the next day, I tactfully suggested
that the troops were tired after two or three days' continuous
duty in the city and deserved to be brought out and given a
rest. I was pleasantly surprised to find this suggestion accepted
immediately by everyone present, including the I.N.A. Gilani.
It was agreed that the troops should be withdrawn the following afternoon, after evacuating the few remaining Hindus
during the morning.

This was more than I had dared to hope for, and the decision was later somewhat modified. The battalion commander
represented to Gurmani that he could not conveniently withdraw his troops so soon and they were eventually permitted to
remain in the city, with the Hindu property at their mercy,
for an extra twenty-four hours.

Nearly all of us who assembled at Gurmani's house that
evening believed that, apart from Marden's wound, the evacuation of the Hindus from the city had been successfully
accomplished without bloodshed. We informed Gurmani
accordingly. Unknown to most of us, a shocking crime was
being perpetrated at that very moment. There was a prominent
citizen of Bahawalpur, named Mehta Nand Kishore, who was
reputed to be very wealthy and had made himself conspicuous,
and perhaps obnoxious, by his staunch championship of Hindu
rights. On learning that the Hindus were to be evacuated from
the city, he had somehow contrived to arrange with the military

for a special lorry to transport him and his considerable bag-
gage to the camp jail. Near the close of the day a special lorry
was duly provided and he and his goods were loaded into it and
driven off at nightfall with an escort towards the new jail. But
they never reached it. After going a short distance the lorry
turned aside and went down to the river. There he was murdered, his body consigned to the waters of the Sutlej, and his
goods divided among his supposed protectors.

The weight of this and of another as yet unknown tragedy
did not oppress me that evening. My thoughts were all of the
future and of the problems of transporting the Hindus safely
from the jail camp to the railway station and thence by train
to Hindumalkot.

The principal railway station of Bahawalpur was on the
main line from Karachi to Lahore, a little less than a mile from
the city. But the shortest route to India, and the only one which
we could use, was the branch line from Samasatta to Hindumalkot and on to Bhatinda. This line passed south of Bahawalpur and there was a small station on it called Baghdad-ul-jadid
about three miles from the city. This was the station at which
the Hindus would have to entrain. But how were we to get
them there? The one train in the day, which we had arranged
should run as a 'refugee special', passed through at 9.20 a.m.
With our exiguous supply of lorries, which, owing to break-
downs, was diminishing rather than increasing, we should not
be able to move appreciable numbers to the station by that
early hour.

Then there was the question of an escort. One train had
already been attacked on this line and Hindus butchered. We
should have to send an escort of troops to repel possible attacks.
But would the Bahawalpur troops be reliable? Or would they
precipitate a massacre?

The feeding of the refugees in the jail camp had also not been
ensured. Nur Mohammad had told me during the afternoon
that he wanted to discuss with me this and other matters connected with the camp; but at that time, amid all the hubbub
of the Hindus streaming in, it was impossible to talk without
interruption. So I agreed to come and see him after dinner, by
which time he hoped the refugees would have settled down for
the night. I got down to the camp about 10.0 p.m. The supply

of more grain was urgent. Nur Mohammad, knowing that I had already gleaned all there was to be had from the mandi, had obtained from leading Hindus a list of temples and other buildings in their wards where sizeable stocks of flour, grain and fuel wood were known or believed to exist. These, if we could lay hands on them before looters seized them, would keep us going for some time. I took the list from him.

Only three or four well-educated Hindus were with him at this hour; the rest had all gone to get what sleep they could. They spoke to me most earnestly about the perils of travelling by rail to India. One and all, they said, wanted to leave the camp and go there, but they had read and heard of terrible train massacres in the Punjab and they did not know how to face the fearful risks of the journey. I told them that they would not have to travel across the Punjab, we would send them out along the branch line running through the State and so could ourselves be responsible for their protection all the way. This seemed to reassure them to some extent, for it was of the Punjab that they were mainly frightened. I also told them that there would be a military escort with every train. They immediately requested that the escorts might be of Gurkha troops. There were a few platoons of Gurkhas in the Bahawalpur Army and we had drawn upon these to provide guards at the jail camp, much to the relief and satisfaction of the Hindus. But I was doubtful whether we could also find Gurkha escorts for the trains. I said that I could not promise this and that in any case a Gurkha escort could not be arranged for the train that was to leave the next morning. I would see what could be done about it in the case of future trains.

I impressed upon them that as we were very short of lorries they must be ready for an early and punctual start the next morning and also see that the lorries were filled expeditiously so that they could make as many trips as possible to the station before the train left. It was agreed to start at 7.00 a.m. Nur Mohammad suggested that tongas should also be utilized for taking the Hindus to the station. I was unnecessarily nervous and did not agree to this. I was afraid that in the explosive atmosphere altercations between the Muslim tonga drivers and their Hindu passengers might lead to outbreaks of violence. In any case I felt that it was too late at that hour of the night to start calling up tongas for the next morning. However, in the course of the next day, I was persuaded by Nur Mohammad that it would be safe to use tongas; and for speeding up the evacuation there was really no other course. He was quite right. The tonga drivers were delighted at the opportunity of doing a roaring trade. The more Hindus they could carry to the station, the better. They had no wish to cause any fracas which might interrupt this profitable traffic.

I left the camp quite late, probably about 11.30 p.m., and went with a chaprassi to the city with the list which Nur Mohammad had given me, in search of the tahsildar. I had been trying to find him all day, but without success. So far as I recollect he was reported to be out on tour, but to be due back that afternoon. To reach his house I had to go through various winding lanes and alleys which were all too plentifully sprinkled with corpses. I did not like stumbling upon them in the dark. When we got there we had great difficulty in rousing him, but at last, after sundry knockings and hallooings, which reverberated in the silence of the night, an answering shout of 'Kaun hai'[1] came from the inmost recesses of the house. We proclaimed our identity, but this did not penetrate to or did not convince the tahsildar. After a long interval he gingerly opened the door and emerged in the darkness covering himself with a double-barrelled gun. He lowered the gun and looked very foolish as soon as he realized who it was. He was profuse in apologies. I thought it very ridiculous for the tahsildar, a Muslim, to show such alarm and take such excessive precautions on being knocked up in the night, and so I was rather severe with him. I asked him what on earth he was afraid of? Did he imagine the city was full of Sikhs? My chaprassi also impertinently interjected some sarcasms and had to be reprimanded. The tahsildar said he had thought we might be robbers. He could not believe that the Revenue Minister would be coming to see him at such a late hour. I told him that he should not carry arms and that it was absurd for Muslims to behave as though they were in danger. He promised not to do it again! Actually he was a very good tahsildar and I liked him. I said I was sorry for disturbing him in the middle of the night, but there was urgent work for him to do in the morning. Handing over to him Nur Moham-

[1] 'Who's there?'

mad's list I directed him to collect the supplies from the places indicated therein and have them sent immediately to the new jail. I told him that this must take precedence over all his other duties and that his primary responsibility during the next few days would be to keep the jail camp supplied with food, fuel and other necessities. He could procure them from wherever he could find them in and around the city. If he foresaw any difficulties, he was to let me know.

A fair proportion of the places shown in Nur Mohammad's list yielded supplies more or less intact. Though there was some delay, owing to lack of transport, in getting them to the jail, they tided us over our immediate difficulties and somehow or other we kept going till the evacuation was over. Later, however, we had to bring in considerable supplies of grain from elsewhere to restock the city.

Since the evacuation of the Hindus from the city was not quite complete, I had decided once again to establish myself for the night just outside the city gate. After leaving the tah-sildar, I made my way there and sat down on my bed. It was a little after midnight. The city was quite still; there were no rifle shots as during the previous night, but from all directions there came the sound of 'tap, tap, tap; tap, tap, tap' as looters hammered away at safes left behind in the deserted houses of the Hindus. Somehow or other I fell in with the I.N.A. officer with whom I had made friends at Bahawalnagar. He had been helping with the evacuation all day and had either settled him-self for the night, like me, just outside the city gate or had strolled over there from the battalion headquarters about two hundred yards away. We sat chatting for some time and then decided, before turning in for the night, to make a round of the city.

We went up the main bazaar and then followed the sound of hammering, first in one direction and then in another; but as soon as we approached, the hammering stopped and the looters eluded us in the darkness. While we were wandering about in this way, a man came running up to us from behind and said that there were some fresh corpses lying in the main bazaar. We were amazed. We had passed up the main bazaar only about fifteen minutes earlier. There had been no corpses there then and since then we had not heard any sound from that direction. We hurried back. There were one or two street lamps in the main bazaar. In the dim light shed by one of these we saw some forms lying in the middle of the roadway. When we got up to them, we found that they were the bodies, still quite warm, of two women and three children. I was stooping down to examine one of the women more closely, when my companion a few yards away exclaimed, 'This one is breathing!' I felt the pulse of the woman near me; it was beating quite strongly. 'This one is also alive,' I said. Just at that moment one of the children, aged about four, sat up and began to talk.

We now guessed that these women must have tried to commit suicide by throwing themselves and their children from the roof of one of the adjoining houses—a fall of twenty-five to thirty feet. For some minutes they continued to feign that they were dead or dying and we could not get them to speak. One of them, the elder of the two, appeared to be quite badly hurt. It was she who at last became a little communicative. We gathered from her that during the day the military had come and taken away their husbands and, being left alone and fearing that the worst would befall them, they had in desperation tried to make away with themselves and their children by jumping from the roof of their house. She also told us that there were some more children, though not hers, inside the house.

This woman was too much injured to rise from the ground. We propped her up and she remained lying there until we could get a lorry to take her to the hospital. The other rather younger woman had only superficial injuries. The smallest of the three children was dead; the second was injured; and the third, who had first sat up and begun to talk, was practically unscathed. We sent a man to fetch a military lorry and another to the hospital to warn them in advance that these patients would be coming. Meanwhile we ourselves went to explore the inside of the house.

We had to go up a narrow passage-way leading from the main street, and then enter the house from the side. In a central room a charming but unexpected sight met our eyes. Laid out on the floor, side by side in rows, each with its own small pillow, were sixteen little children, all fast asleep, sleeping, in truth, the sleep of innocence. Their untroubled slumbers were in strange contrast to the chaos in the city outside and to the agonized despair

of the two women. It was an unforgettable scene. We put out
the light and tiptoed from the room. My companion kindly
undertook to collect these children in the morning and convey
them to the hospital or the jail camp, as might seem best.

A lorry arrived quite soon. We lifted into it the women and
children who had been lying in the road and my companion
went off with them to the hospital. He said that he would make
inquiries at the battalion headquarters about their menfolk.
It was pretty clear that these women and children—some more
women were found in the house later on—were the families
of the captured Sikhs about whom the jamadar had spoken to
me in the afternoon. My companion had, I think, also heard
something about them. The next morning he told me that he
had not so far been able to get any trace of them. Fearing the
worst, I went and spoke to Gurmani. I explained to him that
these Sikhs were said to have been sent over to the battalion
headquarters in the school building. I asked him to tell the
battalion commander to report where they were. The battalion commander, when questioned, denied all knowledge of
them, and the inquiries made by him yielded nothing, or
nothing that was ever conveyed to me or to the outside world.
These Sikhs, about eight in number, just vanished. My I.N.A.
friend quite early on confided to me, with an indignation which,
I believe, was genuine, his suspicion that they had all been
killed. In a day or two, when no clue to them was forthcoming,
this suspicion became a certainty. Where and how they were
made away with was never ascertained, but it seems probable
that by the time the two women threw themselves from their
housetop they were already dead, having been killed and
thrown into the river earlier that night. One of them, Amar
Singh, was cashier of the local branch of the Imperial Bank of
India and had the keys of the strong room containing all the
cash not only of the bank but of the State Treasury. The keys
vanished with him. For days we could not open the strong room
or replenish our stocks of cash, till finally someone came from
Lahore with a duplicate set of keys.

No-one was punished, no-one individually was even blamed,
for this dark deed. The Bahawalpur Army hid the matter in its
own unwritten archives. But I could not rid myself of the sense
of my own responsibility for the tragedy. Knowing as I did the

feeling against the Sikhs and the army's attitude to them it was idiotic to allow my first apprehensions to be lulled to rest because the jamadar told me that the prisoners had been sent to battalion headquarters. Even there they could not be assumed to be safe. In the light of incidents that had occurred in the Bahawalnagar area, I ought to have abandoned all else and gone in search of them as soon as the jamadar spoke to me about them. I have often thought since that in mentioning them to me at all the jamadar was trying to convey to me that I ought to look to their safety. In the few minutes' conversation I had with him, he struck me as a decent sort of man. He must have known that the Sikhs were in imminent danger and, having seen that I was endeavouring to help the refugees, must have realized that I could be the means of saving them. To give an indirect hint by just referring to them would have been typical of his class. But if he meant to give the hint, I was too dull to take it.

The painful task of breaking the truth to the women devolved on me. For several days, in answer to their repeated inquiries, we said that we were still looking for their husbands. But before they left for India—and, owing to the injuries to one of them, they were among the last to leave—it seemed best to put an end to their suspense and to hopes which we knew to be vain. So I told them that all our searches had been fruitless and we had to presume that their husbands were no more.

My narrative has now run ahead of the course of events and it is necessary to go back a little. After sending off the would-be suicides to the hospital in the middle of the night, I went to bed. Next morning I was up early to supervise the transport of refugees from the camp to the railway station. This did not go at all well. When the first lorries arrived, there were no refugees ready to get into them. Though the jail camp was not an alluring spot, there appeared to be a general reluctance to forsake it for the unknown hazards of a railway journey. I began to doubt whether more than a handful of refugees would be induced to take the plunge and go by the first train. Then presently, after about twenty minutes of seemingly fruitless persuasion, there was a sudden rush and a mad scramble to obtain seats. Nur Mohammad and I tried vainly to impose some kind of order. It was utterly useless and we gave it up. Some of the lorries were not really designed for passengers and were not easy to get into. Men, women and children crowded round them, shouting, yelling and weeping, pushing and jostling and banging one another with their luggage without distinction of age or sex. In this confusion parents got into lorries without their children or their luggage, or luggage and children were thrown in first and the owners were unable to scramble up after them. It took ages then to sort this out and send a lorry off without some vital person or package missing. Consequently the lorries made very few trips and we were able to transport barely 1,000 people to the station before the train left.

We had reserved the whole train for refugees. The number that we succeeded in bringing to the station filled but did not crowd it. Muslims in general and the station staff in particular considered that the Hindus were being sent off (at the expense of the Bahawalpur Government) in far too much luxury and comfort. They wanted them to be packed like sardines, to the exclusion, if need be, of all luggage. After the first day their wish on the first point was gratified. With the use of tongas and improved arrangements for loading the lorries we were able to transport two to three thousand refugees daily to the station in time for the train. This usually consisted of seven coaches; but after the first two days we had to agree to the last coach being kept for ordinary passengers and cram the refugees into the remainder. This meant that there was no more luxury travel for them! Many had to cling like locusts to the outside or sit on the roof in the broiling sun or on the buffers. Since the journey to Hindumalkot took the whole day, it must have been terribly uncomfortable and exhausting. But those who travelled in the first train escaped these hardships.

Among these there was a prominent Hindu named Professor Mehta. With a view to allaying the general anxiety the Hindu leaders had arranged with him that he should accompany those going by the first train and come back and report how things went. He left with every profession that he would be seeing us all again the next day. However, having once got safely through to India, he never returned.

While this train was being sent off, the few Hindus still remaining in the city were being evacuated to the jail camp. I went back there direct from the station and spoke to the Hindu leaders about the need to control their people so that in future there would not be such a mad rush for the lorries in the morning. They said that they were themselves ashamed at what had occurred and were determined that the embarkation should be more orderly in future. They soon effected quite a marked improvement.

Not unnaturally they were at this time very querulous and unhappy, and it was impossible to remove all their complaints or to offer them much consolation in their misery. Several of those in the camp had some close relative in some other part of the State and wanted him or her to join them before they entrained for India. A few of these, in what appeared to be especially deserving cases, were fetched in my car and such other private cars as we could muster, but it was not possible to collect them all, still less to scour the countryside for cousins, aunts and yet more distant relations, as we were repeatedly pressed to do. There were also numerous requests for being escorted back to the city in search of some treasured possession that had been forgotten. Since such requests had ordinarily to be refused, a method was soon devised of obtaining an escort on false pretences. Knowing that we were short of grain, individual Hindus would come forward and say that they had several bags of grain stored in their houses and that they offered these to the camp 'as a free gift'—though they were by now hardly theirs to give. We would then depute escorts to take them to the city so that they could point out their houses and the bags of grain. A few of the early offers were genuine; but a large number were found to be bogus. When the house was reached, there would be no sign of any bags of grain; the donor would say that they must have been looted and immediately begin to search for other of his belongings. We soon had to refuse all such offers.

Apart from these petty matters, there was the question of having Gurkha escorts for the trains. I put the Hindus' request to Gurmani. Like me, he was not very hopeful about it. He discussed it, I think, with Marden who was at this time still lying wounded at Gurmani's house. There were overwhelming objections to it. The use of Gurkha troops at the jail camp had caused some murmuring and their use for the escorts would be regarded by the rest of the Bahawalpur Army as a reflection on themselves and might dangerously excite them. Already there had been some signs of hostility towards the Gurkhas and it was felt that in the changed conditions they would have to be disbanded—some initial steps had, I think, been taken. I was quite convinced, and so was Gurmani, that the wisest course was to lay squarely on the Muslim troops the responsibility for escorting the Hindus safely to Hindumalkot. There seemed reason to think that individual units, when entrusted with a specific task such as escorting a train of refugees, would feel in honour bound to discharge it faithfully. Gurmani took the trouble to speak personally to each of the officers deputed to command the escort of a train and impress on him his responsibility.

The Hindus were very far from being satisfied. I could not disclose to them in full our reasons for not providing Gurkha escorts, but I told them that there were in my judgement good reasons and that it was really safer to give them Muslim troops as escorts. In spite of this they went on incessantly pestering me to provide Gurkha escorts until at last I was driven to take an extreme step. I told them bluntly that the matter had been decided in the manner which we judged to be in their best interests and that if they raised it again, I would wash my hands entirely of their affairs and leave them to get to India as best they could without any further help from me. This had the desired effect. Thereafter they became more amenable to my advice and never mentioned Gurkha escorts again except that one of them, a few days later, had the courtesy to tell me that they now realized our decision had been right and that they had been wrong to press us on the point.

Now that the Hindus had been removed from the city we began the usual process of locking and numbering the abandoned houses and shops and listing their contents, if any. Most of the latter were auctioned. The looters had not left much. I felt it necessary to do something to put a stop to the constant hammering at safes, so in the next few days I had them all collected and stored in the compound of the tahsil. About one hundred were found intact; a much larger number had been broken open. There was one which, according to the tahsildar, was reputed to contain 'much gold' and he did not like to have to assume responsibility for safeguarding it; so this one large and very heavy safe was deposited in my house.

One of the items of loot was livestock. During the day following the evacuation of the Hindus from the city the grounds of
the school, which the military had made their headquarters,
gradually became stocked with large numbers of cows, buffaloes
and ponies. These caught the eye of Gurmani who was rather
incensed at this blatant exhibition of their loot by the military.
I was inclined to take a more charitable view of the matter. The
animals left behind in the city by the Hindus, I said, had to be
fed and watered by someone. As Revenue Minister I was
Custodian of Evacuee Property, but I had not yet had time to
attend to these animals and was quite glad that the military
had provided for them in this way. Gurmani was emphatic
that the military intended to appropriate the animals; in any
case, he said, the populace, seeing them tethered in the grounds
of the battalion headquarters, would conclude that they had done
so, and we ought not to permit any such public advertisement
of military misconduct. He therefore asked me to take the
animals over and see about their disposal; and he ordered the
O.C. troops—who rather foolishly disclaimed all knowledge
of them—to hand them over to me. But when the tahsildar, on
my instructions, went to collect them, only a few inferior ponies
were delivered to him. All the valuable milch cattle had disappeared—like the Sikhs—no-one could say where.

I had thought that by midday on September 17th all the
Hindus still remaining in the city had been removed to the
camp with the exception of those we had allowed to stay in the
precincts of the Gosain's shrine. Some time in the middle of the
afternoon, as I was going up the main bazaar, two or three men
stopped me and said that they had heard some shots coming
from somewhere off to the right. On my questioning them,
they pointed to a narrow doorway and said that some soldiers
had gone in that way not long before and they thought that it
must be they who had fired the shots. I then realized that this
was the entrance to the shrine in which late the previous day
some Hindu families, unable to obtain places in the lorries to
go to the camp, had taken refuge. I looked about for some
V.C.O.[1] as I considered it prudent, so far as possible, to handle
the troops through their own officers. I was told that there was
a jamadar a little way down the street. Sending my chap-

[1] Viceroy's Commissioned Officer.

rassi off to call him, I hurried through the doorway and up a narrow flight of wooden stairs. These led to a maze of rooms, dark passages and balconies overlooking courtyards down below. I made my way through some of these, then down some more stairs and up another flight, and was beginning to despair of finding anything when I heard voices and sounds of a scuffle a little ahead of me. Coming out on to a flat roof, I saw three soldiers in an open court below and a crowd of Hindus huddled under the roof of a colonnade running along one side of it. The soldiers had their backs towards me, but the Hindus were facing me and saw me up on the roof opposite to them. Many of them raised folded hands towards me and there was a sort of muffled gasp of 'Sahib a gaya'.[1] Some of them pointed to a stairway at one corner by which I could get down into the court. I ran to it and down the stairs, shouting out in Hindu-stani to an, as yet, imaginary jamadar, 'Come along, this way, jamadar sahib, here they are.'

The soldiers were taken by surprise. I peremptorily ordered them to fall in, and, having got them lined up in a row, tapped one of them on the pocket of his tunic, which was bulging tre-mendously, and asked him what he had got in there. He pulled out an enormous alarm clock. Meanwhile the other two, with the greatest alacrity, began taking out of their pockets a large assortment of watches, rings, bracelets and fountain-pens. Every one of their pockets was stuffed full. They were very apologetic and repeatedly asked to be forgiven and were so naïve and engaging that my anger began to evaporate. One of them even asked if he might be permitted to retain a particular watch as he liked it very much! I was still collecting the booty from them when my chaprassi and a jamadar appeared on one of the roofs above. I pointed out to them the stairs leading down into the court and, as soon as the jamadar arrived, handed over the soldiers to him and went across to the Hindus. There were thirty or forty of them. Some of the men had begun to pluck up courage and had ventured out into the court to watch the soldiers disgorge their plunder; but several of the women were weeping and I now saw that one grey-haired old woman was lying dead on the floor. She appeared to have been shot through the heart. I called the jamadar and showed him the

[1] 'The Sahib has come.'

dead body, saying, 'Look what your men have done.' He seemed rather appalled and, staring down at the old woman, said two or three times, 'Bara zulm hai, bara zulm hai!'[1] I angrily asked the soldiers why they had shot her. They replied that one of their rifles had gone off by mistake. This produced a violent volley of contradiction from the Hindus. I cut short the beginnings of a fierce altercation and told the jamadar to march his men away. I then handed over to the Hindus their watches and other property and asked them whether they wanted to be sent to the jail camp. They said that they had been waiting for someone to take them there but had been altogether forgotten—which was quite true. So I summoned a lorry and they were all sent off.

I was not called as a witness at the court martial of the soldiers. Marden told me later that it had not been necessary to bother me as the evidence of the jamadar had been sufficient. They were given some kind of punishment; but not, of course, in any way commensurate with the crime of robbery with murder of which they had been guilty. It is possible that they were never charged with murder; in any case their story that the woman had been shot by accident would have had to be accepted as there was no-one, except the Hindus, to prove the contrary and, after their evacuation to India, they were not available to give evidence. I made no particular effort myself to secure the condign punishment of these men. Perhaps secretly I felt some sympathy with them or had become infected with the lax spirit of the times.

So far as I know, this old woman, the murdered Sikhs and the wealthy Nand Kishore were the only casualties in the town of Bahawalpur after the decision was taken to evacuate the Hindus. This decision may be fairly regarded as equivalent in effect to agreements of the type often reached during wars in earlier times, whereby a city was delivered over to be sacked by the soldiery, but the lives of its inhabitants were spared. By and large the Hindus were saved from further slaughter, but their property became legitimate spoil. Certainly the appearance of the Hindu quarters and the bazaars of Bahawalpur after the evacuation conformed to my idea of a city that had been sacked. The casualties before the evacuation totalled two hundred and

[1] Literally: 'It's a great tyranny!'

fifty to three hundred, of which about a third were Hindus from the surrounding villages who had sought refuge in the town. Both absolutely and, still more, relatively to population these casualties were lower than at Bahawalnagar and Hasilpur; but the consternation which they caused among the Hindu population was no less and their ultimate effects far greater; for the enforced evacuation from the capital of many of the oldest Hindu families profoundly shook the confidence of the Hindu community throughout the State.

The reader may have wondered how the disturbances in Bahawalpur city originated and what course they took prior to my arrival late in the afternoon of September 15th. I have so far only recorded the very brief explanations of them which Gurmani gave me that same evening. To this day I have not been able to obtain any full or coherent account of what happened. It is certain, however, that the disturbances were pre-arranged. Some of the Hindus were given warning of the coming trouble by Muslim friends or employees. They repeatedly expressed their uneasiness to Gurmani, Gilani and others in authority, but right up to the last moment they were assured by them that there was no cause for anxiety. On the evening of September 13th at exactly 9.0 p.m. there was a loud explosion in the city just outside the principal mosque. This was the signal for the riot to begin.[1] A Muslim mob, which included some of the relatives of one of the Muslim Ministers, debouched from the mosque into the main bazaar and began looting and setting fire to shops and killing any Hindus they came across. A smaller mob emerged from a second mosque and began doing the same in another quarter of the town. A third mob advanced on the city from outside the walls and did great slaughter among Hindus who had come in from surrounding villages and had been accommodated in a large Hindu school. This mob was said to have been led by a lame man on a white horse alleged to be a member of the Gilani family.

At 10.0 p.m. a curfew was imposed; the streets were gradually cleared, the rioting subsided and the city quietened down for the night. Large numbers of troops were brought in during the

[1] During the Mutiny the signal for the sepoys to rise and murder their officers was at many stations given by the firing of a gun or some kind of explosion.

next two days and the city was kept under curfew. The Hindus remained shut up in their houses, too terrified to venture out, while military pickets and Muslim gangs looted such shops and houses as could be easily broken into, killing any stray Hindus that fell into their hands. This was the position when I reached Bahawalpur.

The outbreak of rioting in the city more or less synchronized with a disturbance in the jail. Beginning as a small affair, it developed into an attempt at a mass break-out. The inner wall was breached and it seemed at one time that all the prisoners might escape and join the marauding gangs in the city. Owing to reluctance to fire upon them effectively, it took many hours and a large force of police and military to overpower them and drive them back to their cells.

During the two days of September 14th and 15th when the city was under curfew some endeavour was made to clean up the mess and to clear away the corpses; but the municipal lorry engaged on the latter task broke down before it was completed. By the time I arrived on the scene the dead bodies had been removed from the two main bazaars, but a good many were still lying about in the side-streets and remained there for a number of days. One corpse of a stout Hindu sprawled, completely naked, right across a lane which I went down daily in order to visit the Hindus in the Gosain's shrine. Day by day it became more swollen and bloated. Again and again I and my entourage passed it without comment until one day we came along and found that it was missing from its usual place.

During the period of mass hysteria I found myself in a 'through the looking-glass' world of moral conventions. There was a complete breakdown, or rather reversal, of the ordinary moral values. To kill a Sikh had become almost a duty; to kill a Hindu was hardly a crime. To rob them was an innocent pleasure, carrying no moral stigma; to refrain was a mark not of virtue but of lack of enterprise. On the other hand to try to stop these things was at best folly, at worst a crime. Mild remonstrance, though disliked and despised, could be tolerated, like the babblings in England against betting or blood sports; but effective action was liable to be viewed as a capital offence.

Most of those who in these days robbed and murdered

members of the opposite community might have plausibly put
forward a plea of temporary insanity; for they did not know, or
had forgotten, the real moral character of their actions. A new
scale of values had been introduced and the old one had been
almost universally discarded. Certainly my own indignation at
their misdeeds, though often very great, was constantly tempered
by my awareness of this change in moral values. I was also not
blind to the dangers of an excessive zeal for the usual standards.

Well-to-do Muslims expressed more than once to me their
fear that the sanctity of life and property having broken down,
the mob, after finishing with the Hindus and Sikhs, would
turn upon them. These fears were not realized. Between Muslims
the normal moral code continued to apply and operated everywhere with all its pristine vigour once the Hindus were out of
the way.

The dispatch of the Hindus of Bahawalpur city to India took
six days—from September 17th to the 22nd. Such was my
anxiety for its safe accomplishment that it seemed more like a
fortnight. I used to go to the jail camp every morning and then
from there to the railway station to supervise the entraining of
the refugees. I had an arrangement with Leghari that I would
ring him up on the railway telephone immediately after the
train had left and that he would be at the Bahawalnagar railway
station at that time to receive the call. I used to tell him the
approximate number of refugees we had put on the train that
day and he would transmit the information to Hindumalkot
and also see that there were adequate supplies of drinking-
water and such other refreshment as could be provided for the
parched and exhausted refugees when the train passed through
Bahawalnagar at about 4.30 p.m. Then again in the evening I
would go to the station at a fixed time and Leghari would ring
me up and let me know if the train had passed safely through
Bahawalnagar and reached Hindumalkot. This arrangement
enabled me also to keep in touch with the affairs of the Bahawalnagar area, where another 40,000 Muslim refugees had
arrived,[1] and to give directions quickly to Leghari and Fazlur
Rahman on any matter that they might wish to refer to me.

The Muslim railway officials at the Baghdad-ul-jadid station

[1] These had marched all the way from Hissar and Rohtak districts. They
traversed Bikanir and entered Bahawalpur in the Harunabad area.

were at first rather sulky and did not much like the constant use of their telephone and the trouble that was being taken over the dispatch of the Hindu refugees. But they soon got used to our ways and, after hearing me talking over the phone to Leghari and Fazlur Rahman about measures for the receipt of incoming Muslim refugees, they became quite friendly and obliging and on more than one occasion took much trouble to locate me and call me to the telephone at the station when Leghari wanted me urgently.

Almost up to the last day I remained in constant dread that one of the trains would be attacked, that the escort would fail to repel the assailants with proper vigour and that there would be a massacre of Hindus. At the time of actual entraining I was afraid, not that they would be assaulted, but that they would be robbed or on some pretext relieved of the pitifully small possessions that they were trying to carry away with them. It was mainly to prevent this and other harassment of the refugees that I personally attended the entraining every morning. Muslim feeling in general was against their being allowed to carry away anything at all. There was a sort of idea that all their property belonged really to Pakistan and so should not be taken out of it. Objections were constantly being made that some box or package, which a wretched Hindu had successfully lugged from his house to the camp and then transported to the railway station, was too large or too heavy to go in the train! I overruled all such objections and somehow or other all the luggage brought to the station was squeezed into the train or stacked on the roofs of the carriages. But my rulings were not altogether appreciated. Several times as I stood on the platform watching a train steam slowly from the station, crammed full to overflowing and with men and luggage piled along the roofs of the coaches, Muslim officials would say to me, 'Look how these rich banias are being allowed to leave laden with their belongings, whereas our people are being driven out of India empty-handed.' I had no very adequate answer to this and to some extent I entered into their feelings.[1] So I just used to reply

[1] It must be remembered that under the British 'rule of law', Hindu and Sikh moneylenders and shopkeepers in the Punjab, and particularly the Western Punjab, had been allowed to oppress the Muslim peasantry in the most shameful manner.

that Muslims were not as barbarous as the Sikhs or as mean as the Hindus and were expected to behave more chivalrously. 'That is the reason', they would say, 'why we have always come off worst.'

On one occasion, just before the train was about to leave, my attention was drawn to a sick man lying right at the end of the platform. In a weak voice he asked to be put on the train and said he was not being allowed to go. None of his relations were at hand and I concluded that they had deliberately left him on the platform, thinking he was too ill to travel and wanting to be rid of him. I asked where they were, and after a minute some of them jumped out of the train and came running up. I inquired why they were being so heartless as to leave the poor man behind. With tears in their eyes they replied that they wanted him to go with them, but had been prevented from putting him on the train by someone—I think the guard—who said that they must produce a doctor's certificate that he was fit to travel! There was no doctor at hand and they begged me to detain the train till they could go and fetch one. How easily they could be imposed upon by petty officials! The need for a doctor's certificate must have been thought of by someone who hoped to obtain a good tip for graciously waiving its production. I told them that their sick relation could go without doctor or certificate. The train was already packed, but we made some men get out and climb on to the roof and so found room for him.

Yet it would be wrong to convey the impression by these instances of harassment and the desire to rob the outgoing Hindus that their departure was unaccompanied by any signs of friendliness and good feeling. On the contrary, there was daily quite an attendance of Muslims at the station who came to say goodbye to old friends. They helped them to carry their luggage and embraced them affectionately on the platform; and, as each train left, there was from both sides a great waving of farewell. Sentimental affection for the Hindus subsisted along with the desire to benefit from their plight.

There was a particularly large concourse at the station on about the fifth day when the Gosain and all his people were brought from their sanctuary in the city. No doubt he may have been considered by some to be a pious fraud, but he was quite a figure and a well-established institution in the State. He came down to the station wearing a topi and accompanied by a mass of luggage and the I.N.A. Gilani. The latter had assumed charge of his evacuation—an arrangement that was doubtless highly satisfactory to both parties. He was given a privileged seat in the train and a hearty send-off.

There was one incident at the station—probably on the fourth day of evacuation—that gave me some minutes of anxiety. The train was standing at the platform and the refugees were still clambering into it when an officer of the State Forces on duty at the station came up to me and said that in the rear coach, which was reserved for ordinary passengers, there was a Muslim gentleman from the North-West Frontier Province travelling to Harunabad with a bodyguard of eight Pathans, all carrying rifles. He asked whether I thought it would be safe to let these armed men from the Frontier travel on a train crammed with Hindu refugees. He wanted to know what should be done. This was rather a tricky question and inwardly I did not thank him for posing it, though it was quite right of him to do so. The risk that these Pathans, the servants of some wealthy and respectable Muslim gentleman, would get out of hand and use their arms against the Hindus was small, but in these excited times it was not easy to discount it altogether. Moreover there were the feelings of the Hindus to consider. Word would flash down the train that in the rear coach there were Pathans from the Frontier armed with rifles and this would put many of them in an agony of fear throughout the journey. It was indeed likely that before the train left they would importune me to take the arms away. On the other hand the Muslim gentleman might well regard a request to surrender the arms as a quite un-necessary precaution and an insult to himself. I judged that he might prove a difficult customer for to be travelling about with an armed guard was sheer swank and indicated that he must be a pompous fellow with a great sense of his own importance. If he adopted a stiff attitude and declined voluntarily to give up the rifles and we were compelled to take them away by force, then this might lead to a scene and a scuffle and even worse. We might thus wantonly provoke an outbreak of violence which it was our object to avoid.

All these thoughts raced through my mind as I walked down

the platform towards the rear coach. By the time I reached it I had decided that the rifles must be taken away. So I climbed up into the coupé in which the Muslim gentleman was sitting, apologized for the intrusion and requested to speak to him for a minute. He was a stout elderly man and asked me in rather a surly tone what I wanted. I explained to him that we had a lot of frightened Hindus in the train whom we were evacuating to India and requested him, having regard to their feelings and the prevailing tension, to hand over temporarily the rifles which his men were carrying. I said that we would return them later and that if he let me know when he would be coming back, I would have them ready for him at the station. He refused to agree to my request and questioned my right to make it, so I was forced to inquire whether he had a licence to carry all these arms in Bahawalpur State. (I was quite certain that he had not.) He replied grandly that he held an all-India licence. I pointed out that such a licence was valid only in the whole of what had been British India and was not valid in a State, like Bahawalpur, for which a separate licence was required. I had therefore ample right to request him to surrender the arms, since they were in fact unlicensed; and, though in normal times I would never have dreamed of taking him up on such a formality, I must, in the special circumstances already explained to him, repeat my request to him to give them up. This did not please him and he began to bluster. He said that he was a friend of Sir George Cunningham, Sir Rob Lockhart and other famous figures of the Frontier; that he had travelled all over India and never before been questioned about his arms or asked to give them up; that the Nawab of Bahawalpur knew him well and would be very angry when he heard that he had been insulted in this way.

The officers on the platform outside were now telling me that the train was due to leave. Further attempts at persuasion seemed useless, so I said to him, 'Very well then, Khan Bahadar, if you won't tell your men to hand over their arms, I'll have to uncouple your coach and leave you standing here on the line while the rest of the train goes on without you.' I got down from the carriage and gave orders for the rear coach to be uncoupled. This brought him to reason. 'All right, all right,' he growled, coming to the window, 'I'll give them up,' and he leaned out and told his men in the next compartment to hand over their rifles. They immediately complied. I thanked him for so kindly acceding to my request; but he was not to be mollified. 'Why', he asked, 'does Jinnah employ such bad officers?' I had held myself in so far, but I could not now resist the pleasure of exculpating Mr. Jinnah. He was not, I said, in the least to blame as he had got my services quite by accident and was probably not yet even aware of his misfortune. The blame rested on the Nawab of Bahawalpur and Gurmani. I advised him to complain to the latter as the Nawab was away in England!

I was thankful to have got the rifles away from him quietly and without any scuffle. The train went on its way and reached its destination safely.

By the 21st I began to feel confident that the evacuation would be completed without mishap. There were only twelve hundred to fifteen hundred refugees left in the jail camp, and these were all entrained and dispatched safely to Hindumalkot on the 22nd. In all about fifteen thousand were evacuated by train to India from the city of Bahawalpur. In these trains, and in other escorted refugee trains which we sent to Hindumalkot before and after, there was not a single casualty. This is a tribute to the Bahawalpur State Forces. Whatever criticisms may be made of their conduct in these times, their successful escorting of these trains stands conspicuously to their credit. An attempt was made by crowds of villagers to attack one of the trains—probably on the third day—but the escort promptly opened fire and the crowds were scattered. After that no-one again ventured to play any mischief.

So far as Bahawalpur State is concerned, the evacuation of the Hindus from the capital was a decisive event. It was the signal that the State must inevitably lose all its Hindu inhabitants and become a purely Muslim territory. Up till then this had not been a foregone conclusion. Even if West Punjab was emptied of Hindus, it had seemed possible that Bahawalpur, like Sind to the south where no large-scale migration had yet begun, might retain a large proportion of its Hindu population. As recently as September 11th, I had been thinking and talking in terms not merely of retaining Hindus, but of recovering those who had already left. Now all such ideas were seen to be illusions. A few people, it is true, still continued to think in the old terms, but they were persons far removed from the actual scene of events. Those in daily contact with them and able to sense the popular mood knew that to retain any Hindus would be difficult and dangerous and that to recall those who had left and reinstate them in their property was impracticable madness and would provoke a fresh holocaust.

Conscious of the change that had occurred. I had found time while I was at Bahawalpur to run up to Khairpur and Qaimpur and have a talk with the Hindus of those places. Now that all the Hindus from the capital were being sent away to India they were unanimous that they too could no longer remain in the State and requested me to arrange at once for their evacuation. I discussed the matter with Leghari over the phone. He said that all the Hindus still remaining in Chishtian and other places in the eastern part of the State were also now wanting to leave. He suggested that as soon as the evacuation of Bahawalpur city was complete, we should send them all off by train to Hindumalkot. Arrangements were made accordingly and they were also safely evacuated.[1]

Thus by the close of September the Bahawalpur district—rather more than one-half of the State—had been completely denuded of its Hindu and Sikh population. Only a few stray individuals—the Hindu Minister, a Hindu High Court Judge and some Hindu officials attached to the Palace—still remained. The frenzy of slaughter subsided, for in the Bahawalpur district victims were no longer readily available. But in the Rahim Yar Khan district, so far comparatively tranquil, we still had sixty to seventy thousand Hindus; and Muslim refugees were still pouring into the State. Our troubles were diminished, but not over.

[1] This took over a week as Pakistan was now suffering from a coal shortage and a train from Samasatta to Hindumalkot could only be run on alternate days.

XII

Events in Rahim Yar Khan

I N the closing days of September a serious and unexpected calamity befell us. Normally the monsoon slackens in northern India during September and by the beginning of October has come to an end. But this year was an exception. During the last week of September there was unusually heavy rain throughout the Punjab, quenching to some extent the fires of communal fury, but intensifying the miseries of the refugees. We had just completed the evacuation of the Hindus from Bahawalpur city and I was looking forward to a little respite when I was called urgently one evening to the station at Baghdad-ul-jadid to speak to Leghari over the railway telephone. The news he had to give me was most disconcerting. The rain, he said, had caused a heavy flood in the Sutlej; this had arrived with little warning at Suleimanke, broken through the protective embankments, and breached both the two big State canals, the Sadiqia and the Fordwah, taking off from the Suleimanke headworks. The damage to the Sadiqia was reported to be extensive and the irrigation officers thought it would take weeks to repair it.

Coming on the top of all the troubles of the past month, this mishap seemed to me the last straw. The damage to the Fordwah Canal did not so much matter, for this was only a semi-perennial (six-monthly) canal and was in any case due to cease running in about a fortnight's time. But the damage to the Sadiqia, a perennial canal, was disastrous. The sowing time for the rabi crop was at hand; if the Sadiqia could not be re-opened by about the third week of October, there would be no rabi in the vast semi-desert tract which it irrigated. Moreover in this tract the villagers were entirely dependent on the canal for water for themselves and their cattle. Any prolonged interruption of supplies would force them to migrate.

In normal times such a disaster could never have occurred.

Telegraphic flood warnings would have been sent out from
high up the river, where it debouches from the mountains, and
the staff at Suleimanke would have had at least twenty-four
hours' notice of the flood. They would have immediately started
intensive patrolling of the embankments so that any weak
points revealed by the rising waters could be promptly strengthened and potential breaches closed before they had been effectually opened. But owing to the division of the Punjab the warning system had broken down and Suleimanke received less than
four hours' notice of the flood; and owing to the defects of the
Radcliffe line the embankments on the south of the river were
not patrolled; for except the first hundred yards these now all
fell in Indian territory and the Dogra troops in the area prevented or frightened Muslim canal patrols from venturing along
them.

These embankments, which should have held the swollen
river in its channel and guided it to the headworks, gave way
in several places. The waters poured through the breaches and
piled up against the Sadiqia Canal which, running due south
at right-angles to the river, lay right athwart their course. The
weight of the water caused the bank of the canal to give way;
the water then poured into it, filled it to overflowing and, owing
to the excessive pressure on the banks, caused breaches in them
at intervals over a distance of forty-five to fifty miles. Some of
the water also burst through into the Fordwah Canal, which
for about one mile south of the headworks runs parallel to and
only thirty to fifty yards distant from the Sadiqia.

The breaches in the Sadiqia were biggest and most numerous
over the first ten miles of its length. For their speedy repair—
two or three of them were seventy to eighty feet wide—a large
labour force was required. But in this area no suitable labour
was available. This was the area around Macleodganj Road
where the Muslim cultivators had scattered in panic and the
numerous Sikh colonists had crossed over into Bikanir. In place
of the Sikhs there were now a lot of newly-arrived refugees from
the East Punjab. These poor people had barely settled in their
new homes after their trek when they had been overwhelmed
by the floods and forced to spend days and nights on the roofs
of their houses or in the branches of trees. It was futile to expect
to get hard labour from these unfortunates. The only course

was to bring in labour from elsewhere. Though Roy, the Chief
Engineer, was at first sceptical, I had no doubt that the stout-
hearted Punjabi colonists at the tail of the canal around Fort
Abbas, over a hundred miles away, would readily offer their
labour gratis, if the need for it was explained to them—since
the reopening of the canal was for them a vital matter. The
tahsildar was directed to call for volunteers. There was no lack
of them; rather the difficulty was to provide them with sufficient baskets or other utensils for carrying the earth required to
fill the breaches. The train service between Fort Abbas and
Bahawalnagar had been suspended owing to shortage of coal;
but we persuaded the railway authorities to put on a special
train and transported several hundred sturdy peasants from
around Fort Abbas and Harunabad to the Macleodganj area.
They brought with them their pots and pans and bedding and
we supplied them with flour. The work of repair was admirably
organized by the officials of the Irrigation Department—a
highly efficient body of men—and within little more than a fortnight the breaches were repaired and the canal was running again.

These floods caused great havoc among the refugees strug-
gling in both directions across the Punjab. Many are said to have
been swept away and drowned. The actual number who
perished in this way may not have been large, but the rain and
floods added enormously to the difficulties and discomforts of the
refugees and to some extent undermined their stamina.

During most of the month of September the fury of communal
frenzy had raged unabated in both halves of the divided Punjab. But with October, there began a long period of slow con-
valescence. The remnants of the respective minority communities had by now in most places been herded into camps and
in consequence killings and disorder became less widespread.
Attacks on refugee trains and on columns of refugees moving
by road had not yet been fully mastered, but gradually there
was an improvement; and as, with the movement of refugees
in both directions, the two communities were separated and
withdrawn from proximity to one another, the normal moral
sanctions reasserted themselves, the bonds of society were
renewed and law and order prevailed once more.

But while the disease had burnt itself out at the centre, viz.
the Central Punjab, at points on the circumference, where the

communities were still intermingled, there remained a danger
of fresh outbreaks. In Bahawalpur State we still had many thousands of Hindus in the Rahim Yar Khan district, and until
they could be got safely away to India we could never be certain that they might not occasion a fresh outburst of killing.
They remained a constant source of anxiety. Our other problem was how to cope with the continuous stream of incoming
refugees. Throughout October their numbers and, with the
onset of the cold weather, their needs increased; and the sympathy which they had at first excited turned, through no real
fault of theirs, to indifference and even disgust.

Events in the Rahim Yar Khan district and the resettlement
of refugees are, therefore, the main themes of the two conclud-
ing chapters of this narrative.

A new factor was introduced into the local situation in Bahawalpur by the return of the Nawab. He arrived back in the State
from his summer residence at Farnham, Surrey, on October
2nd. I was at that time in the Bahawalnagar area, coping with
floods and refugees. Gurmani explained to the Nawab all
that had occurred, whereupon he is said to have expressed the
intention of composing a poem in my honour and reciting it to
me when I came to see him! This was a kind thought, but I am
afraid the recitation never took place. Long before I saw him
there had been a clash between us and his poetic ardour cooled.

The exodus from the State of such a large number of his
'loyal Hindu subjects' affected the Nawab keenly. The
courtiers at the Palace represented that Gurmani and I had
'driven them away' and introduced in their place Punjabi
Muslims with no tradition of loyalty to a Nawab or Maharajah. Gurmani and I had, of course, been at the mercy of
events, but it is certainly true that these had not been favourable to the position of the Nawab as an autocratic ruler. In
Bahawalpur, as in many of the Princely States of India, the
minority community felt a particular allegiance to the Ruler,
for they looked to him, and not in vain, for protection from
oppression by the majority. Thus the Hindus who had left the
State were in a real sense 'loyal' subjects of the Nawab. Their
community had been treated by him and his forefathers with
justice and consideration and they felt some attachment to the
Ruler as such. On the other hand the Punjabi Muslims, who

had flooded in as refugees from East Punjab, cared nothing for the Nawab of Bahawalpur and perhaps had hardly heard of him. The exchange of population which had taken place meant, therefore, for the Nawab the loss of loyal subjects and their replacement by others who would be at best indifferent to him.

Not unnaturally the Nawab was strongly opposed to any more Hindus leaving the State. He also expressed the wish that only refugees from Princely States, e.g. Bikanir, Patiala, Nabha, Bharatpur and Alwar, should be received and settled in Bahawalpur since these, being accustomed to personal rule, would more readily accommodate themselves to our conditions and develop a loyalty to the Ruler. This was a reasonable and desirable proposal, but only to a very limited extent practicable. However much we might prefer refugees from Princely States, we had no means of effectively exercising this preference. We had, as a matter of fact, already received a large number of refugees from the State of Bikanir; but this had been due not to our own volition but to the fact that Bahawalpur, being adjacent, was the natural place for them to come to. To some extent we could pick and choose from among the refugees who actually entered our borders, passing on to the Punjab those whom we did not like or were too numerous for us to absorb. But we could not control or even influence the movement of refugees from India and so determine which of them should enter Bahawalpur territory. Within the narrow limits possible, we did tend to give preference to refugees from Princely States; but not invariably as there might be other overriding considerations. For instance, in November several thousand refugees reached us from a small State in south-east Punjab. They appeared to me to be very poor stuff and likely to be a drag on the economy and so, with Gurmani's approval,. they were all pushed over into the Punjab.

The Nawab's views regarding the selection of the incoming refugees did not have much practical effect. But his strong desire not to lose any more of his loyal Hindu subjects affected for some months the fortunes of those still bottled up in Rahim Yar Khan. Here circumstances favoured his views; for, as will be explained later, it was very difficult for us to extricate the Hindus from the Rahim Yar Khan district; nor could they slip away themselves except slowly in small numbers.

The story of the Hindus of the Rahim Yar Khan district runs on right until the middle of 1948. At no time were there widespread disturbances, as in the Bahawalpur district, but there was one bad episode and many small incidents and recurrent threats of a flare-up. At the beginning of September there was a good deal of restlessness in the northern portion of the district and a few stray Hindus were killed. During this period Gurmani sent out Roy and Duncan (the British Superintending Engineer) in a jeep with a couple of Bahawalpur soldiers to run about from place to place and try to nip any trouble in the bud. One incident of their jeep trips requires mention. They were driving along a canal bank in the northern part of the district when they saw ahead of them a bullock-cart standing on a bridge across the canal. There seemed to be some knobbly things sticking out of it which in the distance looked to Roy like swedes or turnips; but this puzzled him, as such root crops are not grown in Bahawalpur. On getting nearer he discerned that the knobbly things were really the arms, legs and heads of human beings—the cart was in fact full of corpses which were being tipped out into the canal. The men with the cart, on seeing who were in the jeep, jumped over the bridge into the canal and were quickly carried away by the current. The two soldiers accompanying Roy and Duncan opened fire on them, but with the usual lack of aim—no doubt in the water they were not easy targets—and they all escaped.

The corpses had been brought from a small village or hamlet not far distant. Roy and Duncan went over to it. At first they could find no sign of life. The whole population of about two hundred seemed to have been wiped out and their bodies were lying about all over the place. The hamlet had been inhabited by Labana Sikhs whose forefathers had been settled there in the last century by the then Ruler of Bahawalpur. The penalty had now been exacted for the crime of being Sikhs! Roy and Duncan thought at first that not a single living soul was left, but they did at last find a woman with an infant in her arms still alive and cowering in the corner of one of the houses. They were the sole survivors.

Apart from this small group of Labanas the total number of Sikhs in the Rahim Yar Khan district was only two to three thousand. Soon after disturbances broke out in the State, they sensed that they were in danger and by the middle of September had all congregated for safety at one or two centres; whereas the Hindus remained for some weeks more scattered throughout the district and pursuing their normal avocations. Gurmani, who, it will be recalled, had assumed responsibility for Rahim Yar Khan, was confronted with the problem of what to do with these Sikhs. The desideratum was to get them away to India as quickly as possible; but to put them in one of the main line trains running through Rahim Yar Khan would have been sheer murder, and we had not enough lorries to transport them all the way by road to Samasatta and then send them down the branch line to Hindumalkot. Gurmani, therefore, proposed that they should be marched out under escort from the town of Rahim Yar Khan to the extreme border of the cultivated area and thence across the desert to the State of Jaisalmir which adjoins Bahawalpur on the south-east and forms part of India. There are well-marked tracks across the desert and at the nearest point the distance from the edge of the cultivated area to the Jaisalmir border is only a day or two's march. It was thought that with adequate preparations the journey would not be too arduous or hazardous. Camels and donkeys could be provided for the women and children. Gurmani consulted me about this proposal a day or two after the evacuation of Bahawalpur city had begun. I felt rather dubious about it, but could suggest no better alternative. My main misgiving was in regard to the escort which was to be furnished by the Bahawalpur State forces. In answer to my doubts Gurmani assured me that the officer commanding it would be one who could be relied upon to do his duty. My doubts were not, however, wholly removed. I said to Gurmani that if the military were to furnish the escort—I would have myself preferred the police to do so—then at least a senior civil officer with magisterial powers should accompany the expedition. I suggested that no less a person than the Deputy Commissioner of the district should be deputed for this purpose. A Muslim officer of the State, Maulvi Faiz Ahmad, held this post and since the outbreak of disturbances had also been given the powers of District Magistrate. Owing to the loss of one eye he had, perhaps, a somewhat villainous appearance, but I knew him to be a man of strong character, well capable of standing up to the military and not likely to be browbeaten or

bamboozled by them. Gurmani, while agreeing that a civil
officer should accompany the column, said that the Deputy
Commissioner could not be spared. There was some force in this
contention as the whole district was at that time rather bobbery;
and so it was settled that the Assistant Commissioner should
accompany the Sikh refugees on their march.

My mind was not at rest and I therefore asked Faiz Ahmad
to keep me in touch with the progress of this expedition. At the
end of September I heard that it had started, and some days
later, when I happened to be at Bahawalnagar, I received a copy
of a report, signed by the Commanding Officer and counter-
signed by the Assistant Commissioner, to the effect that the
whole column had reached the border in safety and good
order and that the refugees had departed with many professions
of gratitude for the excellent manner in which they had been
looked after and protected from all dangers by the escort of
Bahawalpur troops.

The report was written in a vivid colourful style; but somehow or other I didn't believe a word of it. I showed it to Leghari
and asked him what he made of it. He said that he thought it
was quite false and that reports which had reached him from
other sources of his own told quite a different story. He urged
me to make further inquiries and satisfy myself as to the real
facts. Not long after I had occasion to go to Rahim Yar Khan
and while there I questioned the Deputy Commissioner about
the report and told him that it did not ring true to me. He was
a bit cagey at first and put me off, saying that he would talk
to me about it later. After a couple of hours he came back to the
rest-house where I was staying and said that, since I had myself cast doubts on the correctness of the report, he had decided
to reveal to me the truth. The report, he said, was in fact false;
the Assistant Commissioner had now admitted this, and had
made a statement, which was corroborated by other witnesses,
giving an entirely different account of what had taken place.
He had reduced all this evidence to writing and handed it over
to me for perusal.

It was a horrible tale of treachery and violence. The column,
rather over two thousand strong, had moved off on the afternoon of September 26th from a chak near Rahim Yar Khan
where they had all congregated. Before the start there was a

slight contretemps. The Sikhs had thought that they would be allowed to carry with them such arms as they possessed, but they were ordered to surrender them. With the usual Sikh lack of docility they were inclined to resist. They said that the Deputy Commissioner had promised them that they would be permitted to take their arms. Fortunately Faiz Ahmad had himself come along with the Commanding Officer to the chak to see them set off on their journey, and through his intervention the matter was amicably settled and they were persuaded peacefully to surrender their arms. They parted from him with expressions of gratitude and goodwill.

On the first evening, when the column had encamped for the night, trouble broke out. The escorting troops began to search the Sikhs and relieve them of their valuables. A certain Karnail Singh resisted. There was a fight; Karnail Singh and several other Sikhs were shot dead and a number were injured. At once there was a great commotion and outcry throughout the camp. This was awkward for the officer commanding the escort. Rahim Yar Khan was still not far distant. Some of the Sikhs might slip away with news of what had happened and bring the Deputy Commissioner on the scene. The Assistant Commissioner, accompanying the column, talked of sending in a report. The Commanding Officer persuaded him that it was best to keep quiet and hush the matter up, while towards the Sikhs he was most conciliatory. He expressed profound regret for what had taken place, said that it was all a mistake and due to some misunderstanding and promised that nothing of the kind would happen again.

Partially reassured the Sikhs continued on their way; but the next evening when they were approaching the edge of the desert and were already far from any hope of succour the Commanding Officer announced that they would be searched and all their belongings taken away. He justified this on the ground that the Muslims who were being driven out of India were not being allowed to bring any of their possessions with them. The Sikhs protested against this betrayal and breach of all the promises made to them; but resistance was useless. During that night and the following day they were all systematically searched and deprived of everything, including the camels and horses on which some of them hoped to cross the desert. The booty was loaded

H*

on to military lorries and driven away to Rahim Yar Khan. The Assistant Commissioner weakly acquiesced in all these proceedings. He perhaps eased his conscience with the thought that the C.O. was acting under some secret instructions not communicated to him.

The Sikhs could now place little faith in the C.O.'s promises. Nevertheless they were assured that there would be no further harassment; and so they journeyed on. They had now reached the farthest limit of the cultivated area and were starting on their march across the open desert in considerable distress for want of sufficient food and water. After two days they had almost reached the border and halted for the night of September 30th only about two miles short of it. Chauki Kishangarh, the nearest inhabited place in Jaisalmir territory, lay some miles farther on. They expected to cross the border and make their way to this place the next morning. But at about 1.0 a.m. the two leaders of the Sikh column, Bakhtawar Singh and Bhag Singh, were roused from their slumbers and told that they must all make ready to start immediately. They protested to the C.O. and expressed their disquiet and suspicion at being suddenly ordered to march at the dead of night. By way of answer they were both bayoneted and fatally injured.

The rest of the column moved off, but after they had gone a short distance firing was heard ahead and they were ordered to halt. They were told that the firing was coming from a gang of armed Hurs,[1] who were waiting to fall upon them, and that special measures must be taken to ensure the safety of the women and children. This was, of course, all a hoax. A portion of the escort had been sent ahead with orders to conceal themselves behind some sand-hills and let off their rifles. However, on the pretext of an imminent attack by Hurs, of which the firing was supposed to provide the evidence, the women were separated from the men under threats of violence. A selection was then made of the younger women who were in due course distributed among the escort and taken back to Rahim Yar Khan.

Having secured their prey the escort were anxious to be rid

[1] A fanatical sect of Muslims who had turned outlaws and terrorized parts of Sind during the war. Military operations had to be undertaken to hunt them down. At this time small parties of them still caused an occasional incident.

of the men and of the old women and children. So these were
told that, as there were Hurs prowling around, they had better
make a run for it to the border. At the same time the escort
began firing off their rifles indiscriminately—perhaps to suggest
that they were giving covering fire against the bogus Hurs.
Some of the Sikhs ran wildly forward in the direction of the
border; the rest struggled after them under fire from the escort
behind and from the party concealed behind sand-hills to the
front. In the darkness and confusion an unascertained number
were killed or wounded. From the accounts which the Assistant
Commissioner and others were able to give us it was impossible
at that time to judge how many, if any, of the column had survived and made their way successfully into Indian territory.

Some years later I was able to contact in India members of
this ill-fated expedition. Several hundred of them,[1] I learnt, got
through safely to Chauki Kishangarh and reported what had
befallen them. Camels were sent out from there to the scene
of the firing to bring in the wounded, most of whom were ultimately transported to Jodhpur and admitted to hospital there.

In this affair the Bahawalpur escort certainly showed a well-
judged audacity, but they were wrong in supposing that their
dark deeds far out in the desert would remain unknown. The
bringing in of so much booty and so many female captives to a
small place like Rahim Yar Khan could not pass unnoticed.
The arrival of the lorries laden with spoil, though they came in
under cover of night, set tongues wagging; and later the return
of the escort, accompanied by numbers of Sikh women, quickly
gave rise to open scandal. The women's presence could not in
any case have easily been concealed; and it soon became
notorious; for a number of them escaped from their captors
and hid themselves in the tall standing crops just outside the
town. There followed a regular game of hide-and-seek. In
broad daylight soldiers of the Bahawalpur Army were to be
seen hunting these young women from one millet field to
another round the outskirts of Rahim Yar Khan. Some of
them were recaptured, but three or four got away altogether
and were taken in and given shelter in various houses in the
town. The respectable inhabitants of the place were greatly

[1] I should guess at least 600–700 but the numbers given to me were
considerably less.

shocked. They reported the matter to the Deputy Commissioner and soon the full story of the treachery began to leak out.

When the Assistant Commissioner was confronted by the Deputy Commissioner with the damning evidence afforded by the women, he broke down and made a clean breast of the whole affair, pleading his own helplessness in face of the overbearing attitude of the military. It was with some difficulty that the Deputy Commissioner induced him to present himself before me. I felt sorry for him. He was by no means a bad man, but he did not possess the strength of character equal to the sternness and wickedness of the times.

I returned at once to Bahawalpur and informed Gurmani of all that the Deputy Commissioner and Assistant Commissioner had reported to me. He agreed that the Assistant Commissioner should immediately be suspended from service and the Commanding Officer placed under arrest. Orders were issued accordingly and the Commanding Officer, having been duly arrested by the police, was handed over to the military for custody. The Nawab, who had been consulted by Gurmani about his arrest, was reported to be greatly enraged at his misconduct.

Within a week he had escaped—or been permitted to escape by his military guards—and made his way to Multan. At Multan, which is in the Punjab, he was beyond our jurisdiction. We could not have him rearrested there except with the concurrence of the (West) Punjab Government. Gurmani therefore considered—perhaps with some relief—that the matter was closed. But I was not content. I pointed out that the evidence at our disposal against him disclosed offences of robbery, abduction and murder, or at any rate abetment thereof. These were grave offences and we could ask for his extradition. There was no need for any lengthy investigation at this stage. The statements of the Assistant Commissioner and of the women who had escaped afforded sufficient prima facie evidence to justify a request to the Punjab Government for his immediate extradition.

Gurmani agreed to address them. A few weeks later he told me that they had replied with an absolute refusal. They had not asked for further evidence or explanations on any points but had simply rejected the request for extradition out of hand.

At this stage I gave up the unequal struggle. It was said—with what truth we did not know—that a British military officer of very high rank had intervened with the Punjab Government on the C.O.'s behalf. Whether this was really so I never had time to inquire; but even without any well-meant prompting from a distinguished British military officer, it would have been quite natural and in keeping with current sentiment for the Punjab Government to refuse extradition. Despite noble professions there was no real desire to punish those who robbed, raped and murdered the minority communities; rather there was a disposition to punish those who tried to protect them. This was the main reason why I did not press the matter or attempt to persuade the Punjab Government to reconsider their decision. I had shot my bolt.

There were many incidents in those days both in India and Pakistan far exceeding the story of this ill-starred expedition in horror, atrocity and the extent of the bloodshed; but I know of none that surpass it in calculated perfidy. To me it was more painful and shocking than any other incident that took place in the State of Bahawalpur. Partly this was because there was such an absolute and flagrant breach of trust. On no other occasion did the Bahawalpur Army, when solemnly assigned a specific task, let us down so completely. But partly it was because of my feeling of direct responsibility for the disaster. In authorizing the expedition we had, with our eyes open, taken a fearful risk. We already knew the temper of the troops. One battalion had looted Bahawalnagar, another Bahawalpur. We could not expect that the appetites of the remainder would be any less keen. In entrusting the Sikhs to their protection we were handing them over to ravening wolves. Yet we were, I think, justified in doing so as the consequences of keeping them were almost certain to be worse. Our mistake lay, not in taking the risk, but in failing to take the one measure which could have effectively lessened it, and that was to send the Deputy Commissioner along with the column. I have no doubt that if Faiz Ahmad had gone with it instead of the Assistant Commissioner he would have stood up to the military and all the worst episodes would have been avoided. I also believe that if I had urged this course upon Gurmani with the vehemence which the situation required he would have agreed to it. As it was we contented ourselves with an ineffective half-measure; for the Assistant Commissioner, while he assisted in the end in uncovering the villainy, was not a strong enough man to prevent it.

It is only fair to the Commanding Officer and his troops to point out that the temptation to them to despoil the Sikhs must have been very hard to resist. They had so far had no share of the loot; and everywhere in West Pakistan Sikhs were at that time considered fair game. To spare their lives could be accounted a special favour; to relieve them of their property a normal routine. If the Commanding Officer had ever been brought to trial he might have pleaded in his defence that it was impossible for him to keep his men in check. Certainly the incident on the first evening, when several Sikhs were killed, may well have been due to the unauthorized high-handedness of a section of the troops. The systematic searches on the following evening and the seizure of all that the Sikhs possessed were, according to all evidence, ordered and organized by the C.O. himself; but he might have argued that this was the only way of satisfying the troops and avoiding a repetition of violence and further heavy loss of life. Thus far one may find some excuse. But the general deceitfulness of his proceedings and the final transparent ruse, whereby the women were separated from the men and the latter driven in helpless panic and under a rain of bullets towards the border, are very hard to extenuate or defend.

The mistakes of the Bahawalpur Government and the crimes of its employees that have just been narrated may have undesignedly helped to keep the Rahim Yar Khan district comparatively free from disturbances. If the soldiery had been baulked of their prey and had returned hungry from their escort duties, it is likely that they would have contrived to instigate large-scale assaults on the thousands of Hindus who still remained in the district, so as to provide themselves with an opportunity for loot. As it was, they glutted themselves on the Sikh column and were content that the Hindus should remain more or less unmolested. The booty which they had taken from the Sikhs they divided up quietly among themselves; and no questions were asked. Their enjoyment of most of the women was more temporary. In the course of the next year all except twenty-seven were recovered and sent away to India.

During the month of October the Hindus living in the vil-

lages of the Rahim Yar Khan district began gradually to shift
for greater security to the towns. Some planted themselves on
friends and relatives; others took up their abode in serais
or built themselves temporary shelters. This migration was
hastened by a number of small incidents in which Hindus
were robbed or murdered. Most of these were the work of tribes-
men from the Dera Ghazi Khan district across the Indus. With
the fall in the river they took it into their heads to make tip-
and-run raids into Bahawalpur territory, directed against
villages where rich Hindus resided. The lead which they gave
was to some extent followed by the local inhabitants.

It was very difficult to stop these raids or to give effective protection to Hindus in the rural areas. Many of them sought safety
by temporarily embracing Islam. Faiz Ahmad and I were
afforded a good first-hand example of this one morning following a big raid in which several villages had been attacked. We
were motoring along the bank of a small canal running through
the affected area and came to a large village where two or three
Hindus had been killed the night before. As we approached it,
a stream of Hindu women was to be seen issuing from the village
and crossing the canal in the direction of a mosque on the other
side around which a number of people were gathered. Faiz
Ahmad, realizing at once what was afoot, jumped out of the
car and began to reason with the women and try to deflect them
from their purpose. It was like trying to deflect a line of ants.
The women were bent on proceeding to the mosque to be received into the Faith and paid not the slightest heed to what the
Deputy Commissioner was saying. They simply backed away
from him, murmuring snatches of the Koran, and then edged
past him over the bridge. He begged them not lightly to
abandon their own religion; he assured them that it was un-
necessary and that both he and I had come to protect them. It
was all to no effect. The stream divided and flowed on past him
to the mosque.

As a good Muslim Faiz Ahmad took to heart these enforced
and spurious conversions much more than I did. I was only too
happy that these people should be able to purchase so easily, if
not absolute safety, at any rate a feeling of safety. It seemed to
me to relieve us of a good deal of bother and anxiety. These
crude utilitarian views I conveyed in slightly modified form to

Faiz Ahmad, quoting Gibbon's observation that all the various modes of worship may be considered 'by the philosopher as equally false; and by the magistrate as equally useful'.

By the latter half of November virtually all the Hindus had come away from the villages and were concentrated in the four or five towns of the district. The immediate responsibility for their welfare fell on Faiz Ahmad. It was a great and growing burden. Cut off from their normal places of business and livelihood many of them soon began to find themselves in straits; and so to a constant anxiety for their safety was added the problem of how to support them. Naturally Faiz Ahmad wished to be relieved of the burden; while amongst the Hindus themselves the conviction grew that they had no alternative but to abandon their homes and migrate to India. Some of the more wealthy of them made their way down to Karachi and from there took ship or plane to Bombay. Others by bribery managed to get themselves conveyed in military lorries to some railway station on the Hindumalkot line or even to Hindumalkot itself. In this way several hundred and, as weeks lengthened into months, perhaps some thousands slipped away from the State into India. But a hard core of some sixty thousand Hindus still remained. As in the case of the Sikhs, it was impossible without special trains to move them out along the main Karachi-Lahore line which ran through the district; and we had nothing like sufficient lorries to move them up to some station on the Hindumalkot line and entrain them there. Moreover the Nawab was still wedded to the idea of keeping his 'loyal' Hindu subjects and was even thinking of getting back those who had already left! There was no hope, therefore, of persuading him to ask the Pakistan Government to provide special trains; nor, even if asked, was there much prospect of their being able to comply, for Pakistan was short of everything required for running trains, particularly coal.

Help came from another quarter. A large number of Hindu refugees from Bahawalpur State were by this time gathered at Delhi. They were well posted with all the difficulties of their co-religionists in Rahim Yar Khan and during December they began to agitate vigorously for arrangements to be made for their evacuation. Some threatened to fast before the Governor-General's house; others staged demonstrations at Gandhi's prayer-meetings, appearing with placards on which was written 'Save 70,000 Hindus of Bahawalpur'. Gandhi himself, though sympathetic, was not really in favour of extricating these Hindus from Bahawalpur. His whole aim at this time was to stop and even reverse the movements of migration. But the agitation had some effect on the Government of India and one day in December a British colonel, in the service of the Indian Union, arrived at Bahawalpur with an offer of special trains.

The Nawab and Gurmani were both away at Karachi,[1] so the colonel came to see me. I warmly welcomed the offer but I had no authority to accept it. I explained to him the Nawab's attitude and advised him to go to Karachi and try to see both Gurmani and the Nawab personally. I also wrote to the former strongly urging him to prevail upon the Nawab to accept this opportune offer.

It was all to no effect. The Nawab would not let his people go and the offer was refused.

The unwisdom of this refusal was speedily demonstrated. One afternoon early in January I had met Faiz Ahmad at a place called Khanpur to discuss with him various problems regarding the settlement of incoming refugees. While we were so engaged a message was received that there had been a raid on a small town named Ahmadpur Lamma and that a number of Hindus had been killed. This place lay in the south of the district towards the Sind border some fifty miles from Khanpur. We at once bundled into a car and bumped along as fast as we could over some very bad roads, but did not reach the place till after nightfall. Everything was pitch dark and we found our way with some difficulty to the police station, where a small group of lachrymose Hindus were gathered. As soon as our arrival was known, many more assembled, weeping and wailing and begging to be evacuated forthwith to India. Amid all the hubbub it was hard to obtain any coherent account of what had taken place. It appeared however that about twenty armed men from Dera Ghazi Kkan had suddenly arrived that morning and boldly walked up the bazaar, looting every Hindu shop they came to and shooting anyone who got in their way.

[1] The Nawab had a house a few miles away from Karachi to which he often resorted in the cold weather.

The police, recently reinforced and armed with rifles which would really fire, made not the slightest attempt to interfere —'Dar ke mare',[1] the sub-inspector apologetically explained. Finding that there was no resistance the raiders spent a couple of hours leisurely ransacking the shops and selecting their booty, and left quite unmolested about midday.

We turned from this sorry tale to the exhibits—the corpses which the Hindus were itching to show to us; for the corpses were irrefutable evidence in support of their plea to be sent away to India. It was a mercy, they said, that we had arrived before they were burnt so that we could see them with our own eyes. They were all laid out close to the police station, some on charpoys and some on the ground. A number of police constables were also asleep on charpoys and in the dim light of a hurricane lantern it was hard to distinguish the dead from the living. I kept on confusing a constable for a corpse and a corpse for a constable. These blunders were corrected by my eager guides and with their help I successfully established the existence of ten indubitable corpses. We had come to the end of the row and having, as I thought, finished the inspection I turned to the accompanying Hindus and began to murmur some suitable words of sorrow and sympathy. I spoke too soon; for, just as though they were showing off manure pits or other commendable examples of public spirit, they cried out at once with enthusiasm, 'There're some more, there're some more!'

'Enough, enough!' Faiz Ahmad interjected impatiently, 'we've seen sufficient.'

But the Hindus would not be denied and led me over to the other side of the pathway where another six to eight dead bodies were laid out in a row. I was duly impressed by this ocular evidence of the casualties. I could not, however, give any very straight answer to their urgent request for evacuation to India. The Nawab's views being what they were, Faiz Ahmad and I had to be careful what we said. I dwelt, therefore, on the lack of trains and shortage of coal on account of which, with the best will in the world, we could not immediately get them away. But, not to leave them entirely without hope, I said that possibly the Pakistan Government might be persuaded

[1] Literally: 'Being stricken with fear.'

to furnish trains if His Highness the Nawab himself requested them to do so. I advised them, therefore, to see the Nawab. I happened to know that he was due to return that very night from Karachi to Bahawalpur and that his train would be stopping next morning for ten to fifteen minutes at Sadiqabad—a station about eight miles from Ahmadpur Lamma. I suggested that some of them should go and seek audience of him as he passed through.

They did so, but were rebuffed by the personal staff who said that His Highness was unable to see them. With natural annoyance but little tact they then proceeded to march up and down the platform outside his special coach shouting, 'Dule[1] come out, Dule come out!' But 'Dule' remained firmly in his carriage or in his bed—perhaps quite unaware that some of his 'loyal Hindu subjects' wanted to see him.

The news of the raid on Ahmadpur probably penetrated to Delhi pretty quickly. In any case the Bahawalpuris there were keeping up their agitation. On January 10th it was rumoured that they were going to interrupt the actual reciting of the prayers at Gandhi's prayer-meeting. In the event they refrained from committing this awful sacrilege and were warmly commended by Gandhi for maintaining perfect silence during the prayers and expressing their anguish in a restrained manner. He knew, he said, their sufferings, but he had the word of the Ruler that, though he could not bring the dead back to life, the remaining Hindus could live in Bahawalpur in peace and safety, and no-one would interfere with their religion. The Hindu refugees from Bahawalpur may well have wondered what was the basis for these assurances; but Gandhi himself was only too anxious to accept them at their face value. Like the Nawab, with whom he was at this time in correspondence, he wanted the Hindus to remain where they were so that the tide of migration might be stayed. At the same time, however, he could not ignore the mounting pressure of opinion calling for the evacuation of all Hindus still remaining in West Pakistan. Ultimately, therefore, it was agreed between him and the Nawab that he should send an emissary over to Bahawalpur to discuss with the Hindus their position and try to pacify and reassure them.

[1] An honorific title applied locally to the Ruler, meaning literally: 'generous person'.

Failing this, it was recognized that other measures would have to be taken.

Accordingly about the fourth week of January Dr. Shushila Nair, a lady belonging to Gandhi's intimate circle, arrived in Bahawalpur, accompanied by Mr. Leslie Cross, a member of the Friends Ambulance Association. Both of them were bent on persuading the Hindus not to abandon their homes but to remain and face bravely such dangers as there might be. Both of them seemed to have a sincere belief in the propriety and probable success of their mission.

I was away from headquarters when they arrived, so by the time they came to call on me they had already seen most of the other Ministers, all of whom, echoing the Nawab's sentiments, had expressed warm sympathy with their objectives and given them every assurance regarding the safety of the Hindus. It was left to me to strike a harsh discordant note. With the corpses at Ahmadpur Lamma still fresh in my memory I no doubt expressed myself with more vigour than tact. I told Dr. Shushila Nair that so far as I could judge 90 per cent of the Hindus still remaining in the State wanted to leave it as soon as possible. If she tried to dissuade them, she was assuming a very heavy responsibility. Suppose they agreed to stay on and were then the victims of an assault such as had taken place recently at Ahmadpur, their blood would be on her head. What justification would she then be able to plead for endangering their lives? It was all very well to exhort them to face danger courageously, but with what object was she trying to make heroes out of these timid Hindu shopkeepers? I could not see that any public or private purpose was served by inducing them to stay on in Rahim Yar Khan, especially when in the rest of the State and in the surrounding Punjab districts all Hindus had migrated to India.

She said that the Nawab had personally assured her that he guaranteed their safety. I replied that the Nawab would in April go off to England for the summer. Whether from Farnham, Surrey, he would be able to protect his Hindu subjects in Rahim Yar Khan it was for her to judge. I certainly could not underwrite the guarantee.

I am afraid that both she and Mr. Cross were a little put out by my emphatic and uncompromising hostility to the main

objectives of their mission. They did not, however, take it ill
and a few days later, after they had toured the Rahim Yar Khan
district, they called on me again and good-naturedly admitted
that they had quite come round to my way of thinking. Dr.
Shushila Nair told me that at each place which she had visited
the Hindus had been assembled and she had talked to them
alone, putting forward to them all the arguments which she
could think of in favour of their remaining in the State. She
had then at each place asked those who were willing to remain
to hold up their hands. Not a hand was raised. She realized
that the desire to migrate to India was overwhelming and unalterable and that for many of them, unable to follow their
normal avocations, every day that passed was adding to their
distress. In the course of her tour she had also seen and heard
enough to realize that the wealthier Hindus were slipping away
in military lorries to the Hindumalkot line and were paying
through the nose for the privilege.

Everything was now quickly and happily settled. Dr. Shushila Nair went straight from Bahawalpur to Karachi, whither
the Nawab had again betaken himself, and told him she must
advise both him and Gandhi that the retention of the Hindus
in the Rahim Yar Khan district was impossible and that they
would have to be evacuated to India. She renewed the offer
of special trains and also, at my suggestion, proposed that a
liaison officer should be sent from India to help in the evacuation and obviate the possibility of subsequent complaints
and misunderstandings. A few days later I received word that
everything had been agreed to and that she was on her way
back to Delhi. Poor lady! The end of her mission coincided with
a tragedy shocking to everyone but particularly painful to her.
At Lahore on her return journey from Karachi to Delhi she
learnt that Gandhi had been assassinated.

The evacuation was accomplished without any hitch or
unpleasantness. Mr. Anand Deva, the liaison officer, came well
in advance and was most sensible and helpful. I took the opportunity of his presence to have opened more than a hundred
safes which had been recovered intact from the houses of Hindus
in Bahawalpur and stored in the tahsil. Nearly all of them were
found to be empty and the total amount of cash and valuables
which they yielded was quite trifling. One may perhaps con-

clude that the majority of the Hindus who were evacuated from Bahawalpur city succeeded in taking with them their most valuable possessions and that the numerous safes which looters broke open disappointed their cupidity.

It will be recalled that there was one very large and heavy safe which, according to the tahsildar, was reported to contain 'much gold'. He had on this account been unwilling to assume responsibility for it at the tahsil and so it had been deposited at my house and had remained there for about four months. I was personally present along with Mr. Anand Deva when this massive safe was solemnly prised open. I had visions of it containing gold and ornaments worth about a lac of rupees, but the actual yield was much less spectacular. The 'much gold' of popular imagination turned out to be a few currency notes and some jewellery worth perhaps in all about Rs 1000.

The Hindus of Bahawalpur city had been obliged to leave their homes in haste and confusion at less than twenty-four hours' notice. By contrast the evacuation of the Hindus from the Rahim Yar Khan district was a planned and orderly operation and only undertaken after plenty of time for preparation. For weeks beforehand the Hindus had been selling—no doubt at knock-down prices—such of their movable property as could not easily be transported; but they successfully carried away with them their most treasured possessions, including gold and silver ornaments and cash worth in all about two crores of rupees. The process of evacuation extended over a couple of months. Altogether sixteen special trains were run and the number of persons evacuated was about sixty thousand.

So in the end the Nawab's good intentions towards his 'loyal Hindu subjects' were honourably carried into effect.

XIII

Resettlement

I F the massacres of 1947 showed the Punjabis at their worst, the enforced migrations brought out some of the best of their qualities. The fortitude with which they bore the sudden uprooting from their homes and the vigour with which they set about establishing themselves in new ones were such as few other peoples could have equalled. They showed all the cheerful vitality of birds which, when robbed of their nest, will start immediately to build a fresh one. The conditions were harsh, but not too harsh to suppress or even check the surge of life in these sturdy, virile people. I often wondered whether a more sophisticated society would have survived so easily the violent shock to which the Punjab was subjected in 1947. It seemed to me at the time that if the more highly-strung and highly-organized peoples of the western world had had to undergo such a ruthless transplanting, they would have succumbed in large numbers to sheer exhaustion and *taedium vitae*.

The resettlement of the refugees, or 'displaced persons' as they had to be officially termed, was such a gigantic task and took so much of the time and energies of all the Governments concerned that no account of the upheaval of 1947 would be quite balanced without a few pages devoted to this subject. There are several publications[1] which deal with it in some detail. Here I will only describe briefly how the problem presented itself to us in Bahawalpur.

The first really big wave of refugees struck Bahawalpur in the last few days of August. They came from the Ferozepur district of East Punjab and, as mentioned in an earlier chapter, entered the State near Macleodganj Road. At about the same time most of the Muslim inhabitants of the adjoining State of Bikanir moved across into Bahawalpur by various routes. There was then a slight lull; but about September 20th a second smaller

[1] E.g. *Out of the Ashes* by M. S. Randhawa.

wave of forty to fifty thousand refugees poured into the State across the Bikanir border. They had marched all the way from the Rohtak and Hissar districts of south-east Punjab and were in a famished and exhausted condition. Some two thousand of them died within a few days of their arrival in Bahawalpur. Small parties from the same districts and from some of the Princely States south of the Sutlej followed in the next three to four weeks, but by the middle of October the stream had dwindled to a trickle and we concluded that the flow was drying up.

Our plans for coping with this influx were formulated at the end of August immediately after my arrival at Bahawalnagar.[1] At that time we could not tell whether there would be any limit to the number of Muslims forced to leave India. For aught we knew, all of them, or at any rate all those in northern India, might be driven into Pakistan. Certainly many Hindus, in their bitterness at the partition of the country, wanted all Muslims to be expelled and hoped that in this way Pakistan would be smothered at birth. We thought it quite likely that these sentiments would prevail, and during September, as the area of disturbance widened and the Government of India proved incapable of preventing indiscriminate assaults on Muslim lives and property even in Delhi, its own capital, our expectations seemed to be confirmed. It was not till October that the spread of disorder could be seen to be definitely checked. Muslims were still streaming in from East Punjab in accordance with the agreement of September 2nd for exchange of populations between the two halves of the Province; but beyond the confines of East Punjab the Government of India was proving capable of crushing any attempts to harry and drive away the Muslim population. To us in Bahawalpur this successful checking of the assaults on Muslims appeared to be mainly due to Gandhi. We felt that had it not been for his exertions and tremendous moral influence we should have been overwhelmed by a multitude of Muslim immigrants far greater than we could possibly have absorbed. In reality there must have been other forces working in the same direction and certainly Gandhi's efforts were vigorously backed by Nehru—though not equally so by all the leading figures in the Government of India. They were, however, battling

[1] See Chapter IX, p. 158.

against very strong currents of popular opinion, as Gandhi's subsequent assassination all too vividly revealed, and I still believe that his influence with all classes was the decisive factor in halting the disturbances on the Indian side more or less at the borders of the Punjab.

At the end of August we could not foresee that this would be the outcome. We had to be prepared for the worst; and so we thought it advisable to frame our resettlement plans so as to accommodate as many as we could. In the colony areas of Bahawalpur the normal unit of allotment had been the 'square' of twenty-five acres. We decided that we should not allot to any refugee family more than half a square for cultivation and that wherever the canal supplies were reasonably adequate one-quarter of a square or six and a quarter acres should be the unit of allotment. In this way we were able to settle on the land two to three times the number of families that had left it.

Speed was essential if, as we desired, we were to get the refugees on to the land in time to prepare it for the 'rabi' crop. This would have to be in the ground by the middle of November at latest. We made the allotments, therefore, as fast as we could on a temporary six months' basis. The refugees were permitted to gather without payment whatever they could of the standing 'kharif' crops and to hold the land on payment of only the land revenue and water rates until they had reaped the 'rabi' harvest in the following May. Thereafter fresh terms would be settled.

Our principle was to allot land on a uniform basis of one-quarter or one-half of a square per family to all those who owned or cultivated agricultural land in the districts from which they came. We did not at this stage make detailed inquiries about the size of their holdings, but simply tried to satisfy ourselves that those to whom we allotted land were genuine owners or tillers of the soil. We required them to file affidavits to this effect, warning them that we would in due course check the correctness of their statements. This turned out to be a not entirely empty threat, as some time later an agreement was reached between India and Pakistan for an exchange of copies of all the relevant revenue records and so eventually it became possible to verify everybody's claim. Of course a fair number of false affidavits and bogus claims were put in.

Settlement of the refugees in the colony lands evacuated by the Sikhs proceeded at a very rapid pace. The Sikhs had cultivated their holdings themselves and not through tenants and so, with their departure, the land and the villages which they had occupied were left quite vacant and the newcomers could move straight in. Settlement of the old proprietary land owned by the Hindus in the non-colony areas was a slower and more complicated business. This land had mostly been cultivated by Muslim tenants and was often intermingled with other land owned by Muslims. As soon as the Hindus left, the tenants or neighbouring Muslim landowners appropriated it, and it took some time to come to arrangements with the former or to oust the latter. A considerable portion of it had to be left with the tenants.

The settlement of refugees in urban areas followed a similar pattern. In the colony towns, where the buildings were all new and well-constructed and where there were competent municipal staffs, the work proceeded rapidly. The refugees were themselves eager to settle in these towns and in order to accommodate as many as possible we divided up some of the bigger premises. The fixation of rent was comparatively simple as the houses and shops vacated by the Hindus were of a few standard sizes and designs and their valuation for purposes of municipal house tax readily ascertainable.

There was much more difficulty in filling up the old towns with their ramshackle buildings of all shapes and sizes and inefficient or non-existent municipal staff, and several of them remained half-empty throughout the winter.

It was a marvel to me how the incoming Muslims who settled in these urban areas—tradesmen, artisans and ordinary labourers—succeeded from the very start in standing on their own legs with very little help of any kind from the Government. Some of them within a day of arrival dashed off to Multan, laid out their scanty resources on the purchase of wares, and returned to peddle them at the street side pending the allotment of premises. Others began straight away to ply their trades in the roadways, establishing themselves as barbers, cobblers, tailors etc., at whatever seemed a favourable site. It puzzled me how so many more or less destitute people could so quickly find a livelihood by taking in each other's washing. The explanation is that in these colony towns the interchange of goods and services amongst the refugees themselves managed to base itself almost at once on the solid foundation of economic service to the surrounding countryside. These 'mandi' (market) towns fulfilled certain essential functions in the economy of the area, and in the performance of these functions the incoming Muslims were able to step fairly easily into the shoes of the departed Hindus. They were aided by the fact that the harvest was at hand. Large quantities of grain, cotton and oilseeds were about to come into the market and had to be warehoused, bagged, processed or dispatched by rail to other centres. At the same time the cultivators, having received payment for their produce, had money in their hands for buying goods and services in the towns. So the refugees settled into their new quarters at a favourable moment and were soon sustained by the normal flow of economic life which had been only temporarily interrupted.

Most of the grain merchants and other dealers in agricultural produce had been Hindus, but there were a few substantial Muslims in the trade and other local Muslims with a little capital soon set themselves up as grain dealers. We also entered the market wherever necessary, advancing money to agents to buy up stocks on our behalf. There was, therefore, not much difficulty in taking from the cultivators the produce which they had to offer. Only cotton presented a serious problem. This was the principal 'cash' crop in Bahawalpur and the cultivator largely relied on it to provide him with the means of paying his dues to the State Government. Cotton in its natural raw state as plucked from the bush cannot be stocked for any great length of time. The first step is to gin it, that is to separate the cotton from the cotton seeds. Ordinarily most of the crop was bought up at harvest time by the ginning factories, of which there were three or four in Bahawalpur district and about double that number in Rahim Yar Khan. All of them, except perhaps one in Rahim Yar Khan, were owned by Hindus and were worked by them with a predominantly Hindu staff. Those in Bahawalpur district were abandoned during September as a result of the general exodus of Hindus from that district. Some of the factory owners in Rahim Yar Khan also left for India, while those who remained showed no disposition to run their factories. They considered it too dangerous for themselves or their employees to go out into the rural areas to arrange purchases of cotton, nor were they willing to lay out large sums on such purchases when there was no certainty that they would be able to stay on in the State and recover their investment. There was a prospect, therefore, that practically all the ginning factories would remain closed and cotton become unsaleable. How were we to get them working? This was a question which continuously worried us from the beginning of September right on until well into November. It also worried the West Punjab Government. I would say that it was in regard to the working of these ginning factories that the Hindu notion of paralysing Pakistan by withdrawal of essential expertise came nearest to fulfilment.

Somehow or other a solution was found. When it came to a pinch, the Muslims proved to be less lacking in initiative, ingenuity and business capacity than had been imagined and with a little delay enough factories were brought into operation to handle the crop. It became clear quite early on that we should have to provide most of the working capital required. This we did through the State Bank of Bahawalpur at the head of which we were fortunate in having at this time an experienced Muslim banker on loan from the Imperial Bank of India. The difficulty was to find parties, with or without any capital of their own, who had any experience at all of the business and who could be relied on to collect staff capable of starting up one of these ginning factories and keeping it running. There was a danger of being hoodwinked by speculators who, after taking advances for the purchase of cotton and making a show of starting up the factory, would decamp with the money. Even when what seemed to be genuine and reliable parties were forthcoming, the negotiation of terms for the lease of a factory was a tricky business, especially as in some cases they were being simultaneously wooed by the West Punjab authorities and could play us off against each other. The back of our problem was, however, broken when a Muslim who had owned several ginning factories in East Punjab turned up as an applicant for the lease of some of ours. Resisting the blandishments of West Punjab, he did a deal with us and by shifting the Muslim personnel he had brought with him from one factory to another he managed by December to get three or four of the biggest ones into operation. Other lesser fry started up a few more and so we scraped through. We were in such straits that the lessees got the factories on very easy terms and probably some of them made a small fortune out of the one season's working. I was, however, so thankful to see smoke coming out of the factory chimneys and bullock-carts unloading cotton in the factory yards that I did not care if we had dropped a few lacs of rupees in lease money.

The reader may have wondered under what authority we disposed of the land, houses, shops, factories and other premises left by the Hindus and Sikhs. From the very outset we felt the need of some legal basis for our proceedings and in the last few days of August I began to draft an ordinance regarding the custody of evacuee property. To my intense relief I was spared further labour for just about this time the West Punjab Government issued an excellent ordinance on this very subject. It was simple, lucid and comprehensive and with a few modifications could easily be adapted to our needs. We duly promulgated our version of it. It provided *inter alia* for the appointment of the highest revenue authority (in the Punjab the Financial Commissioner and in Bahawalpur the Revenue Minister) as Custodian of Evacuee Property with Deputy and Assistant Custodians under him whose orders were ultimately appealable to him. This gave our proceedings a legal basis and to some extent a judicial character.

By the second half of October we had taken in as many refugees as we could for the moment readily absorb. There were still a number of nooks and crannies into which, with time and careful arrangements, more could be fitted; but for the time being we could not cope with any more. So far we had been fairly lucky, as we had succeeded in passing on to the West Punjab large numbers whom we could not readily accommodate or did not like the look of. We were helped by the fact that for most of the refugees Bahawalpur was only a first haven of refuge and not the ultimate goal. They were really making for the Punjab and most of them were willing of their own accord to proceed there, particularly if no immediate and attractive accommodation was made available to them in Bahawalpur. We refused quite firmly, despite pressure from several quarters, to open any regular refugee camps in the State. At one or two places we made temporary transit arrangements, but we did not undertake to look after, except for a few days, any for whom we could not permanently provide. So we kept the refugees on the move and those who seemed disposed to linger were politely but firmly pushed across the Sutlej into the Punjab.

Everything seemed to be settling down nicely when suddenly at the end of October almost without warning the Government of India began dumping on us at Macleodganj Road thousands of refugees brought there by train from districts around Delhi. Some eighty thousand were deposited in this way during the first half of November. At about the same time the Maharajah of Bikanir wrote to us saying that 150,000 refugees bound for the West Punjab had entered his State from the Hissar and Rohtak districts and that he proposed to pass them into Bahawalpur in the Fort Abbas region, whence they could proceed to the bridge across the Sutlej at the Pallah headworks, instead of conducting them northwards through his own State to the bridge at Suleimanke which was their shortest route. He gave as his reason that there were a number of Sikhs in the north of Bikanir (including many who had recently migrated from Bahawalpur) and he was afraid the column of refugees might be attacked if it passed through that area.

We could not but agree to receive them and give them passage through the State, though we did not like it. To have this column on our hands while simultaneously thousands of unwanted guests were detraining at Macleodganj meant a great strain on our resources; and we feared that many of the column, wearied of their journey and no longer in danger of attack, might halt permanently by the wayside and become our liability. However the column proved to be well-disciplined, and fortunately much of the Bahawalpur territory through which they had to pass was so little removed from sheer desert that they were glad to press on to the Punjab. As they approached Pallah and entered country that was more smiling and attractive, I mobilized all available tongas, donkeys, ponies and camels to assist them over the last laps of their journey. They thanked me profusely for this help, little realizing, I hope, how far from disinterested it was.

The refugees decanted at Macleodganj were more of a

burden. The Government of India insisted on dumping them there because it was easier and safer to do this than to take them by train through the Central Punjab and push them over the frontier between Amritsar and Lahore. The arrangement was most unwelcome to us, and unwelcome also to the Governments of West Punjab and Pakistan, as it meant that at a time when there was an acute shortage of coal in Pakistan, trains had to be provided to move these refugees from Macleod-ganj into the West Punjab by a long and circuitous route via Samasatta and Multan. An attempt was made to get us to accept responsibility for them. This we declined to do. Our stand throughout was that the Government of Bahawalpur, unlike that of West Punjab or the Federal Government of Pakistan, could not be held responsible for refugees. We had not asked for the creation of Pakistan or even been consulted about it, and there-fore anything that we might do to mitigate its consequences by settling refugees within the State was purely *ex gratia*. We had by this time already absorbed nearly two hundred thousand and could not for the present take on any more.

The West Punjab Government had to accept this position and assume responsibility for the refugees at Macleodganj. But they accumulated there much faster than trains could be provided to move them to the Punjab and for two to three weeks we had large numbers on our hands. However, ulti-mately we got rid of most of them.

We were not alone in passing on refugees to others. The feelings of pity and sympathy which they had initially evoked had become deadened by repeated excitation, and by this time Provincial Governments and district authorities were all alike trying to shift the burden from themselves. The West Punjab Government were particularly overwhelmed and anxious for relief. Owing to weak administration the whole refugee prob-lem had come to appear to them much more intractable than in fact it was. There was no danger now of all the Muslims in northern India being driven out. The flow had been checked and the numbers to be accommodated were, therefore, more or less limited to the Muslims from East Punjab and the adjoining Princely States. Room for all of them could in reality be found fairly easily in the West Punjab, but owing to delays and corruption in the allotment of land and houses this fact was obscured and huge numbers collected in refugee camps or in squatting places of their own choosing where the misery and squalor were appalling. The West Punjab Government, erroneously thinking that most of the available land had already been allotted to bona fide refugees, were at a loss how to empty these camps and were disturbed because in some of them there had been minor demonstrations and cries of 'Pakistan Murdabad'[1] and 'Jinnah Murdabad'. They appealed to the Pakistan Government for assistance and early in December the latter called a conference in Lahore to consider the whole problem.

At this conference a general, if cynical, hope was expressed —though not officially recorded—that with the onset of the really cold weather, due in two to three weeks' time, a good proportion of the refugees would die of pneumonia and so relieve us, partially at least, of our difficulties. But we could not rely on these forces of nature, nor in the event did they give us much aid—the refugees proved remarkably tough. The West Punjab Government had another quite simple solution for the problem and that was, with the backing of the Pakistan Government, to persuade other Governments to take a large number of the refugees off their hands. I was afraid that the Government of Bahawalpur might be one of those expected to come to the rescue and was relieved to find that, with very little persuasion from me, it was generally accepted that we had done our part and could not for the moment be expected to do any more. The two Governments specially earmarked for relieving the Punjab of refugees were those of Sind and the N.W.F.P., particularly the former. Sind had so far escaped the main deluge and had only received some few thousand refugees, arriving by sea and air from Bombay. There was a general belief that they had vast areas of land available for allotment. This was not altogether correct, as a large proportion of the non-Muslim population had not yet left the province. However, Sind were more or less told that they would have to take half a million refugees from the Punjab. They did not clearly accept this liability, but they seemed to acquiesce in the necessity of doing something.

It was proposed to make a start by sending 150,000 refugees on foot to Sind complete with all their bullocks and carts. It would be a long trek and for 125 miles their route would lie

[1] 'Down with (death to) Pakistan.'

through Bahawalpur, so our co-operation was desired. We were expected to prepare camping grounds, arrange for water supplies and provide stocks of food, fodder and fuel. Though I was sceptical of both the need and the practicability of the plan, I undertook to do all that was required of us. Suitable halting places were selected, officers deputed to be in charge of them, stocks of fuel etc. laid in and complicated changes made in the rotation of the canals so as to ensure water supplies at the right places and at the right time. After several postponements a date was finally fixed for the commencement of the march. Everything in Bahawalpur was in readiness. But nobody came. The refugees refused to budge from the Punjab and the whole project of sending 150,000 of them on foot to Sind collapsed ignominiously.

The refugees were quite right in their obstinate refusal to move; and slowly it dawned on the West Punjab Government that there was ample land available for accommodating them and for compensating them in full for land abandoned on the other side of the frontier. Ultimately it turned out that, after meeting all just claims, there were several hundred thousand acres surplus.

In Bahawalpur Rao Fazlur Rahman had reported quite early on that owing to the mistakes or corruption of the subordinate revenue staff there had been many cases of over-allotment and double-allotment, and of wrong allotment to persons who were not owners or cultivators of land or were not refugees at all. So in January and February we undertook a thorough scrutiny of all the allotments so far made as a result of which several thousand acres were found to have been improperly allotted and became available for further settlement of refugees. We also took this opportunity to do some reshuffling of the refugees so as to group together those from the same district or belonging to the same tribe, and also so as to ensure that the border areas would be occupied by stout-hearted cultivators with martial traditions who would not run away at the slightest alarm. These reallotments were worked out by the middle of March and scheduled to take effect at the end of May after the 'rabi' harvest had been gathered. It was hoped that after this reshuffling all the allotments would in fact become more or less permanent and that none of the refugees would have to shift

I

again. But it was impossible at this stage, when there had been no proper verification of claims, to make permanent allotments and so for the time being they were made on a yearly basis.

In the latter half of February I made an extensive tour through the eastern parts of the State where the refugees were most thickly settled. I had rather dreaded it as I feared that I would everywhere hear nothing but complaints and be assailed with requests which could not be granted. But not at all; everywhere the refugees had settled down amazingly contentedly and were full of thanks for all that had been done for them. They were particularly grateful to the inhabitants of adjoining villages who had lent them bullocks or ploughed and sowed their lands for them and in numerous other ways assisted them to find their feet in their new quarters. They were looking forward to a good 'rabi' harvest and seemed already to have forgotten all their tribulations of a few months earlier.

I have painted on the whole a rosy picture of the refugees. This is because in Bahawalpur we escaped the worst scenes of misery. At Vehari and Arifwala and, no doubt, several other places in the Punjab, hundreds of refugees sat day after day by the roadside huddled together, half dead or dying, in squalor, filth, utter wretchedness and dumb despair. In Bahawalpur too, though the conditions were nowhere so bad, we had a few black spots. Macleodganj Road was one of them. From the very outset this place had continuously a large floating population of refugees. Though certain facilities were available there and we had a competent staff in charge, at times the numbers outran our resources and the refugees suffered considerable privations. Another bad spot—probably the worst in the State—was Samasatta. This was a railway junction and nothing more. There were some railway quarters and a number of railway sheds and warehouses and a very small bazaar, but no regular town or municipal services. Large numbers of refugees entering the State at Macleodganj Road came on by train to Samasatta and waited there to catch some train going northwards to the Punjab. For about six weeks, from the end of September till well into November, a floating population of about two thousand refugees squatted and defaecated near the station and along the railway lines. During about half this period there were on an average six deaths daily—mostly old people and infants.

Very soon the mess and filth in the station precincts became indescribable as there was no-one to clear it up. We then bribed some of the municipal staff of Bahawalpur city with large bonuses to come out periodically in lorries and clean the place up and some improvement was effected. But we were not able to do much for the refugees halting at Samasatta and the condition of many of them was pitiable.

One should also not forget the emotional suffering of the refugees, forced to quit all of a sudden and for ever the familiar scenes of childhood and youth or, maybe, of a lifetime. One scene, riveted in my mind, typifies for me this measureless and meaningless suffering. I had gone over to Macleodganj Road—probably one day in October—in response to an urgent call from Rao Fazlur Rahman. The flour mill at that place had run out of oil and was about to close down, the Muslim owner or his agent having given no warning of any shortage until his stocks of oil were on the point of exhaustion. Fazlur Rahman was faced with the imminent prospect of having no flour to offer to the incoming refugees, and he wanted my authority for requisitioning one of six tank wagons, fully laden with oil, which happened to be standing at the station *en route* from Karachi to India. Together we dragooned the station staff into uncoupling one of these wagons and handing it over to us. Having secured this supply of oil and given orders for the flour mill to be restarted, we turned our attention to the refugees, large numbers of whom had newly arrived by train from India. They were squatting disconsolately along the line for several hundred yards on either side of the station and seemed so stunned by their misfortunes as to be incapable of speech or movement. As we were strolling about among them, trying to reassure them and cheer them up, a long train of open trucks drew into the station from the west, crammed with Hindu refugees from Multan who were being evacuated to India. Thus the two separate sets of refugees, driven in opposite directions by the same impalpable forces, met at Macleodganj station, and for fifteen minutes gazed at each other in lugubrious silence. Not a word was exchanged and the sense of cumulated misery was overpowering. As those standing in the trucks looked down at those sitting by the track and those sitting by the track looked up at those standing in the trucks, an expression of half-dawning comprehension crept into their gloomy, bewildered faces and seemed to say, 'So you're also in just the same plight! God help you!' Then the train started again and steamed slowly out of the station with its load of misery, while the other lot of refugees continued sitting dazed and speechless by the side of the line. All alike had been driven from their homes by the exigencies not of war but of freedom. It did not make sense, but it had to be endured.

XIV

Summing Up

I N this chapter I shall attempt to answer two questions, which may have suggested themselves to the reader, and then conclude with some general remarks regarding the responsibility for these events.

The two questions which I shall try to answer are:

(i) Were the happenings in Bahawalpur typical of the disorders elsewhere?

(ii) Could these massacres and migrations have been prevented?

There is no doubt that the outbreaks of violence in Bahawalpur, even in the eastern part of the State which was most affected, did not compare in scale or savagery with those in the Central and Eastern Punjab. At one stage the Indian press made great play with the Bahawalpur disturbances and produced some ingenious calculations to prove that no less than seventy thousand Hindus and Sikhs had been killed in the State. There were special reasons for this propagandist arithmetic. In some of the Princely States of East Punjab, notably Patiala, Kapurthala and Faridkot, the slaughter of Muslims had been particularly heavy and this had been given great prominence in the Pakistan press. India was tempted to reply with a *tu quoque* and the Bahawalpur disorders, considerably exaggerated, provided convenient material. In actual fact the total casualties in the whole of Bahawalpur State (including the Sikhs from Rahim Yar Khan district killed on the way to Jaisalmir) cannot, on a liberal estimate, have exceeded three thousand, and V. P. Menon's description of it as 'a paradise compared with East Punjab' was not wide of the mark.

In Bahawalpur there were no terrific holocausts such as took place at Sheikupura, where several thousands of Hindus and Sikhs were killed in a few hours, and no large-scale train

261

massacres. On three occasions small parties of Hindus were murdered while travelling in trains within Bahawalpur territory, but there was no successful systematic hold-up of a refugee train, followed by an overpowering or seduction of the armed guard and a wholesale slaughter of all the passengers. Several such sickening outrages were perpetrated elsewhere. There were also in Bahawalpur none of the grosser excesses—no deliberate mutilation of men or women, no sadistic rapes as distinct from seduction, no parading of women naked through the streets such as was widely reported to have occurred in a town in East Punjab.[1]

In general the disturbances in Bahawalpur resembled closely both in scale and character those in the immediately adjoining districts of south-west Punjab. The resemblance was due to a similarity in the composition and temperament of the population, while differences in these same respects gave a somewhat different colour to the disturbances in the Central Punjab. In Bahawalpur and south-west Punjab loot rather than blood was the dominating motive of the majority community. Non-Muslims who resisted the pillagers or got in their way were liable to be bumped off and occasionally, when the Muslims were roused to fury by the sight of injury to any of themselves, blood flowed freely. But there were very few instances of an organized hunt for victims and a delight in killing for its own sake. The Muslim population was less interested in blood than in the quiet enjoyment of Hindu property and Hindu girls.

In the Central Punjab, on the other hand, particularly among the Sikhs, there was a positive lust for blood and consequently casualties were much higher. Individuals boasted—not without exaggeration—of the numbers of the opposite community they had slain. Casualties resulted not merely from chance encounters or sudden gusts of anger but from systematic butchery and hunting down of victims. Many witnesses attest how in East Punjab murderous-looking Sikhs armed with large kirpans prowled about the platforms of railway stations sniffing

---

[1] It should be noted that a similar story was current during the Mutiny when forty-eight young women were reported to have been paraded naked through the streets of Delhi, ravished in broad daylight and then murdered. This story was classed by Lecky among the 'Fictions connected with the Indian Outbreak of 1857'.

for blood, and when a train halted, searched the carriages for Muslim travellers and, if they discovered any, stabbed them to death. The historian of Lahore records how in the early eighteenth century during the commotions that marked the break-up of the Mogul empire, the Sikhs laid waste the Punjab from Ambala to Lahore. 'They butchered, bayoneted, strangled, shot down, hacked to pieces, and burnt alive every Mohammedan in the place.'[1] History repeated itself in 1947.

The greater ferocity displayed in the Central as compared with the south-western Punjab was in part just a reflection of the differing temperaments of the respective populations. Even in ordinary times the number of murders reported to the police in districts like Lahore, Amritsar and Ferozepur exceeded a hundred per district per annum. There were similar high murder rates in some of the Muslim districts of north-west Punjab. But in the districts of Bahawalpur and south-west Punjab the rate was more like ten than a hundred per annum. The relative docility of the peoples of this area gave a milder character to the disorders.

Apart from this difference of temperament, the more even distribution of the population between the two communities in the central districts was conducive to greater and more widespread violence. Here there was considerable intermingling of Muslims and non-Muslims not merely in the towns but in the rural areas also. In all these central districts Sikh and Muslim villages existed side by side while quite a number had mixed populations. Thus once warfare broke out between the two communities it involved the whole countryside and was very difficult to control. In a number of instances whole villages or sections of villages were practically annihilated.

Moreover the more even the balance between the two communities, the greater the force required for the one in the majority to assert its mastery. The Sikhs were determined to overpower the Muslims on their side of the frontier and to drive them away; and they had armed themselves well for this purpose. But since the Muslims were very numerous in the east-central districts of Amritsar, Ferozepur, Gurdaspur and Jullundur and initially had no thought of leaving their homes, the Sikhs had necessarily to employ force and terror on a consider-

[1] *Lahore, its history,* by Syed Mohammad Latif.

able scale in order to dislodge them; and this in turn set going corresponding Muslim violence in the adjoining districts across the frontier.

The same conditions did not obtain in Bahawalpur or in the western districts of the Punjab generally. Here not only were the Muslims in an overwhelming majority, but, outside the colony areas, the population of the countryside was almost exclusively Muslim. The non-Muslims were concentrated in the towns. In the rural areas there was only a sprinkling of Hindus and Sikhs—shopkeepers, moneylenders and petty officials—and, save for the Sikh colony 'chaks', there existed very few villages with a wholly or largely Hindu or Sikh population. The Sikh 'chaks' in Bahawalpur were nearly all near the eastern border and, as mentioned earlier, their inhabitants at the very outset of the trouble slipped away into Bikanir State with little loss or molestation. The only instance in Bahawalpur of a whole village being wiped out in the style of the Central Punjab was the isolated hamlet of Labana Sikhs whose fate has been recounted on page 230.

Of the Hindu and Sikh shopkeepers scattered about the villages in small numbers, some were killed, some submitted to forcible conversion, but the majority, sensing their danger in time, made their way to the nearest town where there were larger numbers of their own community and more hope of protection from the authorities. Thus the disorders in the villages, never very considerable, tended to subside rapidly through the elimination of the few non-Muslims, and the towns, large and small, with all that they offered in the way of Hindu property to loot, became the main centres of trouble. In the larger towns disturbances were the work of the local Muslim inhabitants. In the smaller towns the Hindu shops and quarters were liable to be attacked by mobs of Muslim villagers from the surrounding countryside, often with the connivance of the Muslims inside, as happened at Khairpur, Qaimpur, Macleodganj Road and Hasilpur and was attempted at Minchinabad.

This was the general pattern of the disorders both in Bahawalpur and throughout most of western Punjab, but towards the north, where the Muslim population was by nature more turbulent, the violence tended to be greater.

The herding of members of the minority community into

keeps or camps where they could be more easily safeguarded was a common feature throughout the Punjab, and our jail camp outside the city of Bahawalpur had its counterpart in places great and small from Delhi to Rawalpindi. We were lucky in being able to evacuate all the inmates of our camp within a very few days so they suffered no serious or prolonged privations. This was not everywhere the case.

Throughout the Punjab—and not merely in Bahawalpur—the forces of law and order proved unreliable. Their general apathy and at places active connivance in loot and murder were a principal cause of the magnitude of the disorders. The behaviour of the police and military in Bahawalpur in these respects was not unrepresentative and by no means below the general level elsewhere—indeed, so far as I can judge, the Bahawalpur troops behaved far better than some of the forces in the Sikh States of East Punjab. But in Bahawalpur we were at this disadvantage, that we had nothing to fall back upon. The States in East Punjab had the Government of India behind them, and the Government of India, finding many of its forces unreliable, could and did call in Gurkha and Madrasi troops who were more or less uncontaminated. We had no option but to do the best we could with the Bahawalpur Army. Pakistan was hardly in a position to help us and its own troops were largely infected with the general contagion.

These troubled times afforded to officials of all ranks unparalleled opportunities for illicit gain and some of them may have felt, like Clive, astonished at their own moderation. Money could be made both from the outgoing and from the incoming refugees. The former, if they had any resources, were naturally willing to pay for safe evacuation, and they could also be called upon to pay for the privilege of taking some of their belongings with them. The theory was put forward—and being so beneficial to dishonest persons quickly gained wide acceptance—that an evacuee must not take away anything valuable from the territory he was leaving on the ground that 'it belonged to Pakistan' or to India as the case might be. On this absurd pretext evacuees could be searched and their property misappropriated, or they could be compelled to pay a heavy toll. This system of semi-legalized robbery and extortion, of which there were many traces in Bahawalpur, flourished extensively in

I*

both halves of the Punjab. An unmolested evacuation such as was arranged in the Rahim Yar Khan district in 1948 would have been hardly possible in 1947.

Much of the movable property left behind by evacuees in shops, factories, business premises and houses fell into the hands of plundering mobs; but articles which they could not easily carry away or dispose of, such as furniture, carpets and cars, were often appropriated by high-ranking officials and their friends either by open seizure or on the plea, true or false, that the owners had consigned them to their care. The inclination to profit from the misfortunes of others was widespread and showed itself in the highest as well as the lowest strata of society. One story illustrative of the general depravity, which particularly shocked Nur Mohammad—a man of rather old-fashioned views—was that of a well-known Muslim prostitute of Delhi. It was said that in return for a large sum of money an influential Muslim family, who were in a position to arrange for their own evacuation by air, permitted her to pose as one of their daughters and take her seat along with them in the plane.

The incoming refugees desired to be allotted and put in possession of vacated land, houses, shops etc., so that they could settle down quickly and begin to earn a livelihood. Those who possessed ready cash or could borrow from relations and friends on the side of the border to which they had migrated, bribed and tipped patwaris and other petty officials according to the custom of the country. This went on in Bahawalpur as elsewhere, but in Bahawalpur the incoming refugees were probably settled more promptly and with less harassment than elsewhere because we had the advantages of an autocratic government, which could take decisions promptly, and of an efficient 'settlement' staff all of whom could be switched at once from their ordinary duties on to 'resettlement' of refugees.

Big money often changed hands when it came to the allotment of factories, mills, and other commercial or industrial undertakings. There were prospects of large profits for anyone with the ability to restart these abandoned establishments, and incoming refugees with business experience and access to banking facilities were prepared to pay handsomely for quick possession. Amid all the golden opportunities for peculation in those days here was the real bonanza for political bosses and high-ranking officials.

Against the general inhumanity and collapse of moral standards must be set numerous individual examples of kindness and compassion, loyalty to friendship, devotion to duty, and courage in shielding and sheltering those whose lives were in danger. In this and in other ways there is a parallel with the Mutiny ninety years earlier. Unfortunately these examples of virtue were not widely appreciated and sometimes received even from the Governments concerned less than lukewarm approbation. While the Governments of India and Pakistan were both genuinely anxious to do the right thing and bank down the fires of hatred, the two new Governments of East and West Punjab were both appreciably influenced by the popular passions to which they were more directly exposed. Consequently officials who were slack in the performance of their duty or even guilty themselves of horrible crimes were allowed to go unpunished, while the few who vigorously and courageously resisted the general frenzy were in several instances frowned upon or victimized.

Most civilized societies have been liable to occasional pogroms. What occurred in the Punjab in 1947 was qualitatively a not uncommon phenomenon; but it was unusual in so far as it affected so many people simultaneously over such a wide area and resulted in such a very heavy death roll. In India the nearest well-authenticated precedent to frenzy on such a scale is afforded by the Mutiny. The parties to the conflict at that time were different, Hindus and Muslims being ranged on one side and Christians of all kinds—European, Eurasian and Indian—on the other; but the passions aroused were much the same and caused the adherents of all three religions alike to sink to the crudest savagery. The mutineers set the standard by shooting their British officers and then murdering their wives and children. This roused in the British such a burning spirit of revenge that British troops, when they got the opportunity, slaughtered 'niggers' indiscriminately without regard to guilt or innocence, age or sex. These ferocious reprisals provoked further outrages by the sepoys, including the hideous massacre of women and children at Cawnpore, and this in turn stimulated the British to more fearful acts of vengeance. Thus one atrocity or the report of it led to another and prompted the irrational massacre of quite innocent persons. A young English Assistant Commissioner, whose sister had undoubtedly been murdered in Delhi by the mutineers, believed that she had first been stripped naked and outraged. The thought of this so worked upon his feelings that on the recovery of Delhi by the British, 'he had put to death', according to his own admission, 'all he had come across, not excepting women and children'. The less sophisticated Punjabi, inflamed by similar provocations, real or rumoured, perpetrated in 1947 many like insensate deeds of violence, though he has probably left no such clear written record of his vengeful exploits.

This review of some of the general features of these massacres and migrations may be rounded off with a few overall statistics. Reliable figures are not available in regard to all matters, but it can be stated compendiously and with certainty that while Muslims lost the most lives, Hindus and Sikhs lost the most property. As regards the number of persons compelled to migrate, reasonably accurate figures are available. Between August 1947 and March 1948 about four and a half million Hindus and Sikhs migrated from West Pakistan to India and about six[1] million Muslims moved in the reverse direction. A great part of this huge migration took place within the short space of three months, that is between the middle of August and the middle of November.

The Hindus and Sikhs who left West Pakistan were as a whole decidedly better-to-do than the Muslims who entered it. The latter were mainly peasants, artisans and labourers with a comparatively small admixture of big landowners and business-men. On the other hand among the Hindu and Sikh refugees there were a considerable number of landlords and capitalists, big or small, and numerous persons holding administrative or clerical posts in industry, trade, banking, and insurance, while the Sikh peasantry, who had to leave the 'colony' areas of West Pakistan, were more prosperous and had larger holdings than the Muslim peasantry of East Punjab. This is reflected in the available statistics. In West Punjab alone the land abandoned by Hindus and Sikhs amounted to 6·7 million acres against 4·7 million acres abandoned by Muslims on the other

[1] Seven million according to Pakistan authorities.

side of the border. Figures regarding the total value of immovable property left on either side are less reliable. In the years immediately after Partition exaggerated claims were made by both sides, but according to more recent and more moderate estimates of the Government of India Rs 500 crores represents the value of property left by Hindus and Sikhs in West Pakistan while the corresponding figure for the property left in India by Muslims who migrated to West Pakistan is put at Rs 100 crores. Even if the disparity was not as much as the five to one indicated by these figures, it was certainly very considerable.

Estimates of casualties are largely a matter of guesswork. During and immediately after the disturbances it was freely stated that millions had lost their lives. Even a later and more sober estimate made by an Indian High Court judge puts the figure at about half a million.[1] An English journalist, Andrew Mellor, thinks[2] that the number killed is unlikely to have been less than two hundred thousand and may well have been far more. The other extreme is represented by an estimate, attributed to Nehru, that twenty to thirty thousand people had been killed in the Punjab. My own guess, based on some rough calculations[3] originally made in December 1947, is not widely different from that of Andrew Mellor. Slightly varying his conclusion I would say that the number killed is unlikely to have been more than two hundred thousand and may well have been appreciably less. This, though lower than most estimates, is an enormous total for civilian casualties in time of peace.

I turn now to the second question, 'Could these massacres and migrations have been prevented?' To answer it one has to be clear about their cause. Succinctly stated their cause was the decision to create Pakistan by dividing the Punjab and thus dividing or threatening to divide the Sikhs. The question, therefore, resolves itself into two parts, viz.:

(i) Could Pakistan have been avoided altogether?
(ii) If not, could the Sikhs have been peacefully accommodated in some agreed way?

These two parts of the question are closely interconnected,

[1] *Stern Reckoning*, by G. D. Khosla, p. 299.
[2] *India since Partition*, p. 45.
[3] See note at the end of the chapter.

but for purposes of analysis it will be convenient to consider
them separately.

In this narrative the course of events leading to the creation
of Pakistan has been traced only from the year 1937; for though
Pakistan had its roots much further back in history, as is apparent from the ideas expressed by Sir Syed Ahmad in the nineteenth century, it was only after 1937 that it became a live
political issue. I propose, therefore, to examine whether its
avoidance was possible only from 1937 onwards and not to dig
down deeply into the events of an earlier period. As regards pre-
1937, I will dwell only on one significant fact, namely that
Gandhi's rise to ascendancy in Congress was more or less coin-
cident with Jinnah's estrangement from it.

In 1917 Jinnah was a member and keen supporter of Congress, noted primarily as an Indian rather than a purely Muslim
Nationalist. At that time he was pooh-poohing the threat of
Hindu domination. 'Fear not,' he said, 'this is a bogy which
is put before you to scare you away from the co-operation and
unity which are essential to self-government.' So long as Congress was led by men like G. K. Gokhale, who spoke the familiar
language of Western liberalism and constitutionalism, Jinnah
felt at home in it. But the growing influence of Gandhi at the
end of World War I set it on unconstitutional paths and simultaneously gave it a more pronounced Hindu complexion. To
these developments Jinnah could not reconcile himself. He
parted from Congress in 1928.

Jinnah's dislike of Gandhi—that 'Hindu revivalist' as he
called him—was deep-seated; and he distrusted profoundly his
methods of non-co-operation and organized agitation. They
'have already caused split and division', he wrote to him in
1920, 'in almost every institution that you have approached
hitherto,' and he predicted that they would 'lead to disaster'—
as indeed they did as regards Hindu-Muslim unity, the preservation of which was an objective which at that time both of
them shared. The fact is—as Jinnah seems dimly to have perceived—that with Gandhi's decision not to co-operate with the
British and to launch a campaign of civil disobedience the seeds
of separation were being sown. Civil disobedience involved an
appeal to the masses, and an appeal to the masses by an organization headed and symbolized by Gandhi was necessarily

an emotional, semi-religious appeal to the Hindu masses and
not to the Muslims; for Gandhi with all his fads and fastings,
his goat's milk, mud baths, days of silence and fetish of non-
violence was pre-eminently a Hindu. He himself claimed to be
'a Muslim, a Hindu, a Buddhist, a Christian, a Jew, a Parsee'.
But this claim did not cut much ice; indeed who but a Hindu
could entertain such a preposterous hope of being all things to
all men?

Gandhian leadership of Congress was highly successful in
securing for the nationalist movement popular backing from
the Hindus; and popular backing was considered necessary in
order to bring pressure on the British to relax their hold on
India. Whether this view was correct is open to question. It
may well be that the British could have been induced to leave
just as quickly if Congress had stuck to strictly constitutional
methods and had consistently co-operated with the British instead of doing the reverse. However this may be, under Gandhi's
leadership Congress took the opposite course and, instead of
remaining just an organization of the intelligentsia, deliberately
sought to enlist wide popular support. But to appeal to the
masses was to run the risk of rousing the latent Hindu-Muslim
antagonism that existed at mass level. Congress, it is true,
achieved in the N.W.F.P. a limited and deceptive success among
the Muslim masses, and it continued to enjoy the support of a
few distinguished Muslim intellectuals. But in general the more
Gandhi became the idol of the Congress and the more Congress
diffused itself among the masses, the more the Muslims as a
whole stood aloof from it, viewing it coldly as an essentially
Hindu institution.

The danger that his methods would provoke Muslim antipathy was not adequately appreciated by Gandhi who, with
the normal Hindu tendency to prefer dreams to facts, ideals to
reality, could not divest himself of the belief that Congress—
more particularly Congress as personified by himself—could
and did represent everybody, or at any rate everybody that
mattered. This fatal self-deception had already by 1937 done
serious, though not irreparable, damage to the cause of national
unity. What was ultimately to prove worse, Gandhian policies
had also alienated Jinnah who instead of being friendly to
Congress was by now potentially, though not as yet actually,

hostile. No-one, of course, could have foreseen that he would
prove such an implacable foe. Unknowingly, however, Gandhi
had helped to transform him from a keen nationalist into the
chief architect of Pakistan.

At the beginning of 1937 all this was still in the womb of
time. Jinnah had no considerable following and his prospective
importance was not at all apparent. The question 'Can Pakistan be avoided?' could hardly have been asked, since Pakistan
was not yet envisaged as even a remote possibility. Though
Hindu-Muslim differences were fairly acute, even Jinnah and
the League had not suggested that division of the country was
an appropriate or possible solution of them. At this stage Pakistan was still quite easily avoidable. When were the mistakes
made which caused it in a few years to become absolutely unavoidable?

When a boat is being carried downstream by the current of a
river towards a weir or dangerous rapids, it is difficult to fix
the precise moment at which all efforts to save it become vain
and nothing can prevent it from being swept to disaster. At a
distance from the fall the rowers, if they realize in time the
danger ahead of them and exert themselves, will be strong
enough to make head against the current. Even if they neglect
this opportunity and let the boat drift down to where the current
is too much for them, there may still be time to steer it to the
safety of the bank. But there comes a point, not exactly identi-
fiable, when the force of the current will take complete charge
and draw the boat irresistibly to destruction.

So it was with Pakistan. In 1938 the current making for it
was quite discernible, but was not yet too strong to be resisted.
By 1942 it had gained tremendously in strength, but there still
seemed to be ways of avoiding its worst effects. Even as late as
1946 it appeared at the time that there was a slender chance of
steering clear of an absolute division of the country. By the end
of that year division was seen to be inevitable.

The crucial years were 1937–42. It was in this period that
mistakes were committed and opportunities let slip which made
unavailing the later efforts to avoid the division of the country.
First came Congress's mistake of declining to form coalition
governments with the League in those Provinces in which they
had a majority. The mistake was very natural, perhaps un-

avoidable, and by no means fatal. It could have been retrieved.
But Congress did not perceive the importance of retrieving it
because they did not appreciate how deep and widespread were
the fears which it had aroused among the Muslim intelligentsia.
Yet they had sufficient warning. The immediate rallying of all
Muslims to the League banner and the doubts which Muslims
began to express about submitting to a permanent Hindu
majority at the Centre were very plain danger signals. Congress
did not read them.

The outbreak of war afforded a splendid opportunity of
repairing the damage that had been done. On the plea of a
national emergency Congress could have retraced their steps
and sought to join with the League in coalitions both in the
Provinces and at the Centre. If Congress had entered into such
working partnerships with the League while moderate men were
still in control of the Muslim masses both in Bengal and the
Punjab, the forces of disruption could have been checked. But
Congress elected to follow the barren path of non-co-operation
—non-co-operation with both the British and the League—
and resigned office in all the provinces in which they held it.

From the point of view of preserving Indian unity, this was
perhaps the most foolish step Congress ever took. In fairness
it must be said that several Congress leaders consented to it
with reluctance and misgiving; and Gandhi's own initial instinct was against it. If the British had shown more generosity
and imagination the scales might have been tipped the other
way. But the chance was missed and Congress, blind to the
importance of reaching accommodation with the Muslims
while there was yet time and obsessed by their struggle with the
British, gave up office and with it the prospect of coalitions with
the League. Within six months Jinnah and the League had
committed themselves to the demand for Pakistan.

In so far as Jinnah really wanted Pakistan, despite all the
calamities which it would necessarily entail, he cannot be held
to have been guilty of a mistake in demanding it in 1940. If,
however, as seems probable, he did not at this stage really intend to follow the demand through to its logical conclusion,
then it was a grave—a criminal—error to raise such a dangerous
slogan, and men like Sikander, who clearly foresaw the dangers,
were also much to blame for weakly consenting to it. If they

were unable to dissuade Jinnah from his course, they should have broken with him at this time instead of giving their tacit blessing to a demand for the absolute division of the country.

Probably the last chance of averting an absolute division came in 1942 with the 'Cripps' offer. If it had been accepted, Congress and the League would at any rate have participated together in the defence of India against the Japanese and the partnership might have prevented an absolute break later. The chance was not taken.

After this all further rescue operations were probably vain. It seemed at the time that the Cabinet Mission of 1946 had an outside chance of saving the unity of India and that this was thrown away through the bad judgement first of Gandhi and then of Nehru. In retrospect this chance appears to have been illusory. The constitution-making machinery proposed by the Cabinet Mission might have been brought into operation, if it had not been for the mistakes of the Congress leaders; but it could hardly have produced an agreed constitution for a single Indian Union. Congress and the League were by this time such poles apart, so much the slaves of their own slogans and animosities, so much imbued with mutual hostility and distrust that the Constituent Assembly as envisaged by the Cabinet Mission, if it had ever started to function, would have broken up in confusion and strife.

To sum up: A general lack of wisdom and statesmanship in the years 1937–42 made Pakistan unavoidable. Thereafter British efforts to preserve the unity of India were sincere and well-conceived—it is difficult to see what more they could have done—but passions had been too deeply aroused for human reason to control the course of events.

I pass to the second part of the question. If Pakistan became unavoidable, could the Sikhs, nevertheless, have been peacefully accommodated in some agreed way? The answer depends on whether one considers that agreement between the Akalis and the Muslim League was inherently possible or inherently impossible. On this opinions may well differ. But one thing is certain. If any possibility of agreement did exist, it was effectively destroyed when the League was excluded from power in the Punjab in the spring of 1946. The formation of the Khizar-Akali-Congress Government so infuriated the Punjabi leaguers

—never very reasonable at the best of times—that thereafter they could never be brought even to attempt to reach agreement with the Sikhs.

Agreement, if at all possible, could only have been reached on the basis of avoiding altogether the partition of the Punjab and reconciling the Sikhs to its inclusion as a whole[1] in Pakistan along with the whole Sikh community. This is what the Muslim leaguers themselves originally wanted, and it might have been made acceptable to the Sikhs, if the League had shown some disposition to safeguard their interests. But the League made no effort at all to conciliate them and there was no-one to act as mediator. Khizar and the moderate Muslims were regarded as traitors and the British were suspect for having connived at the formation of the Khizar Ministry.

It may be thought that agreement might have been reached for a division of the Punjab on the basis of a planned transfer of population. In the circumstances as they actually developed an arrangement of this kind was out of the question. The League claimed the whole of the Punjab for Pakistan and would not think in terms of division till the very last moment. But by that time such violent passions had been aroused and so much blood had been spilt in the Punjab and elsewhere that delicate negotiations for an agreed transfer of population could not possibly have taken place.

There are good reasons for thinking that an agreement on these lines was in any case inherently impracticable. It was no mere coincidence but in the very nature of things that the proposal for the division of the Punjab should find both parties in a very angry mood; for neither party wanted division and each was bound bitterly to blame the other for being the cause of it, the Sikhs holding the Muslims responsible because of their insistence on Pakistan, the Muslims holding the Sikhs responsible because of their refusal to be included in Pakistan.

Apart from this, the great disparity between the assets owned by the Sikhs (and Hindus) in West Punjab and those owned by the Muslims in East Punjab would have been a well-nigh insuperable obstacle to an agreed and planned exchange of populations. The Sikhs would have pressed for the dividing line to be shifted westwards—at the very least, west of Lahore—

[1] Minus, possibly, some predominantly Hindu areas in the south-east.

so that both the transfer of Sikh population and the loss to themselves on the transfer would be diminished. It is, however, difficult to imagine that the Muslims would ever have voluntarily surrendered Lahore or indeed agreed to any dividing line materially different from what they were entitled to on a population basis. Nor would they have consented to pay compensation for any disparity of assets. In reply to such a demand they would have contended that they had no wish to turn out non-Muslims from Pakistan, all of whom were quite welcome to remain and enjoy their property.[1]

For these reasons even in the most favourable circumstances it would hardly have been practicable to negotiate an agreement for the division of the Punjab on the basis of an exchange of population. But suppose it had been, would the populations in those circumstances have moved at all? A negotiated settlement would have implied a calm, peaceful atmosphere. In such conditions millions of people do not abandon for ever their ancestral homes in response merely to official requests and propaganda. Some strong compulsion is required to make them move—the compulsion of fear, famine or the harsh unchallengeable fiat of a Stalin or Nebuchadnezzar. A forcible transfer by government decree in Russian or Babylonian style was hardly conceivable in India at that time. The political leaders and the people at large had been too long accustomed to the mild easygoing ways of the British to employ or submit to such official coercion. The transfer took place in fact—and probably could only have taken place—under the impulse of fear and at the point of the sword.

So the conclusion is that, once Pakistan became inevitable, there was little or no chance of promoting an amicable Sikh-Muslim settlement which would have prevented a holocaust in the Punjab. If any chance existed at all, it vanished when the Sikhs were permitted to combine with Khizar in forming a Government to the exclusion of the League. This fatal step precluded all possibility of a peaceful solution of the Sikh problem.

It will be clear from the previous discussion that by the time

[1] The real urge for transfer of population came from the Sikhs—despite the fact that many of them individually would lose so heavily by it—because they did not want their small community to be split between India and Pakistan. This is discussed further on pages 280–1.

Lord Mountbatten arrived in India it was far too late to save
the situation. The creation of Pakistan had become unavoidable, and this in turn in the circumstances which had developed
was bound to involve a conflagration in the Punjab—indeed the
first premonitory outbreaks had occurred shortly before his
arrival. No last-minute miracle could prevent this conflagration; on the other hand by lack of decision and dilly-dallying it
might easily have been made far worse than it actually was.
The vigour and speed with which Lord Mountbatten acted had
at least the merit of confining it to the Punjab. Nevertheless
there has been criticism, particularly of this very speed of
action which was in reality a merit. The critics say that he
rushed ahead without realizing the probable consequences and
that if he had not been in such a hurry to wind up British rule
in India—antedating by some ten months the time limit set by
the British Government—the division of the Punjab could have
taken place with less carnage and in a more planned and
orderly fashion. This criticism may have gained a certain plau-
sibility from the fact that the magnitude and severity of the
disturbances in the Punjab in August–September 1947 seemed
to take the authorities in India by surprise. That this was in
fact the case is confirmed by the frank admission of Mr. V. P.
Menon already quoted.[1] Some trouble in the Punjab was expected, but it was optimistically believed that a Boundary
Force (quite inadequate both in numbers and composition)
would be able to control it. Here undoubtedly there was a miscalculation. But the question arises whether, even if Lord
Mountbatten had foreseen more clearly what was going to
happen in the Punjab, he could have done any better than he
did. While he and the topmost leaders of Congress and the
League may all have misjudged the Punjab situation, quite a
number of people acquainted with that Province were fully
aware, especially after the March disorders, that its proposed
division must end in a catastrophe. But none of them were
able at the time to offer any practicable suggestions for averting
or even minimizing it; nor have those who were wise after the
event indicated any alternative course of action which might
have promised better results.

All the suggestions that have been put forward really amount

[1] See page 94.

to this, that instead of rushing through the Partition in two and a half months while the Punjab was seething with passion, Lord Mountbatten should have stuck to the time-table originally laid down by the British Government and so enabled the Punjab to be brought under control and tranquillized before the final division took place. If this had been done, the withdrawal of British authority, it is contended, and the setting up of two new governments for the two halves of the Province could have been effected in a more organized manner and in a calmer atmosphere. Tempers would have cooled and there would have been less disposition for Muslims and non-Muslims to set upon one another. There would also have been time to sort out all the Muslim and non-Muslim police, magistracy and other civil officials and settle them in their appropriate stations in West and East Punjab well in advance of the formal Partition, instead of all this reshuffling synchronizing, as it actually did, with the Partition itself, so that at the crucial moment civil officials were still in transit to their posts or had only just reached them and the whole administration in a state of turmoil.

This sounds very plausible; but it all rests on the false premise that the means and the time were available for controlling and tranquillizing the Punjab. In fact they were not, and so the course proposed was a quite impracticable one. After the March disorders, to re-establish law and order firmly in the Punjab required the proclamation of martial law, which would have been politically difficult, and the employment of overwhelming and *reliable* military forces, which simply did not exist; while to assuage the tempers that had been aroused required far more time than the twelve to thirteen months which the British Government's schedule allowed.

As regards military forces it must be remembered that the bulk of the Indian Army was drawn from just those areas and races of northern India in which communal passion was at its height. An attempt to hold down the Punjab with such forces would have been worse than useless. It would have ended at best in a fiasco, like the plan for a Boundary Force, at worst in a civil war in which the armed forces were themselves engaged.

Other comparatively neutral elements of the Indian Army, e.g. Gurkhas, Mahrattas and Madrasis, would have been quite insufficient in numbers for the task, and to have employed them to the exclusion of the rest would have been fraught with political and practical difficulties. In order to muster enough dependable forces, it would have been necessary to bring out to India a large number of additional British troops. In the summer of 1947, with the British scheduled to quit India for good by June 1948 and barely able to scrape together enough troops for occupied Germany, this was plainly not feasible.

But let us suppose that somehow or other enough forces could have been assembled during the summer of 1947 to enable the Punjab situation to be firmly gripped, would this have afforded any solution of the problem? Would tempers have so much cooled and the Province been so much tranquillized by June 1948 that its division and the withdrawal of the controlling forces could have been accomplished comparatively peaceably? At the time there was certainly no reason to think so. On the contrary it seemed clear that any temporary over-awing of the Punjab by a tremendous show of strength—if that were possible —could only put off the evil day at the risk of making it far worse when it ultimately came. I expressed this view in connection with the proposal for a Boundary Force. If it was weak, the Sikhs would simply ignore it—which is what actually happened. If on the other hand it was strong enough to be effective, the Sikhs would bide their time and wait for its withdrawal before launching the attack on the Muslims of East Punjab for which they had long been preparing. The same would have applied to any other short-term measure for holding down the Punjab. There was not the slightest hope of the Sikhs meekly swallowing the insults and outrages which they had suffered and allowing all their revengeful feelings to evaporate in the short space of twelve months.

But apart from these feelings of revenge there was another factor which would have made it impossible to prevent a violent explosion in the Punjab by mere postponement of its division till June 1948. This factor was none other than the determination of the Akali leaders to ensure the survival of the Sikhs as a compact, coherent, undivided community. In the situation which had developed by 1947 this basic objective of Sikh policy could only be realized by the forcible expulsion of Muslims from East Punjab; for only so could accommodation be found on the Indian side of the frontier for the two million Sikhs who would otherwise be left in Pakistan. So in falling upon the Muslims in East Punjab *vi et armis* in August 1947 the Sikhs were not only gratifying their desire for revenge, but also helping to secure a more rational objective—the integral survival of the Sikh community. The migratory movements that were thus set going became, no doubt, largely spontaneous and instinctive, the natural product of fear and danger, but there lay behind them, as the original source of the initial impulse, this rational motivation. To grasp this is to grasp an important clue to the understanding of these events. The determination of the Sikhs to preserve their cohesion was the root cause of the violent exchange of population which took place; and it must have operated with like effect even if the division of the Punjab had been put off for another year.

The Sikhs would, no doubt, vehemently disclaim the part here ascribed to them. They would contend that the root of the trouble was the Muslim desire to expel *all Sikhs* from Pakistan and in support of this would cite the Muslim attacks on Sikhs in March–April 1947. There is, however, little to show that these attacks in the spring of 1947 had any far-reaching strategic motive or were anything more than ill-timed ebullitions of Muslim hooliganism. Jinnah had, it is true, at one stage suggested in general terms an exchange of population, but one cannot infer from this that the Muslims entertained any plan or intention of forcibly expelling all Sikhs or all non-Muslims from Pakistan. I know of no reliable evidence of such a plan or intention, and all that I myself saw and heard in those days was entirely inconsistent with its existence. Moreover such a plan would have been highly dangerous to the Muslims themselves, as it would have been to risk inviting as a reprisal the extrusion into Pakistan of *all* Muslims from India, and Pakistan would not have been large enough to hold them. That this might actually happen was a fear that oppressed us on the Pakistan side of the border during the weeks which followed the beginning of the migratory movements.

For the Sikhs, on the other hand, the preservation of their cohesion was a natural, intelligible objective. It had long been uppermost in the minds of influential Akali leaders. Even as far back as 1942 they had been thinking in terms of concentrating all Sikhs on the Indian side of the border, if the Muslims insisted on Pakistan. When, therefore, Pakistan became inescapable and the Mountbatten Plan for dividing the Punjab —and so the Sikhs—was announced, they accepted it, but, in order to meet it, privily perfected their own plans for Sikh concentration. They were, of course, led to hope that, because of 'other factors', the dividing line would be fixed farther west than it was and consequently that the number of Sikhs from the Pakistan side to be accommodated in East Punjab would be smaller and the Muslim assets available for distribution among them greater than actually proved to be the case. In a measure they were deceived and befooled. But though the Radcliffe line disappointed them, they were committed in advance to accepting it and had no option but to put their plans for Sikh concentration into operation. In order to drive out the Muslims from East Punjab there was need initially for force and terror. The Sikhs, thirsting for revenge and with large stocks of arms at their disposal, were well prepared physically and psychologically for this part of the programme and it did not require many days of their ruthless methods to make all Muslims wish to leave. The other half of the programme, the inflow of Sikhs from the Pakistan side of the border, followed partly as a natural chain reaction without plan or preparation. But not entirely; large numbers of Sikh colonists of the Montgomery and Multan districts, like most of the Sikh colonists in Bahawalpur, left their villages and trekked away to India, unscathed and in good order, before anyone had touched them or the disturbances had spread to their areas. I have no doubt that this was the result of previous Akali propaganda. The only considerable body of Sikhs who did not immediately move were the Sikhs of the colony district of Lyallpur. Protected by their own strength and the efficiency of the Muslim Deputy Commissioner—who did his duty but got into trouble for it—they stood their ground until September when they were evacuated with very little loss.

The policy of concentration ensured the survival of the Sikhs as a single distinct community, but at the cost of much blood and enormous sacrifices by individual Sikhs. If the objective was legitimate—and the Sikhs, being the most homogeneous, integrated and self-conscious community in India, could claim as much right to survival as the Muslims—the policy is defensible. Nay, what else could the Sikhs do? Circumstances which others had created threatened their existence as a distinct community, and their leaders cannot justly be blamed for adopting this policy, despite the bloodshed which it entailed, but only for the brutal savagery with which it was carried out.

Thus—to resume once more the main thread of the argument —Sikh desire for revenge and Akali determination to keep the Sikh community together would have prevented any gains being derived from a temporary postponement of Partition. Holding down the Punjab by overwhelming force till June 1948, if it had been possible, would only have meant deferring till a year later the upheaval of 1947. Even the supposed advantages of having administrations far more ready to assume responsibility in the two halves of the Punjab than was the case in 1947 would have been unappreciable. For the troubles were uncontrollable in 1947 not because Governments and officials were insecurely seated in their saddles, but because the forces of law and order were themselves unreliable. This is well illustrated by our experience in Bahawalpur. The Government and government officials remained practically unchanged. A stable administration, hardly at all affected by transfers or losses of non-Muslim personnel, was available to cope with the troubles. Yet in a situation far less difficult than that in the Central Punjab we failed to prevent disorders because the police and military could not be depended upon. This was also the fundamental weakness in the Punjab and, unless passions had subsided, would have produced the same results in 1948 as in 1947.

Postponement of Partition by ten months could have done no good; and it carried with it dangers of its own. Sparks from suppressed fires in the Punjab were liable to ignite combustible materials in other parts of India. Any delay in separating the armed forces might give occasion, in the excited state of feeling, for clashes between Muslim and non-Muslim units with incalculable consequences. The three parties who had agreed to the Mountbatten Plan might resile from it, if they were given too much time for reflection. Furthermore, from the purely British point of view there was the danger that the drastic measures which would be necessary for keeping the peace in the Punjab would earn them the odium of all three communities and that

they would in the end leave the country amid general exe-
cration.

All things considered, it must really be accounted a mercy
that Lord Mountbatten did not foresee more clearly the magnitude of the calamity that threatened the Punjab. Had he done
so, he might have fumbled and faltered, casting about vainly
for means of avoiding it while the whole country drifted into
civil war. As it was, by driving ahead at top speed with his
plan for Partition he successfully divided the country and the
armed forces before they could be engulfed in universal strife,
and the Punjab alone had to pay in blood the price of freedom.

While Lord Mountbatten may be absolved from blame, the
claim, often put forward, to great merit for the manner of our
departure from India rings somewhat hollow. It is true that the
disturbances of 1947 were more or less confined to the north-
west of the sub-continent and that the tribulations of the Punjab
meant no more to central and southern India than did the
horrors of the Spanish civil war to the rest of Europe. Yet that
the ending of the British Raj, which we had so long foreseen and
so long proclaimed as our goal, should involve a last-minute
division of the country which we had ourselves united, the
sudden rending in twain of two large well-knit provinces, the
precipitate, enforced migration of well over ten million people,
and casualties of the order of 200,000 does seem to argue a
singular want of prevision and failure of statesmanship.

For this the British bear a good share of the responsibility.
The complacency shown by them from 1937 to 1942, when the
demand for Pakistan was first gathering strength, has been
commented upon in earlier chapters. It is possible, though by
no means certain, that if from the outset the British had made
it quite clear that they would never countenance Pakistan, the
division of the country would have been avoided. But it was
very difficult, if not impossible, for them to do this. By the time
the demand for Pakistan was actually put forward by the Muslim
League, World War II had already broken out and the main
Hindu political organization, Congress, was standing aloof in an
attitude of passive hostility. In these circumstances the British
could hardly have been expected to risk antagonizing also the
principal Muslim political party by turning down their demand
out of hand. They were also precluded from doing so by the

repeated assurances given earlier that the wishes and interests of the minorities would not be lightly overridden. The most, therefore, that the British could do at this time was to temporize and to use their best endeavours to bridge the chasm that had opened between Congress and the League. The latter they certainly failed to do in the period 1937 to 1942.

But to understand fully the British responsibility one has to go back further. The root of the trouble lay in the decision to introduce parliamentary democracy into a society which was far from homogeneous and riven with the deep Hindu-Muslim cleavage. The irrevocable step was taken with the Montagu-Chelmsford reforms at the end of World War I. Ten years earlier the liberal Secretary of State, Lord Morley, when introducing his own Morley-Minto reforms, had said that he would have nothing to do with reforms which directly or necessarily led to the establishment of a parliamentary system in India. But by 1919 the tide running in favour of parliamentary democracy was too strong to be resisted. Almost everywhere sceptres and crowns were tumbling down and being replaced by democratic institutions. The Indian intelligentsia, deeply imbued with the ideas of English liberalism, could not think of freedom from foreign rule in any other terms; and even English opinion, lacking for the most part any real insight into Indian conditions, tended to view with equanimity, if not enthusiasm, the export of parliamentary democracy to India. And so there was introduced into a vast country of illiterate peasants, belonging to diverse races and religions and held together only by geography and common subjection to British rule, a system of government which, while it has served the English and some closely kindred peoples well enough, has elsewhere been—and doubtless will continue to be—a constant source of strife, disunity and disruption.

The inherent dangers of this British-sponsored experiment would have been lessened if the British, having once launched it, had hastened to transfer all political power to Indian hands before the constant appeals to the gallery inseparable from democratic processes had time to inflame feelings and accentuate the Hindu-Muslim division. But the British, fighting a stubborn rearguard action, conceded power in the inter-war period only slowly and reluctantly. While it is not true, as is often alleged against them, that in this period they deliberately promoted divisions, they certainly took advantage of the divisions that existed in order to justify the prolongation of their rule, and they failed, until quite near the end, actively to promote unity. Their hesitation to part with power in the inter-war period gave time for the communal situation to deteriorate and the cry of Pakistan to be raised. If in 1929, when the Montagu-Chelmsford reforms came up for review, they had boldly decided to treat Dominion Status as an immediate and not a distant objective and had set about with some determination to frame a constitution on this basis with merely a few transitional safeguards, then by the early thirties a Central Government representative of the major Hindu and Muslim parties would have been installed in power before anyone had occasion to think of Partition. And once the country had virtually reached the goal of independence as a unity, that unity would have been preserved at least for some time; for, apart from the bias of sheer inertia in favour of the *status quo*, the Muslims of the Muslim-majority provinces, with wide control over their provincial affairs, would have had no strong motive for secession. What might ultimately have been the outcome is a matter of speculation, but at least the British would have brought their rule in India to a blameless close.

If therefore the British ever care to ask wherein lay their responsibility for the massacres and migrations of 1947, the answer may be succinctly given. It lay in their belief in the virtues of parliamentary democracy and their reluctance to part with power.

Responsibility did not rest only with the British. Countless Indians and Pakistanis of every walk in life share the guilt for these events. Of those in a position of authority His Highness the Maharajah of Patiala was for many weeks regarded in West Pakistan as one of the blackest villains. Startling tales were in circulation of the atrocities alleged to have been committed by Patiala troops at his orders or instigation, and it was reported that these crimes were so weighing upon his conscience that terrible dreams visited him nightly and prevented him getting any rest. At that time we did not trouble to ask ourselves how any authentic information about the Maharajah of Patiala's dreams could possibly percolate to Bahawalpur. The reports about them, so comfortingly suggestive of divine retribution, were acceptable and were readily accepted. Nevertheless I was very loath to believe that the Maharajah, whom I knew and liked, was really responsible for the crimes attributed to him. Knowing from my own experience how difficult it was in those days to control the armed forces, I preferred to think that he had been powerless or, at worst, insufficiently determined to curb the violence of his Sikh troops. Some time later I inquired the truth of the matter from a friend on the Indian side of the border who knew something of events in Patiala. He substantially confirmed my assessment of the Maharajah's responsibility and went on to point out that he and many others like him were largely the victims of circumstances and that real responsibility rested higher up and ultimately, and in greatest measure, on two persons—Gandhi and Jinnah.

This may be an over-simplification, yet it conveys the essential truth. As the acknowledged leaders of the Hindus and Muslims they undoubtedly share, though perhaps not equally, the main responsibility for the catastrophe in which their leadership resulted. In the ultimate analysis the cause of the disaster was their common worship of the new god—the National State. Utterly dissimilar though they were in temperament and outlook, they resembled each other in this, that both alike were high priests of this modern Moloch—a god which the Akalis in their humbler, cruder way also served—and both, though with different degrees of reluctance, were prepared in the last resort to sacrifice countless victims at the altar. The National States which they had in view were different, but the motivation was basically the same. Western nations should feel no surprise or indignation at this blood-stained worship, seeing that they themselves at the bidding of the same god have accepted the slaughter of two world wars.

Jinnah's responsibility is the more obvious and was certainly the more deliberate. It is a measure of his guilt, but also of his greatness, that without him Pakistan would never have come into being. His career affords a striking illustration of the influence of a single individual—and also of sheer chance—on the broad course of history. Only Jinnah, and none of his lieutenants whether singly or combined, could have mastered all the Muslims of the Punjab and Bengal, dominating or overthrowing their own leaders, and swung them in favour of a policy and objective to which they were originally quite opposed. Yet Jinnah would never have had the opportunity to seize the lead and make Pakistan the goal of all the Muslims had it not been for the accident of fate which removed from the scene in 1936 the great Punjabi Muslim, Sir Fazl-i-Husain, at the comparatively early age of fifty-nine. Sir Fazli was the founder of the Unionist Party, a staunch Muslim, a staunch Punjabi, but also a staunch Nationalist. Like Jinnah he was a man of integrity, and in ability, force of character and renown he was more than his equal. If he had lived to lead the Unionist Party for another ten years instead of dying prematurely and giving place to lesser men, Jinnah would not have been able, and would not even have attempted, to win over the allegiance of the Punjabi Muslims and Pakistan would have remained an 'impracticable students' scheme'. But fate decreed otherwise and by removing Sir Fazli gave Jinnah his chance.

The responsibility for first putting forward 'Pakistan' as the well-nigh unanimous demand of the Muslims rests squarely on Jinnah. It was he who, despite the misgivings of Sir Sikander and many others, transformed it from an esoteric fancy into a powerful political slogan. Even if originally he made the demand only as a tactical move, he stuck to it thereafter so uncompromisingly—only at the time of the Cabinet Mission showing a disposition to accept something less—that a settlement on any other basis became virtually impossible. By his stubborn attitude and refusal to negotiate with anyone except on his own terms he made sure of getting Pakistan, but also of getting it in the worst possible form—a truncated, 'moth-eaten' Pakistan brought into existence by an unnatural division of the Punjab and Bengal with all the miseries that flowed therefrom. At no stage did he show signs of uneasiness at the probable consequences of his policy or seriously attempt to avert them; on the contrary, by consistently rebuffing the Sikhs, he ensured that the partition of the Punjab would take place with the maximum horror. To what extent in all this he acted with his eyes open is not definitely known. Possibly in regard to the facts of the Punjab situation he deliberately preferred to remain ignorant so that knowledge might not inhibit him from the course he wished to pursue. Great achievements

in action, whether divine or diabolic, require a certain ruth-
lessness.

It would be too uncharitable to presume—as some have done
—that Jinnah, in pressing the demand for Pakistan, was
actuated solely by vainglory and desire for personal power. He
must have persuaded himself that some larger interests were at
stake. Though not a religious man or deeply steeped in Islamic
culture, he may well have genuinely believed that to safeguard
the interests of the Muslims as a separate community and to
preserve their distinctive character and way of life from insidious
Hindu encroachment were objectives of supreme importance.
Whether he was right in so believing, a non-Muslim perhaps
cannot fairly judge. In any case we move into the sphere of
value judgements where there are likely to be differences of
opinion. Englishmen had no doubt that to escape Hitler's
domination was worth a destructive war. Likewise Jinnah and his
Muslim associates might maintain that to save their community
from Hindu domination was worth the miseries of Partition.

But was Partition really necessary in order to secure
the objectives which he had in view? It is here that the
correctness, perhaps even the integrity, of his judgement may
be questioned. He was right, no doubt, in distrusting Hindu
professions. They might say that Muslims were their brothers,
but would in fact treat them as less than stepbrothers. A few
leaders might be sincere in their intentions, but the ingrained
exclusiveness of most of the high-caste Hindus was bound to
assert itself, so that at most only a few hand-picked Muslims
would be embraced as brothers and the rest relegated to the
position of outcastes. An excellent illustration of what treatment Muslims might expect from the Hindus, if the latter had a
free choice, was afforded in the Punjab. In that province most
of the commercial, industrial and banking establishments were
controlled by Hindus. In none of them was any Muslim employed except in a menial capacity as a coolie or watchman
or as an artisan. Well-paid posts and positions of profit were not
open to outsiders, but were filled on the basis of family, caste
and other similar connections according to the deeply-embedded
habits and traditions of Hindu society. That society was not
going to change its nature overnight at the pious wish of a
Gandhi or a Nehru. Hindu professions were widely different

from Hindu practice, as all Muslims knew. Jinnah's distrust of
them was both genuine and well-founded. But it does not
follow that he was right in thinking that the creation of Pakistan was necessary in order to safeguard Muslim interests. Many
staunch Muslims, who shared his distrust of the Hindus and
had Muslim interests at heart no less than he, were far from
convinced that these could only be secured by the division of
India into two separate National States. Since Muslims were in
a majority in several large provinces, it was felt that, with provincial autonomy and constitutional safeguards at the Centre,
they would become too powerful an element in the Indian
Union for the crafty Hindus to override or circumvent their
interests, however much they might desire to do so. Thus
in the opinion of these Muslims—and in 1940 they were certainly a majority—the creation of Pakistan in the sense of a
separate National State was unnecessary.

On the purely political plane—and in the long run this might
have been all that mattered—they were probably right.
Probably, too, in 1940 Jinnah himself recognized that they
were right and did not intend to press the demand for Pakistan
to the extreme limit. But later the tide of events which he had
himself set going, reinforced by his own and his associates'
personal ambitions, persuaded him that he could accept
nothing less than Pakistan, even though all he could get was the
husk without the kernel and at a cost in human suffering which
he had not initially foreseen.

Whatever judgement may be passed on Jinnah by the moral-
ist, he must ever be venerated by Pakistanis as the man to whom
their State owes its very existence. Nor can outsiders withhold
admiration. To have transformed in little more than seven
years the chimerical idea of Pakistan into a living political
reality was an astonishing achievement. Alike in his tenacity
of purpose and in his calm, cold acceptance of consequences
which would have deeply troubled the conscience of an ordinary man he showed qualities of greatness.

Gandhi's responsibility, though less direct and less deliberate
than Jinnah's, was nevertheless very considerable. He did not,
like Jinnah, wittingly follow a policy calculated to lead to
bloodshed, but unwittingly, as has been pointed out in earlier
chapters, he contributed in many ways to this outcome. More-

K

over, as many of his utterances made clear, in pursuit of the cherished goal of Independence he was prepared, despite his proclaimed dislike of violence, to risk both bloodshed and anarchy, albeit with more reluctance and self-questioning than Jinnah.

The mistakes made by Congress under Gandhi's leadership were due basically to the Gandhian facility for self-deception. Over-conscious of his own good intentions, he clung till too late to the fallacy that Congress could and did represent all Indians including the Muslims. Obsessed by the supposedly evil intentions of the British and unaware that his own methods of appeal were calculated to provoke Muslim antipathy he shut his eyes till too late to the menace of Muslim separatism. It was easy to blame everything on the British and to persuade one-self that with their departure Hindus and Muslims would embrace as brothers. It was easy to decry the League leaders as relics of an outworn feudalism and to believe that owing to the primacy of the economic motive—one of Nehru's pet doctrines which was to be abundantly disproved—the Muslim masses would disown them. With these consoling beliefs Gandhi allowed himself to be deceived. They did not accord with facts, but they obviated the need for facing them, until at last the facts themselves confronted him in all their stark-ness, leaving no room for escape from partition, massacres and migrations.

There was no-one to whom this outcome gave more grief than Gandhi himself. The independence for which he had striven so long seemed hardly worth having when these were its first fruits. The extent of his own responsibility for them he may not have recognized, but at least it can be said of him that he made heroic efforts to atone for his mistakes. The closing months of his life showed his character at its noblest. Unbroken in spirit by the shocks to his own hopes and ideals, he laboured to combat the frenzy that had been aroused with a sincerity and courage which cost him his life but entitle him to be looked upon as a saint and a martyr. Gandhi, indeed, may be classed with those Christian saints of the dark and middle ages who combined astute political manoeuvring (and a certain amount of humbug) with genuine moral earnestness and a courage sustained by more than mundane convictions.

The division of India and its entry into the scale of nations as two sovereign States instead of one, though it accords with twentieth-century trends, seems absolutely contrary to the broad long-term interests of the human race. The dispassionate philosopher, no less than Ghandhi, must deplore that Hindus and Muslims insisted on thinking of themselves as separate peoples. But practical statesmen have to bow to the logic of facts. The original formulation of the demand for Pakistan may have been a mistake and the obstinate adherence to it a blunder as, in their hearts, many of those who are now Pakistanis at one time believed. But by 1946 the creation of Pakistan had become the least of possible evils, and in the following year this was wisely, if regretfully, recognized by all parties concerned. It is indeed fortunate that the final attempts to retain some semblance of political unity failed and were abandoned, for in the state of feeling that had been reached in 1946 a single Union of India would have been a house divided against itself and the end would have been a civil war far more devastating in its effects than the severe but short-lived blood-letting in the Punjab. The whole sub-continent and a whole generation would probably have foundered in Chinese chaos. As it is, ordered life has been successfully maintained both in India and Pakistan and in some directions considerable progress has been achieved.

Will these two countries, within a measurable distance of time, come together again in some form of political union? This is a question which those who knew India before Partition necessarily ask themselves. Few of them, perhaps, would now expect to see such reunion within their own lifetime. The longer India and Pakistan remain separate sovereign States, the more they must tend to grow apart and develop personalities of their own which will be resistant to coalescence. With the passage of years the old bonds between the two populations are gradually being loosened and their old common culture effaced. Within the present century a voluntary reunion under democratic forms seems wholly impossible. Such reunion could come about, if at all, only under an authoritarian system which permits differences only within an iron frame of basic uniformity and rigidly enforced discipline. There is at present only one political system in the world which fulfils these requirements.

Note on Casualties

I N December 1947 I made some calculations regarding the number of persons killed in West Punjab and Bahawalpur. I had a pretty accurate knowledge of the casualties both in Bahawalpur State itself and in the immediately adjacent West Punjab districts. Regarding several other districts I had good information from old subordinates, especially among the magistracy and police, with whom I was in touch. I was thus able to reach fairly precise figures for about half the districts of West Punjab and on the basis of these to make intelligent guesses regarding the remainder. These calculations led me to a certain figure for the total casualties from August onwards in West Punjab and Bahawalpur. I found that Sir Francis Mudie, the Governor of West Punjab, had independently arrived at exactly the same result. The figure was 60,000.

I had no detailed information about casualties elsewhere, but knew that in East Punjab, including the Punjab States, they had been considerably heavier than in West Punjab. I assumed at the time that they might have been about twice as heavy, i.e. 120,000, and that therefore the casualties in the Punjab as a whole, including Bahawalpur and other Punjab States, were about 180,000. Making allowances for outlying areas, where casualties were comparatively lighter, e.g. the States of Bikanir, Alwar and Bharatpur on the one side and the N.W.F.P., Baluchistan and Sind on the other, I concluded that 200,000 would be a fair estimate of the total casualties. Subsequent inquiries have led me to think that the casualties in East Punjab, though undoubtedly higher than in West Punjab, were not, as I had assumed, twice as high and that consequently my final figure of 200,000 was somewhat inflated.

Index

Abdullah Shah, compound of, 129, 132, 172, 183

Abul Kalam Azad, Maulana, 23, 41, 55, 58

Afghanistan, 157

Ahmad, Sir Syed, 11, 12, 63, 270

Ahmadpur Lamma, 241, 243, 244

Ajmal Hassan, Mir, Clerk of Court, 153

Akali, Akalis, 31–7, 50; canvass idea of Khalistan, 69 (footnote); 71, 73, 83, 84, 86, 92, 122, 274; determination to preserve Sikh cohesion, 279–281

Alexander, Rt. Hon. A. V. (Viscount), 43

Alwar State, 110, 229, 293

Amar Singh, cashier, 208

Ambala, 117, 119, 263

Amritsar, 31, 33–6, 38, 74; riots in, 78, 80–2; 88, 94, 96, 109, 110, 117, 119, 120, 263 district, 90–2, 116, 120

Anand Deva, liaison officer, 245, 246

Arifwala, 122, 258

Ashiq Hussain Qureshi, Major, 109–10

Assam, 14, 17, 19, 40, 45, 57, 48, 52, 61

Atari, 120

Attlee, Rt. Hon. Clement (Earl), 62, 63, 65, 76

Attock district, 78

Aurangzeb, 16, 30

Babar, Lt., 163, 178, 181, 185

Bagh Ali, 180–2

Baghdad-ul-jadid, 203, 218, 225

Bahawal canal, 123, 124, 133

Bahawalnagar, 108, 111, 123, 124, 132, 133, 135, 138, 140, 144, 146–51, 154, 155, 159, 161, 165, 168, 169, 173, 174, 176, 178, 179, 182–5, 187–9, 191, 195, 196, 209, 216, 218, 227, 232, 237, 248

Bahawalpur, Nawab (Amir) of, 83; position in the State, 99–102; 103–6; accedes to Pakistan, 107; 141, 144; assumes title of Amir, 157; 222, 223; returns from England, 228; wishes to retain Hindu subjects, 228, 229, 240–4; agrees to their evacuation, 245; enraged at misconduct of army officer, 236

Army, State Forces, 104, 108, 123; reported to be unreliable, 135; conduct at Bahawalnagar, 139–40, 144–5, 148; shoot Sikhs, 185; detachments of sent to Suleimanke headworks, 186–7; in Bahawalpur city, 191–4, 198–200; withdrawn from it, 202; 204, 208, 211; escort refugee trains, 223; escort Sikh column to Jaisalmir border, 231–8; 265

Bahawalpur city, 110, 133, 141, 148, 149, 158, 182–4; disturbances in, 189–224; 225, 231, 237, 241, 245, 246, 259, 265

district, 103, 141, 142, 183; evacuation of Hindus from, 224; 230, 251

State, 7–9, 83, 87, 88, 94–6; description of, 97–111; 114, 116, 122; first disturbances in, 124–54 passim; 156, 157; misconduct of railway personnel in, 165; 166, 174, 176, 177, 185; improvement of situation in, 187; 222, 228–31, 237; refugees from, in Delhi, 240–3; 247, 249, 256–8; survey of disorders in, 261–6; 281, 282, 293

Bakhtawar Singh, 234

Baldev Singh, Sardar, joins Punjab Cabinet, 36; goes to London, 60; accepts Mountbatten Plan, 66; 70; persuades Khizar to form a Coalition Ministry, 71, 73; 84–6, 96

Baluchistan, 19, 45 (footnote), 50, 51 (footnote), 293

Beas river, 35 (footnote), 90

Bengal, 14, 17, 19, 22, 24, 40, 45, 47, 48, 66–70, 74, 81, 273, 286, 287

East, 58, 68, 79

West, 68

Bengal Government, 58, 68

Bennett, Sir John, 115

Bhag Singh, 234

Bhandari, P. C., 74

Bharatpur State, 110, 229, 293

Bhatinda, 159, 164, 166, 167, 170, 203

Bihar, 59, 74, 79

Bikanir State, 97, 99 (footnote),

133, 150–2, 159, 163, 166, 169, 173–5, 187, 218 (footnote), 226; refugees from cross into Bahawalpur, 173, 229, 247; 248, 254, 264, 293

Maharajah of, 254

Bombay, 13, 57, 240, 256

Bombay Resolution, 57, 59–61

Boundary Commission, 67, 69, 88, 107

Boundary Force, 94, 95, 119, 123, 277–9

Burewala, 114

Cabinet Mission, Cabinet Mission Plan, 8, 36, 42–64 passim, 65, 67, 70, 74, 274, 287

Calcutta, 58, 68

Cawnpore, 267

Central India Horse, 32

Chamberlain, Neville, 37

Chenab river, 35, 50, 90

Chhotu Ram, Sir, 40

Chishtian, 123, 132, 135, 137, 138, 151, 171, 172, 182, 183, 187, 224

Chuni Lal, Rai Bahadur, 174

Churchill, Winston, 70

Congress, Indian National, 12–18; fails to conciliate Muslim League, 23–8; 33, 40–4, 46, 49, 52–7, 59–65; accepts Mountbatten Plan, 67; 70; unresponsive to Sikh ambitions, 85; 93; attitude towards Rulers, 105–6; 107, 270; Jinnah's alienation from, 271; mistakes of, 272–274, 290; 277, 283, 284

Constituent Assembly, 48, 51, 56–62, 66, 274

Craik, Sir Henry, 33

Cripps, Sir Stafford, 26, 43, 49, 56

Cripps offer, mission, 26-7, 54, 274

Crofton, Sir Richard, 102, 104, 108, 156

Cross, Leslie, 244

Cunningham, Sir George, 222

Curzon, Lord, Viceroy, 101

Darling, Sir Malcolm, 25 (footnote)

Dacca, 58

Daultana, Mumtaz, 120

Delhi, 29, 45, 50, 63, 65, 73, 83, 94-6, 106, 110, 117, 240, 243, 245, 248, 262 (footnote), 265, 266, 268
    Senior Superintendent of Police, 88

Dera Ghazi Khan district, 239, 241

Dera Nawab, 101

Derawar fort, 173

Duncan, Superintending Engineer, 103, 230

Dunga Bunga, 169

Durrani, Lieutenant - Colonel, 104, 105

Dyer, Brigadier-General, 80-1

Eustace, J. C. W., 115-16

Faiz Ahmad, Maulvi, Deputy Commissioner, 103, 231-4, 237, 239-42

Faridkot State, 261

Farnham, Surrey, 106, 228, 244

Fateh Chand, Dewan, Hindu Minister, 194, 224

Fazilka, Sub-Divisional Officer of, 180-1

Fazl-i-Husain, Sir, 287

Fazl-ul-Haq, A. K., 22, 40

Fazlur Rahman, Rao, Assistant Settlement Officer, 158, 160,

163; grapples with refugees, 177-9; 181, 182; reports on Suleimanke headworks, 185-6; 218, 219; regroups refugees, 257; 259

Ferozepur district, 97, 111, 117, 159, 162, 180-2, 247, 263
    headworks, 88, 91, 99, 186 (footnote)

Fordwah Canal, 133, 178, 225, 226

Fort Abbas, 150, 161, 169, 173, 227, 254

Gandhi, M. K., 24; secures rejection of Cripps offer, 27-8; 37, 42, 45; shows sympathy with Sikhs, 50; 51, 52; secures rejection of proposals for Interim Government, 54, 56; 59, 61, 63, 64, 70 (footnote), 79; allays passions in Bengal, 81; resists evacuation of Hindus, 240-5; assassination of, 245, 249; checks assaults on Muslims, 248; his leadership of Congress alienates Jinnah, 270-1; 273, 274, 286, 288; mistakes of, 290; 291

Gilani, ex-army officer, 104, 105, 192, 193, 201, 202, 221

Gilani, High Court Judge, 184, 189, 191, 216

Glancy, Sir Bertrand, 71-2

Gobind Baksh, alias Nur Mohammad, 137, 171, 172

Gokhale, G. K., 270

Government of India Act 1935, 12, 13, 19, 21, 24, 58, 71

Grand Trunk Road, 36, 119

Gurdaspur district, 263

Gurkhas, 104, 204, 211, 212, 265, 278

Gurmani, Nawab Mushtaq Ahmad, 83, 84, 86–8, 90, 94, 102, 103, 105–7; reassures minority communities, 108; 109, 110, 114, 119, 124, 125, 127, 129; indignant at looting, 131; 132, 134, 135, 138, 140–2; speaks to military officers, 143–6; 148, 157, 165, 174, 182; opposes evacuation of Hindus, 183–4; 187, 189; deplores inadequacy of military and police, 190–1; 192, 194, 201, 202, 208; disinclined to furnish Gurkha escorts, 211–12; 213, 216, 223, 228; evacuation of Sikhs to Jaisalmir, 231, 232, 236, 237; 241

Harijan (newspaper), 50
Harunabad, 108, 150, 161, 169, 173, 189, 218 (footnote), 221
Hasilpur, 132–7, 171, 172, 187, 197, 216, 264
Hindumalkot, 159, 160, 164, 165; description of, 166; 167, 170, 172, 175, 176, 185, 197, 203, 212, 218, 223, 224, 231, 240, 245
Hindustan Times, 54
Hissar district, 218 (footnote), 248, 254
Hunter Commission, 188
Hurs, 234–5
Hyderabad State, 107

Imperial Bank of India, 165, 208, 252
Indian Mutiny, 216 (footnote), 262 (footnote), 267
Indian National Army (I.N.A.), 104, 124, 148, 192

Indian (Native, Princely) States, 13, 26, 45, 46, 104, 127, 156; refugees from preferred by Nawab of Bahawalpur, 228–229; 248, 255, 261
Indus river, 97, 239
Iqbal, Sir Mohammad, 11 (footnote)
Ismay, General Lord, 86

Jaisalmir State, 97, 231, 234, 261
Jenkins, Sir Evan, 115
Jinnah, M. A., 12, 13, 16; describes Pakistan Resolution as a tactical move, 21; 22–30, 37, 38; seeks to overthrow Khizar, 39–41; claims to speak for all Muslims, 41–3; 44–6, 48; accepts Cabinet Mission Plan, 49–51; 52, 53; charges Viceroy and Mission with breach of faith, 56; 57, 59, 60, 63, 64, accepts Mountbatten Plan, 66, 68; views on exchange of population, 69; 72; lack of sympathy with Sikhs and ignorance of the Punjab, 37, 82–4, 87; 94; not hostile to Rulers, 105; 118, 223, 256; estrangement from Congress, 270–1; 272, 273, 280; responsibility for Pakistan, 286–9
Jodhpur, 235
  Maharajah of, 107
Jullundur, 119, 178, 263

Kahrore, 123
Kapurthala State, 261
Karachi, 88, 107, 110, 114, 144, 203, 240, 241, 243, 245, 259
Karanpur, 187

Karnail Singh, 233

Kashmir, 19, 107

Kasur, 188

Khairpur, 126–8, 132, 136, 151, 155; lawlessness around, 169–71; looted, 172; a third attack forestalled, 173; improvement at, 182–3; evacuation of Hindus from, 224; 264

Khalistan, 69 (footnote)

Khalsa National Party, 32 (footnote), 36

Khanpur, 241

Khizar Hyat Tiwana, Malik Sir, becomes Premier of the Punjab, 38; expelled from League, 39; 40, 41; loses heavily at the elections, 43; heads a Coalition Ministry, 71–4; 75; resigns, 76–7; 180, 274–6

Khosla, G. D., 269 (footnote)

Kishangarh, 234–5

Lahore, 29, 32–4, 36, 50, 75; outbreak of rioting in, 77; 81, 86, 88, 90, 92, 94, 96, 107, 109, 110; state of on August 15th 1947, 114–17; 120, 203, 208, 240, 245, 255, 256, 263, 275, 276
district, 95, 114

Lecky, 262 (footnote)

Leghari, R. K., Superintendent of Police, 138–40, 146, 147, 150–2, 154, 159; at Minchinabad, 160–2; 164, 166; endures bitter reproaches, 167–9; 171, 173, 177, 178, 182; angry at shooting of Sikhs, 185; 189, 218, 219, 224, 225, 232

Liaqat Ali Khan, 16, 59

Linlithgow, Marquis of, Viceroy, 18, 25, 26

Lockhart, Sir Rob, 222

London, 60, 63

Ludhiana, 117, 119, 170

Lyallpur district, 35, 281

Macleodganj Road, 150, 158–160; looted, 162–3; horrible incident at, 164; 165, 167, 171, 175; refugees pour into, 177–80; 187, 226, 227, 247, 254, 255; a black spot, 258; 259, 264
village, 163

Madhopur headworks, 91

Mahratta Light Infantry, 123

Mahrattas, 143, 278

Mailsi, 123

Majithia, Sir Sunder Singh, 36

Mamdot, Nawab of, 90

Manohar Lal, Sir, 118

Marden, Brigadier J. H., 104, 123, 135, 137, 139, 148, 191, 197; is wounded, 201–202; 211, 215

Mehta, Professor, 210

Mellor, Andrew, 269

Menon, V. P., 66, 94, 96; visits Bahawalnagar, 174–7; 261, 277

Minchinabad, 150; attack on beaten off, 160–2; 177–9, 187, 264

Moghulpura, 116

Mohammad Ali, naib-tahsildar, 91–2

Mohammad Latif, Syed, 263 (footnote)

Montagu-Chelmsford Reforms, 284–5

Montgomery district, 35, 50, 114, 281
town, 121–2

Morley-Minto Reforms, Lord Morley, 284

Mountbatten, Admiral Lord Louis (Earl), Viceroy, 18, 65–7, 81; on transfer of population, 93; persuades Rulers to accede, 106; 277, 278, 283

Mountbatten Plan, 65–70 passim, 84, 281, 282

Mudie, Sir Francis, 293

Multan district, 50, 78, 79, 114, 121, 123, 162, 196, 281
  city, rioting in, 78; 202, 236, 250, 255, 259

Muslim League, 13–18; rapid slide towards Pakistan, 21–25; 29, 33, 39–41; success at elections, 43; 44, 46, 47, 49, 51–4, 56, 57, 59–65, 68, 70; excluded from office in Punjab, 71–4; contest with Punjab Government, 75–7; fails to mollify Sikhs, 82–3; averse to settlement with Sikhs, 84–6; 92, 93, 107, 108, 143, 180, 272–7, 283, 284, 290

Mussouri, 52

Nabha State, 229

Nair, Dr. Shushila, 244–5

Nand Kishore, Mehta, 202, 215

Nazimuddin, Khwaja Sir, 40

Nebuchadnezzar, 276

Nehru, Pandit Jawaharlal, 18, 42, 53; demolishes Cabinet Mission Plan, 56–7; 58, 60, 63; accepts Mountbatten Plan, 66; 79, 248, 269, 288, 290

Noakhali district, 59

North West Frontier Province (N.W.F.P.), 14, 19, 40, 42,

43, 45 (footnote), 48, 50, 52, 66, 102, 104, 137, 155, 221, 256, 271, 293

Nur Hussain Shah, Commissioner of Police, 104, 124, 125, 127, 128; joins pursuit of looters, 130–2; disapproves of shoe-beating, 131; takes gloomy view of situation, 140; 148, 183, 189; absents himself from meeting, 192

Nur Mohammad, Khan Bahadur, Settlement Officer, 103–4, 149, 171, 184; takes charge of jail camp, 195–6; 200, 203; advises use of tongas for evacuation, 204–205; supplies list of stocks of grain, 204–6; 209, 266

Okara, 120

Oliver, Deputy Commissioner, 103, 104

Pakistan, 7, 8; first idea of, 11–13; 15, 19; Sikander's dislike of, 20–3; 26, 27; Sikhs' view of, 29–31, 34–7; 39, 40, 45, 46; as Sovereign State rejected by Cabinet Mission, 47, 49; 51, 57, 63, 66–9, 72, 79; possibility of inclusion of Sikhs in, 82–7; 91, 94, 96; accession of Bahawalpur to, 105–8; 110, 118, 125; danger of collapse, 154–5; 157, 164, 180; coal shortage in, 224 (footnote), 255; 237, 248, 249, 252, 256, 265, 269, 270, 272–7, 280, 281, 283, 286–9, 291

West Pakistan, 9, 11 (footnote), 172, 238, 243, 268, 269, 285

Pakistan Government, 93, 110, 144, 157, 255, 256

Pakistan Resolution, 21, 25, 38, 40

Pallah (Islam) headworks, 99, 106, 121–3, 179, 254

Panjnad, 97
headworks, 99, 103, 105

Pannikar, Sardar, K. M., 174–6

Patel, Sardar Vallabhai, 53, 79, 174, 176, 177

Pathankot, 91

Pathans, in Bahawalpur Army, 104, 144; cause massacre at Hasilpur, 136–7; 155, 172, 221

Patiala State, 33, 159, 229, 261, 286
Maharajah of, 285–6

Pethick-Lawrence, Lord, 43, 56

Pindaris, 143

Princes (Rulers), 14, 18, 19, 105, 106

Punjab, 7–10, 14, 17, 19, 20, 22, 24, 29–41 passim, 42, 43, 47–50, 52, 61, 66–96 passim, 97–100, 102, 103, 106, 108–111, 114–23 passim, 132, 133, 137, 140, 144–6, 154; train massacres in, 169, 204, 262; 187, 225, 227, 249, 253, 254, 262–7, 273, 275–83, 286–8, 291
East Punjab, 9, 35, 68, 79, 84, 85, 90 (footnote), 95, 97, 111, 119, 132, 145–7, 155, 175; Bahawalpur a paradise compared with, 177, 261; agreement for exchange of populations, 181; 202, 226, 229, 247, 248, 252, 255; savagery in, 261, 262, 265; 267, 268, 275, 278–81, 293
West Punjab, 20, 30, 38, 79, 81,

82, 84, 85, 88, 90; warning to Hindus in, 93; 111, 117, 118, 132, 179, 181, 223, 252–4; refugee problem in, 255–8; 267, 268, 278, 293

Qaimpur, attacked and looted, 128–31; 132, 136, 151; lawlessness around, 169–71; 172, 182; evacuation of Hindus from, 224; 264

'Quit India' demand, rebellion, 27–8, 40

Radcliffe award, line, Lord Radcliffe, 91 (footnote), 111; defects of, 186, 226; 281

Rahim Yar Khan district, 103, 106, 176, 224, 225–46 passim, 251, 261, 266

Rajagopalachari, C., 26, 27, 45

Rajputana, 97, 98, 106

Randhawa, M. S., 247 (footnote)

Ranjit Singh, Maharajah, 30, 31 (footnote), 97, 144

Ravi river, 35 (footnote), 50

Rawalpindi, 78, 265

Red Shirts, 15, 40

Rees, Major-General, 94

Rohtak district, 218 (footnote), 248, 254

Roy James, Chief Engineer, 103, 227, 230

Sadiqabad, 243

Sadiqia canal, 152, 154, 173, 178, 185, 225, 226

Samasatta, 159, 169, 187, 203, 224 (footnote), 231, 255; a black spot, 258–9

Shaukat Hyat-Khan, 82

Sheikupura, 261

Short, Major, 31–3; works for Unionist - Akali alliance,

34–6; accompanies Cabinet Mission, 43; 49, 84, 85, 86; arrives in Delhi, 96; visits Bahawalnagar, 174–7; visits Bahawalpur, 184

Sikander Hyat-Khan, Sir, joins the League, 17; 19; foresees dangers of Pakistan, 20–3; 24; in touch with Congress leaders, 25–6; 29, 32, 33; distrusts Akalis, 34; 36; death of, 37; unwilling to stand up to Jinnah, 38; 39, 82, 273, 287

Sikander-Baldev Singh pact, 36, 37, 49, 73

Simla, 18, 40, 46, 47, 114–17
Conference, 40, 42

Sind, 13, 14, 19, 40, 45 (footnote), 48, 50, 84, 97, 105, 110, 223, 234 (footnote), 241, 256, 257, 293

Stalin, 276

Suhrawardy, H. S., Chief Minister of Bengal, 58, 68, 70 (footnote)

Suleimanke headworks, 88, 99, 106, 133, 179, 181, 185, 186, 225, 226

Sutlej river, 35 (footnote), 90, 97, 122, 172, 179, 181, 203, 225, 248, 254

Sutlej Valley Project, 98–100

Tara Singh, Master, 31, 77, 93
Tipperah district, 59

Unionist Party, Unionists, 15, 17, 33, agreement with Akalis, 36; 37; decline of, 39–40; 41; defeat of, 43, 49, 71; 73, 83, 180, 287
Government, 32–4, 37

United Provinces (U.P.), 15, 17, 164

Vehari, 258

Wagah, 36, 120
Walker, Colonel, 115
Wavell, Field-Marshal (Earl), Viceroy, 40–2, 57–60 passim; dismissed, 65, 69
Wyatt, Woodrow, 43

Zafrullah Khan, Sir Mohammad, 88, 90, 96, 107